The Soviet-type Economies

The Social Insect Conquest

THE SOVIET-TYPE ECONOMIES

Performance and Evolution

ROBERT W. CAMPBELL

Indiana University

THIRD EDITION

HOUGHTON MIFFLIN COMPANY · BOSTON

Atlanta   Dallas   Geneva, Ill.   Hopewell, N.J.   Palo Alto   London

Printed in the U.S.A.

Library of Congress Catalog Card Number: 73-9410

ISBN: 0-395-17231-4

Contents

Preface

The goal of this book is to treat in a simple way a most complex phenomenon — the Soviet-type economy and its variants. There are numerous ways to analyze the economic system of the socialist world — as a system of institutions for effecting the allocation of resources, as a set of institutions and policies in interaction with a set of economic ideas, as a vehicle for an economic development strategy exhibiting both an abstract logic and a concrete record of growth. It can also be considered as a social system in hostile competition with other species of economic organization; one which changes even as it succeeds in displacing them, and which is not immutable even in its own homeland as it changes its own environment through growth.

The book attempts in some measure to encompass all these approaches, and although it can be considered a revision of the author's *Soviet Economic Power,* it is far broader than that earlier work in the range of questions considered.

Trying to force such a treatment into a book of this size may require a compromise among the objectives of being concrete enough to communicate the reality of the phenomenon, abstract enough to provide generalizing power and perspective, and comprehensive and systematic enough to convey the variegated structures of the socialist economies. But surely after fifty years of experience with the Soviet-type economy, and after its spread to a dozen nations, the task today is to see it in these broader terms and to assess its role and its future in the company of the world's economic systems, rather than to focus on the Soviet economy alone.

This change should make the book more useful than the previous versions for courses in comparative economic systems, economic history, and economic development, and for courses concerned with Marxist and socialist economic thought and their relation to economic history and economic systems. For courses on the Soviet economy, most instructors will want to supplement it with materials that provide more detailed descriptions of institutions, statistical information on growth, and analyses of current policy issues in the USSR than have been included here.

The author's aim has been to concentrate on analytical issues and concepts of permanent usefulness in interpreting the functioning and performance of the economies of the socialist world that will outlast the vagaries of year to year performance, constantly changing institutional features, and evolving lines of policy. Even with these limitations, there are enough overlapping issues here to undermine logical, straightforward organization; I can only promise that, if the customers will stay to the end of the performance, all will be revealed in due course. We will start with an examination of the prototype, the economy of the USSR, and will attempt in Chapter 1 to assess what kind of system it is by considering its origins. Chapters 2 and 3 will describe how the classic Soviet-type system functions in solving the fundamental economic problem of allocating scarce resources among competing ends. Chapter 4 describes the performance of the Soviet economy in terms of growth and productivity; Chapter 5 outlines the spread of the system to Eastern Europe and its performance in these new environments. Chapter 6 reinterprets this phenomenon as a strategy of growth in relation to the standard difficulties of economic development, and also looks at China and Cuba in

this light. Chapters 7 and 8 deal with some current developments in the socialist economies — the revolution in their
understanding of economics that has liberated them from
dogma inherited from Marx and from Stalinist obscurantism,
and the current struggle to reform their economies in the light
of these insights. Chapter 9 speculates about the direction in
which these changes may be leading them, and about the nature
of the socialist system of the future.

I wish to thank Professors Norton Dodge of the University
of Maryland and Warren Eason of Ohio State University for
their many helpful and constructive comments.

Robert W. Campbell

I

The Soviet Approach to Industrialization

1

Ideological and Historical Background

The Soviet Union proclaims itself a socialist society and professes Marxism as its official ideology. Unfortunately, this does not tell us much about the kind of economic system the Russians have constructed or the kind of economic policy choices Soviet leaders have made. Marx's analysis was mainly concerned with the future development of nineteenth-century industrial capitalist countries — not with the task of propelling a peasant society into the twentieth century. It is true that the Soviet leaders take great pains to interpret and justify their acts by appeal to Marx but, as I hope to demonstrate further on, this is mostly rationalization after the fact. The vague Marxist goal of achieving communism is something they can make ritual obeisance to, but their motivations and preoccupations grow out of more immediate problems. Thus, it is useful to reject the Marxian label as a point of departure and to formulate a new definition. The definition I propose is that the Soviet economy is totalitarianism harnessed to the task of rapid industrialization and economic growth.

It is probably fair to say that the triumph of a proletarian revolution in the Soviet Union was a great doctrinal mistake. Without trying to discuss the correctness of Marx's analysis

of historical forces and the causes of historical change, we
can confidently assert that he was not thinking about proletarian revolution for Russia. In his overall scheme of things, the
historical forces at work in Russia had not yet made it ready
for socialism. The Bolsheviks did not win power in the Soviet
Union because they followed the prescriptions of the science
of Marxist socialism, but because they ingeniously amended
and modified his analysis. It was by introducing a strain of
voluntarism into the Bolshevik version of Marxism that Lenin
made the revolution a success. And he made it a success not
because he acted on the basis of Marxist concepts and analysis,
but because he himself was a creative and forceful political
thinker and strategist. The Russian Communists were brought
to power not because of the historically inevitable growth of
working-class power which Marx supposed would accompany
the maturation of capitalism but in the virtual absence of such
development. They triumphed because of Lenin's successful
forging of a program that kept the peasantry on his side, or
at least neutral, and by his development of the Communist
Party and of other organizational and institutional devices for
manipulating and controlling political forces. Lenin and the
Communist Party he led were not made by the revolution — rather, they made the revolution.

   When the Bolsheviks had achieved power, they found
themselves in an anomalous situation. In strict Marxist terms,
they didn't really belong in power. The social basis for their
power was absent; they had misinterpreted Marx and followed
an adventurist policy. Nevertheless, they held control of the
country. Some Bolsheviks rationalized their situation by de-
claring that the Russian Communists had perhaps prematurely
moved out ahead on one front of the worldwide socialist
struggle, but that the industrialized countries would soon
follow their lead. This development would vindicate the Bolshevik revolution and erase the anomaly of their position.
Others thought that they could not hope to preserve the full
socialist revolution in Russia. They would make a heroic effort,
point the way, and then let their effort go down as a glorious,
path-breaking example from which others might draw inspira-
tion and guidance.

The events of the first year or two after the revolution suggested that the socialist revolution in Russia could not endure. The hoped-for revolutions in the major capitalist countries did not materialize. The few socialist regimes that did come to power were soon overthrown, and civil war and foreign intervention made the prospects for the survival of a socialist regime within the Soviet Union look somewhat doubtful. Even when the withdrawal of foreign troops and military victory in the civil war made the prognosis better, the Bolshevik regime came face-to-face with the opposition of the peasants, a problem that theoretically should not exist in a true Marxist revolution. Presumably, in a country ripe for socialist revolution, peasant agriculture would already have virtually disappeared. Actually, the peasants, no longer fearing the return of the landowning class, increased their resistance to the requisitions of agricultural produce that the Bolsheviks were demanding. When this happened, the Party faced the grim prospect of losing even the support of the small urban proletariat, which it could no longer supply with food. When, in 1921, the workers combined with the peasants in opposition to the Bolsheviks in the famous Kronstadt revolt, it was clear that the regime had lost the support of even its staunchest supporters. It looked as though Russia had indeed not been ripe for the triumph of a socialist revolution.

The New Economic Policy

But Lenin was more concerned with political power than with Marxian logic, and was not prepared to sacrifice the revolution just because the Marxist prerequisites for it were absent. Faced with the disaffection of the working class, in whose name he claimed to speak, he analyzed the situation carefully and then repudiated almost entirely the policies of the previous three years. Beginning in March 1921, he persuaded the Party to introduce a series of decrees, designated the New Economic Policy (NEP), which restored a considerable measure of capitalism to the Soviet economy, particularly in agriculture and trade. His idea was that by this strategic retreat the Party could keep control of the country but stimulate its recovery from the destruction and disorganization of the war years. Once the economy was functioning again, the Party could resume its advance toward socialism. And, indeed, it worked as planned. The NEP was a success in terms of economic reconstruction and it gave party leaders a breathing spell in which to analyze their situation and determine how to proceed.

Consider the Party's position at this juncture. The Bolsheviks were supposedly a proletarian party whose power was based on the support of the industrial urban working class. But, in fact, an industrial working class scarcely existed in the Soviet Union. Moreover, Marxist ideology suggested that they would inherit an industrialized, highly productive country in which the workers were in the majority; a country in which the workers were accustomed to the discipline of an industrial society and possessed the skills necessary to an industrial society; a country in which the people were educated and urbanized. These were more or less essential preconditions for ushering in the era of abundance that the socialist revolution was to make possible. These conditions clearly did not exist in the Soviet Union. Consequently, the leaders were in a precarious position inside the country, and in an even more dangerous position in the world as a whole. The USSR's relatively primitive level of economic development made it very weak vis-à-vis the hostile capitalist powers. So if the Bolsheviks were to remain in power and preserve the socialist nature of their revolution, the logic of the situation clearly demanded that they create the prerequisites for their existence and survival. They had to effect a rapid industrialization, both in order to generate political support and to become strong enough to defend themselves against a hostile and economically advanced capitalist world.

Obvious as this analysis is from our vantage point almost fifty years later, it was not completely understood at the time. For a while, there was argument among the Bolsheviks about whether they should try to preserve socialism, and it was some time before they completely convinced themselves that their survival depended on industrialization. Moreover, it was not completely clear to them that they would have to industrialize in a serious, large-scale way, and that this task would pose almost insurmountable problems. Nevertheless, by the middle Twenties agreement had been achieved among the Bolshevik leaders on the necessity of remaining in power and on the need to industrialize.

The Great Industrialization Debate

Agreement on the need to embark on a program of industrialization and economic growth directed attention to a whole series of controversial issues. How were they to industrialize? How fast? Where would the resources come from?

These issues were central to many of the policy problems the regime faced and constituted the principal substance of economic and political debate and maneuvering in the Twenties. They can probably be understood best presented as a simple two-sided argument between rival factions in the Communist Party. To be sure, this is an oversimplified approach. Many of the protagonists were not consistent in their positions over time. They changed their arguments or changed the emphases of their positions. Also, many subtle distinctions are obscured in this simple dichotomy; less influential groupings of opinion must be ignored here. Despite the disadvantages of this approach, however, it is a useful method of outlining the essential problem.

The Rightist Position. One of the two main positions in this argument was that of the group identified as the moderates, or Rightists, who controlled official government policy during the NEP. This group took the premises and rationale of the NEP as their point of departure. As we have already seen, the NEP was a strategic retreat, an attempt to accommodate to the weakness of the Party vis-à-vis the peasants and, to a certain extent, the workers. During the period of War Communism that preceded the NEP, the regime had found itself in an impasse in which it could retain the support of the workers and keep the urban economy functioning only by forcibly requisitioning grain from the peasants. But the regime was simply not powerful enough to pursue this policy indefinitely. The peasants had too many defenses. First of all, the peasants were scattered over such a wide area that it was difficult to enforce demands for grain. Even if the Party mobilized enough strength to impose its policy of forceful requisition for a while, the peasants could simply cease to produce. The Bolsheviks were not strong enough to win in a frontal attack on the peasants. It was this situation that convinced Lenin in 1921 that the Party must beat a strategic retreat and that the NEP, with its more liberal policy toward the peasants, must be introduced. The essential goal was to get the economy operating again, and this meant — above all — the restoration of agricultural production. The only possible way to accomplish this was to restore the peasant capitalist as the motive force and the market system as the regulator. By restoring a money economy — limiting arbitrary exactions from the peasant and permitting him to sell his grain on the open market and to buy goods from the urban economy through a trade system restored to private hands — the NEP would encourage the growth of food supplies and of agricultural raw materials, on the one hand, and the restoration of industry on the other. These two halves of the economy would be joined by a restoration of private trade. Each half would find a market and a source of supply in the other. Moreover, the growth of agricultural output would again make possible some exports to the world market, which would give the Soviet Union foreign exchange with which to buy the equipment and raw materials essential to restore industrial production.

The NEP was, not surprisingly, a great success. The recovery from War Communism was essentially a problem of putting existing production capacity back into operation. The peasants had to be persuaded out into the fields again to plow and plant. In industry, it was a matter of drawing the workers back into the cities and the factories, and of getting machinery repaired and rolling again. Of course, it was not as simple as it sounds. All of these restorations depended on one other. For the process to start, there must be fuel for the factories, seed, and draft animals. The rudimentary planning apparatus then in existence could do nothing with this problem, but it is the sort of problem that the market system handles superbly. Given a free hand, capitalists and traders mediate between supplies and demands with great flexibility. And as long as they are not afraid of government expropriation, they work hard at it. There was rapid restoration of the economy during the NEP period. Industrial output had by 1921 fallen to less than a fifth of the prewar level, but by 1926 it had regained the lost ground. Similarly in agriculture, at the beginning of the NEP the total area planted to crops had fallen by more than a third from the prewar level and output had declined to less than half the prewar level. Four years later, agriculture had regained the prewar levels, both in terms of output and sown area.

As the prewar level of production was reached, the Party's problem came less and less to be avoiding economic collapse and retaining control of the country. Emphasis now shifted to charting economic policy.

The Rightists' position was essentially that the policy of the NEP should simply be extended indefinitely into the future. They argued that it would be compatible with further growth, even when the economy had been completely restored to prewar levels of output. The Rightists recognized that the economic problem would then take on a new dimension, that of increasing capacity. That is, to continue the process of growth, it would become necessary to make new investments, rather than simply putting existing capacity back into operation. The Rightists argued that funds for investment would be obtainable by means of the following mechanism. As industrial output grew, there would be provided a flow of goods that could be exchanged with the peasantry for additional agricultural produce, which would in turn provide raw materials for the growing industry and food for the growing industrial labor force. The peasantry, protected from arbitrary requisitions and more or less unmolested by the government, would gladly produce this surplus. As this process continued, industry would reduce its costs; this would produce profits that could be plowed back into industrial expansion. As the peasants prospered, they would begin to generate savings, which the state could borrow or otherwise tap to augment the profits of industry for investment in industrial expansion. The process could not be forced, but it would work and would not threaten the political stability of the regime.

Thus, one of the important themes of the Rightist position was emphasis on agriculture. Expansion and improved agricultural efficiency were greatly emphasized as prerequisites for the industrialization program. A prosperous agriculture was necessary to insure an adequate flow of raw materials and food to the expanding industrial sector, and also to provide a market for industry as it expanded. If industry was to grow, there had to be a market for its output; the increasingly prosperous peasantry would provide such a market. This is only the skeleton of the Rightist argument, all of whose main points were supported in detail with additional arguments. But the best way to gain a fuller appreciation of the thinking of the Rightists is to contrast it with the arguments of their opponents. Let us now turn to the position of the other side.

The Leftist Position. During most of the NEP period, there were opposition groups within the Party which disagreed in various ways with the ideas and policies of the Rightists — who, as we have said, were responsible for government policy. One strain of opposition was propounded by the Leftists, whose principal figures were Trotsky, Zinov'ev, and Kamenev. But the theoretical basis of their arguments was largely the work of the economist Evgenii Preobrazhenskii.

The opposition found flaws in the reasoning of the Rightists which they thought would doom their proposed policies for industrialization. They argued that policies that had admittedly been successful in accomplishing the restoration work of the NEP would not work as a method of further industrialization once industry was completely restored. One half of the Leftists' argument concerned the investment requirements of industrialization. They insisted that the investment required was far greater than the Rightists realized. The amounts of accumulation that would be required for further industrialization greatly exceeded those that had been needed during the restoration period. In support of this emphasis on the problem of accumulation, the opposition advanced a number of arguments:

(1) During the NEP years, it had been possible to achieve large increases in output from relatively small amounts of investment because the investment was mostly for repair and

restoration. The problem had been simply to patch up a capital stock that was already of considerable size. This would not be true in the future.

(2) The situation in the late Twenties was such that, in actuality, the Soviet economy was eating into its capital — fixed assets were wearing out faster than new investment replaced them. This process could not continue indefinitely; the country would have to pay later for its capital-consumption binge.

(3) Much emphasis was given to the idea that industrialization would necessitate investment throughout all branches of the economy. There would have to be investment on a broad front to get the economy over the hump and started on the path of rapid economic growth. For instance, there would have to be investment in transportation to move the increased volume of output; there would have to be investment in the cities to provide housing, schools, and medical care for the growing industrial labor force. (This point, incidentally, is strongly supported by the experience of countries that are planning for development today.)

(4) Closely associated with this argument was the idea that, if industrialization were to be completely successful, the planners would have to use the latest developments in technology. For instance, electricity would have to be used to provide the motive power for industry; very large, specialized plants would have to be built and equipped with the most modern machinery. If the planners tried to patch up and extend existing methods of production, industry would remain backward, inefficient, and unproductive. A successful industrialization policy would require that industry be reconstructed on a modern level. But all these measures for making industry very productive were highly "capital-intensive." That is, they would require the investment of relatively large amounts of rubles to raise industrial output by one ruble's worth.

(5) Another related point was that the branches of industry that produce steel, machinery, and other commodities required to carry out an investment program are, in general, quite capital-intensive in contrast with the branches of industry that produce consumer goods. To build the blast furnaces to produce the steel to make the machines to make other machines

that ultimately produce consumer goods is a long, drawn-out process. In short, Preobrazhenskii explained very eloquently all the reasons why industrialization inevitably requires that labor and other resources be tied up for a long period of time before they finally produce something that people can put in their mouths or on their backs.

The other half of the Leftists' argument had to do with the possibilities for financing these investments. They were skeptical about being able to drain off from a thriving agricultural sector enough resources to finance these large outlays. It was true that the peasantry had provided large amounts of resources or funds to finance the industrialization that had begun under the tsarist regime. But these contributions had been achieved only by a peculiar system. The tsarist regime had collected large monetary payments from the peasants in the forms of taxes and "redemption payments," i.e., payments on the loans the government had advanced the peasants when it abolished serfdom and settled land on them. So the peasants had been forced to sell their grain to get money, even when they had not had an adequate supply to feed themselves. The grain thus poured on the market was cheap enough so that large amounts of it could be sold on the world market. These exports gave Russia a foreign trade surplus that enabled the Russian government to accumulate gold, go on the gold standard, and pay interest on foreign debt. These two phenomena — the gold standard and a foreign trade surplus — provided in turn the kind of security that induced foreign investors to finance Russian industry and to lend funds to the Russian government. The regime then spent these funds for direct investments in industrialization and as subsidies to encourage private investment in industry. Thus, the tsarist regime had worked out an effective scheme for putting much of the burden of industrialization on the peasantry.

But, the Leftists argued, since the peasants were now freed of the compulsion of the old system, they would never provide the resources for industrialization. They would, in effect, eat up the grain that had previously gone this roundabout route to build new factories. Or, if the government tried to exchange large amounts of industrial goods for grain, this would aggravate the shortage of goods and make the urban worker unhappy. The peasants would never voluntarily part with that much grain — nor would they save any money that the government could borrow to finance industrialization. Stated briefly, the position of the Leftists was that industrialization would require tremendous savings that would have to come mostly from the peasantry, but that the peasants would never voluntarily make such a sacrifice if the government continued to follow a policy of encouraging peasant agriculture.

Each side found vulnerable points in the arguments of the other. The Rightists tried to argue that the big capital needs that the Leftists emphasized so heavily could be partially offset by exporting grain to the capitalist world in exchange for machinery and equipment. In other words, they could let the capitalist part of the world worry about accumulating the capital required to build factories to build the machinery. This approach would short-circuit the process of capital accumulation and so obviate some of the need for investment.

They also argued that if the Leftist policy were followed, the new industry would suffer a crisis of overproduction. If income were taken away from the peasants to finance the investments needed for industrialization, the peasants would not be able to buy the increased output of industry. There is a certain inconsistency in this argument since, if the increased output were to consist of investment goods, there would be nothing to sell the peasants anyway. But in the context of Russian experience, it was a natural objection to make. The inadequacy of the domestic market to absorb big increases in output had traditionally been an obstacle to industrialization in Russia.

But the most persistent and effective point in the argument of the Rightists was that the policy of the superindustrializers, as the Leftists were sometimes called, was dangerously adventurist. If their vision of the process of industrialization were to be translated into action, it would destroy that alliance with the peasantry on which the NEP was based. Lenin's analysis of the peasant problem, though made in the dark days of 1921, was still relevant. It was still necessary for the survival of the regime to avoid alienating the peasants in this predominantly agricultural country. If the peasants were now squeezed too hard to finance industrialization, they would again resort to the revolt and noncooperation they had engaged in at the time of the civil war. If this happened, there was a danger that socialism in Russia would be finished. Actually, it was on the basis of this issue that Stalin, in cooperation with the Rightists, was ultimately able to destroy the power of the left opposition and to purge the Leftists from the Party.

The Leftists made counterarguments on many of these issues. The really crucial question, as we have seen, was the relationship with the peasants; the position of the Leftists was that the policy of encouraging agriculture would result in the strengthening of the most capitalist elements in the countryside. The Soviet peasants were not all alike with respect to their political allegiances and economic characteristics. It was customary to classify them as poor, middle, and rich, depending on how much land they farmed, whether they owned equipment and horses, and whether they hired labor or worked for other peasants. The conditions of the NEP encouraged this differentiation. The more ambitious, able, and thrifty — or, from another point of view, the shrewdest and most ruthless —expanded their land holdings, their share of the total output, and their power over other peasants. They also accounted for an increasing share of the grain that was put on the market. The poorer peasants with smaller holdings tended to eat most of what they produced. The richer peasants, or *kulaks,* as they were called, were uncompromisingly capitalistic in their orientation. The Leftists argued that if the official line toward agriculture were continued, the *kulaks* would be in a position to strike against the regime. They would do so by withholding grain, the supply of which was coming more and more under their control. Toward the end of the Twenties, this argument was given added force by the course of events. During 1928 grain deliveries fell alarmingly from previous levels as peasants failed to offer the amount of grain the government had expected. (By this time, unfortunately, the Leftists had already been purged from the Party and were unable to exploit this concrete evidence in support of their position.)

Who Was Right?   What was the outcome of this debate? Had the argument shown what the proper policy for industrialization should be? On the theoretical level, it looked as if both sides had virtually proved that the program of the other would never work. Thus, the result of the argument was essentially to pose clearly all the contradictory aspects of the industrialization problem and to demonstrate the nature of the dilemma the regime faced. The Rightists had shown the reasons why the regime must go slowly in its industrialization program; the Leftists had demonstrated the absolute necessity of proceeding very rapidly. It was not that one side was right and the other wrong in its analysis, but that the situation itself posed a contradiction. Each side in the debate had painstakingly illuminated one horn of the dilemma.

From the vantage point of today, this debate seems to foreshadow the experience of later entrants in the industrialization race. Many underdeveloped countries are today debating the courses they should follow in trying to industrialize, and all find that in one way or another they face the same dilemma the Russians faced at the end of the Twenties. The intractability of this problem for the planners of countries now seeking to industrialize underscores the seriousness of the difficulties the Russians faced, and helps explain the willingness of some to look for radical solutions.

As we know, Soviet industrialization was not just a subject for theoretical debate. Despite the theoretical demonstration by these two groups that industrialization must founder on one or the other obstacle, a way was found out of the impasse. The Soviet Union did launch and carry out an ambitious and successful industrialization program. How did this happen? What was missing in the arguments of the two sides in the industrialization debate?

Stalin's Way Out

To understand this part of the story, one must turn from the thinkers to the doers — and in this period the main doer was Stalin. Although Stalin had used the debate over industrialization as a device for destroying his enemies and entrenching himself in control of the Party, he had not contributed much to the theoretical analysis of the problems of industrialization. But at the point when the two sides of the problem seemed to be closing in on the Soviet regime, he maneuvered the Party into risking the use of force on the peasants. His answer to the problem of the relationship with the peasant was collectivization — a radical change in the institutional setting within which the problem was to be handled. Stalin more or less evaded the dilemma by pushing forward the collectivization of agriculture and so putting the peasant in a situation in which he could not fight back. On this issue, as always, it was Stalin's practice to speak from both sides of his mouth, and his statements on the purpose and rationale of the collectivization are somewhat vague. In retrospect, it seems fairly certain that he decided to put the peasants in collective farms where it would be much easier to force on them the sacrifice required by industrialization. In the collective farms, decisions about the division of agricultural output into consumption and transfers to the urban economy would no longer rest with the individual peasant, but would instead be under the control of representatives of the regime. And the consolidation of millions of peasant households into a much smaller number of collective farms would make the problem of control much simpler.

Collective farms had always been regarded as desirable, and were considered the form that agriculture would eventually have to take in a socialist country. There had already been some experiments in introducing collective farms as a "socialist" way of organizing agriculture. But the opinion generally held was that collectives would only gradually come into being, and that they would take over ultimately as the result of a process of competition. The peasants would join collective farms voluntarily when it was demonstrated to them that they were a superior framework within which to carry on their agricultural endeavors. Much was said, by Stalin as well as others, about the technical efficiency of large-scale collective farms. It was hoped that they would be so much more productive than individual peasant farms that there would be enough output to increase the amount going to the state as well as the amount left for the peasants to consume. Part of the reason for the hesitation about pushing the organization of collective farms was the awareness that a large investment would be required to make them efficient. This investment demand, on top of the investment requirements of industry, would aggravate the problems of capital accumulation, and the planners were eager to avoid this burden if possible. So, at the end of the Twenties, influential opinion and official actions seemed to indicate that agriculture would be collectivized only slowly.

By 1928 it looked as though Stalin had adopted ideas from both sides of the argument. He had called for the establishment of a very ambitious industrialization program in the First Five-Year Plan. As the planners worked out successive drafts of the plan, he demanded higher and higher goals. Planners who insisted that further upward revisions in the goals of the plan were unrealistic were purged and replaced by more pliant types. The First Five-Year Plan finally adopted in the spring of 1929 was a superindustrialization plan that went far beyond what even Preobrazhenskii would have thought feasible. Its goals for investment and growth in the nonagricultural labor force indicated that the peasants would have to bear great sacrifices. But at the same time Stalin was essentially following the NEP approach to the question of relations with the peasants. The First Five-Year Plan set very modest goals for the collectivization of agriculture. It stated that "in the course of these five years, individual peasant farming will play the principal part in the production of agricultural commodities," and this decision was embodied in the projection that state and collective farms would increase their share of the sown acreage only from 2 percent in 1926–27 to 13.4 percent in 1932–33. Thus the plan appeared to formalize a policy toward the peasantry that differed very little from the general line of the Party in the NEP period.

When the inconsistency between these two aspects of the plan — the inconsistency the Leftists had emphasized so strongly — began to be evident in 1928, Stalin shifted his position and brought the Party along with him in the decision to risk all-out war with the peasants.

From the fall of 1928 on, grain collections proceeded very unsatisfactorily, amounting to much less than in previous years. It appeared that the peasants were attempting to say *nyet* to the sacrifice the industrial planners wanted them to make. So the time had come to face up to, and find some way of dealing with, the dilemma that had been so carefully explored in the industrialization debate. In 1929 Stalin ceased talking about the virtues of voluntary cooperation in collectivizing agriculture and the technical efficiency of collectives, and instituted a drive to force the peasants into collectives so that the supplies required for industrialization could be extracted efficiently. This was to be a war that would destroy once and for all the peasantry's ability to interfere with industrialization.

Despite the original modest goals for collectivization that had been established in the First Five-Year Plan, there was begun in 1929 a program to collectivize agriculture completely. In the fall and winter of 1929–30, the drive was greatly intensified, and the number of peasant households in collectives rose from about 1 million on June 1, 1929, to a little over 14 million on March 1, 1930. This war with the peasants was not won easily. It was waged by means of terror and repression, which trusted Communists from the cities were mobilized to carry out. The army and secret police were used, and class hatreds within the villages were played on in order to enlist some of the peasants on the side of the regime. The peasants were forced into collective farms willy-nilly; those who opposed the collectives were killed or deported. Altogether some 5 million persons were deported or shot. Collectivization was the most intensive experiment in repression and terror that the regime had ever engaged in.

Naturally, this frontal attack created havoc in agriculture. The peasants fought back with large-scale destruction of agricultural capital; they burned buildings, slaughtered their livestock, and ate up whatever grain supplies were on hand. As the process unfolded, it began to look as if the predictions of the Rightists about the dangers of pressing too hard on the peasantry were about to come true. But despite their adverse effects on productivity and efficiency, the collective farms were an effective device for forcing the peasants to hand over output to the regime. The grain was obtained, even though the peasants who had produced it might subsequently starve. The long-run consequences of collectivization have been most unfortunate, as will be shown later. Also, there is some reason to believe that the grain problem of 1928 was not in fact a sign of peasant political resistance, and might have been soluble by more rational procurement prices. But in the short run, Stalin's collectivization program worked, and made possible a flow of food and agricultural raw materials to permit the drive toward the goals of the First Five-Year Plan to continue.

This approach of ruthlessly remodeling any institutions that stood in the way of economic growth was paralleled in the treatment of the labor unions and in the attitude toward wages. For a while after the revolution, Soviet labor unions had some real power and functioned as devices for expressing and implementing the views of the workers on economic life. At an early stage they gave the workers some voice in the management of enterprises, though this phase was short-lived. Under the New Economic Policy, they still retained some vitality and power to express the workers' feelings and to defend them against the policies of industrial management. Union leaders were permitted to serve as spokesmen for the workers' point of view in the inner councils of the Party, and so were able to exert some influence at the highest levels of economic policy. But the continued autonomy of the unions posed certain threats to industrialization. The workers generally favored an egalitarian approach to wage policy, which interfered with motivation and productivity, and were always asking for increases in wages and consumption. Indeed, during much of the NEP period, workers had managed through the unions to obtain wage increases that were larger than productivity increases. Moreover, the union leaders in the Party had generally favored gradualist policies in the industrialization debate. When the industrialization drive began in earnest, it was thought necessary to eliminate even the limited authority and power the unions still had. They were purged of their leadership, and thus lost any ability to defend the workers' point of view at the highest level. The unions were not actually abolished, but were placed firmly under Stalin's control. They retained certain neutral administrative responsibilities, such as administration of the social insurance program, but were essentially transformed into another of those Soviet "transmission belts," like the Soviet press, whose function is to pass down to the masses decisions made by the Party.

Economic Growth: A Basic Obsession

This brief narrative has sketched in only the barest outline of the process that culminated in the First Five-Year Plan and the collectivization of agriculture. The story is really much more complex. For more details on this crucial period in the formation of the Soviet economic system, the reader should consult some of the works listed in the bibliography at the end of the book. The main objective of this summary has been to demonstrate the implacable determination of the Bolshevik regime to force the pace of Soviet economic growth to the utmost, and to emphasize the early date at which this decision was made. The long discussion in the Twenties made it clear to the Soviet leaders that it was necessary for them to industrialize rapidly, that this would involve considerable sacrifice, and that it would thus require the use of strong pressure on the population by the regime. It was in the name of industrialization that the totalitarian terror machine was perfected. This was the purpose that justified the killing or deportation of 5 million peasants and the destruction of the power of the labor unions. In a larger sense, rapid industrialization was made the justification for the imposition of complete totalitarian dictatorship on the population of the country and was even part of the rationale for remodeling the Party itself along more totalitarian and monolithic lines. To enforce the decision to industrialize, and to eradicate the possibility of argument about it or about the sacrifices involved when questions began to arise, opposition groups were purged from the Party and toleration of different viewpoints or of open discussion, even within the Party, was prohibited.

This obsession with the need for rapid growth has diminished only slightly over the years. Stalin spent a great deal of his later life trying to justify the industrialization decision, and all the sacrifices it entailed, and insisting that the process must continue. The aim of rapid growth has been institutionalized in the slogan "to overtake and surpass the capitalistic countries." This is a cliché that the reader of Soviet propaganda, the speeches of Soviet leaders, and even the serious economic literature of the Soviet Union repeatedly encounters. And it has been thrown at the Soviet citizen until it is as immutable a part of his environment as the rising and setting of the sun. Undoubtedly some Soviet citizens resent this goal that the regime has chosen for them, but at the same time many identify themselves with it and consider it a legitimate objective for their society. The Soviet leaders, and to a considerable extent the Soviet population, see themselves engaged in a heroic struggle to overcome economic backwardness and to catch up with the capitalist countries in the shortest possible time. Current doctrine, as expressed in the program of the Communist Party adopted at the 24th Party Congress, proclaims that the principal economic task of the next decade or so is to complete the building of the material-technical basis of communism and to create the era of abundance that will usher in the communist millennium.

In trying to understand "what kind of thing the Soviet-type economy is," therefore, and in trying to assess how it works and what it can accomplish, one should never forget that the objective of rapid economic growth is a goal that the Party leadership set for the Russians forty years ago and that this has been their primary obsession ever since. As we will see later, this attitude has been exported with the system when other countries adopted Soviet-style planning. Indeed, one of the remarkable things about Soviet-style planning has been that its appeal to underdeveloped countries has been its supposed efficacy in accelerating economic development.

2

Basic Institutions of the Soviet-type Economy: (I)
Administering the State Production Establishment

To achieve the goals described in Chapter 1, the Soviet leaders designed a special kind of political and economic order. The central and most distinctive institution of this system is what I will call the *state production establishment* — a kind of supercorporation charged with running the economy, under unified management and for a centrally determined purpose. This corporation is closely integrated with two other structures — the state and the monopoly political party. The state production establishment is charged not simply with the job of production, but with production for goals set by the political leadership, and it is able to use all the instruments of state power, as well as economic instruments, to serve this purpose.

Sectoring of the Soviet-type Economy

This corporation owns most of the capital stock of society — the factories and other production facilities. It also owns another of the trio of primary factors of production — land, in the broad sense encompassing all natural resources, such as coal deposits, rivers, and oil, as well as land proper. To operate these facilities, the state production establishment,

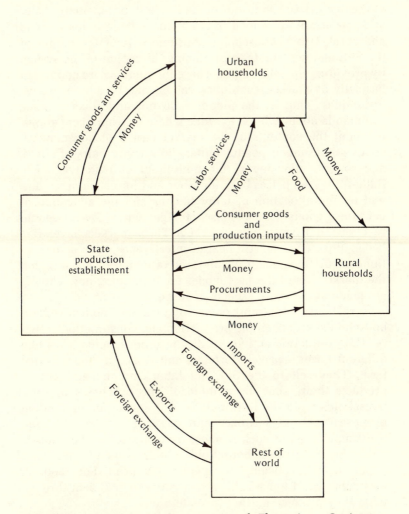

Figure 2.1 Macro-economic Sectors and Flows in a Soviet-type Economy

which we will hereafter refer to as the SPE, depends on *households,* which constitute another basic sector of the system. The relationship between the SPE and households is illustrated in Figure 2.1, which somewhat resembles the familiar circular flow diagram of a market economy, modified to fit the distinctive conditions of the Soviet-type economy. Actually, it is useful to distinguish two kinds of households — urban and rural. Urban households consume part of the output of the SPE and contribute to producing the output of the system by providing the labor input. These interactions are controlled basically by market techniques, rather than by administrative techniques. That is, the planners do not undertake to issue commands about who is to work where at what occupations, or about the contents of the market basket of consumption goods — how much peanut butter, how many pairs of shoes, and so on — allocated to the household of Ivan Ivanovich. Rather, they set prices both for labor and for consumer goods, and let the allocation of labor to jobs and the allocation of consumer goods among households get settled by household reactions to prices in these markets. These markets have often been subjected to a great deal of interference, such as restrictions on the movement of labor, or rationing of housing, but the market is still the best model for explaining how choices get made about these aspects of resource allocation.

Rural households (more or less identical with collective farm households) also combine production and consumption activity. The production activity of the rural households takes two different forms — private farming, and work on the collective farm. They sell to the SPE not labor, but the agricultural products their labor has produced. The purchases of rural households from the SPE include both goods for production purposes such as fertilizer and gasoline for tractors, and consumption goods such as shoes. In contrast to urban households, however, rural households obtain from the SPE only a part of the consumption goods they need. For food, in particular, rural households are largely self-sufficient through what they produce on their private plots.

These interactions of rural households with the SPE have not in most Soviet-type economies been left to the operation of market forces. The prices used in these transactions have usually been so manipulated to the disadvantage of rural households that, if it were left to them, rural households would withdraw somewhat from the link with the SPE to be even more self-sufficient than they already are. Hence the state has had, to a considerable degree, to inject its commands into the decisions of rural households, telling them, for instance, how much they have to deliver to the SPE. To back that up, the planners also have to specify how much of various products the collective farms are to produce, and how they are to produce them. But that approach has never worked as well for agriculture as for steel mills. The planners find it much more difficult to plan these orders rationally for agriculture, and much more difficult to enforce them. The relationship with rural households is thus a blend of the same freedom of action that urban households have to respond to the prices established for these transactions, and attempted direction by the planners of the level and form of rural households' production activity. Note, however, that the rural household sector is not quite coterminous with "agriculture" as a sector of production, since another institution for agricultural production — the state farm — is much more firmly under the direction of the state production establishment, uses hired labor, and is planned and controlled basically like any other unit of the SPE.

Another distinctive feature to be noted is the interaction between the rural households and urban households through the collective farm market. Rather than consuming all the produce of their private plots, collective farm households may sell it to urban households for money. This is an important feature of the Soviet-type system, and urban households obtain through this channel a considerable part of the foodstuff they consume, especially eggs, meat, fruit, and vegetables. This interaction is also organized basically on market principles, and indeed the collective farm market is one of the most nearly free markets in the Soviet-type economy, with prices set by the interaction of supply and demand.

Finally, Figure 2.1 also indicates that part of the output of the SPE may be sold abroad and that the SPE acquires some of the inputs to its production activities through imports.

In addition to characterizing some of the basic institutions of the Soviet-type economy, this sectoring is highly relevant to understanding the Soviet development strategy. These institutions are designed to generate a surplus for purposes of investment. Consider the actual resource flows. The SPE takes the labor provided by urban households and the agricultural materials provided by rural households, and combines them with other inputs in its gigantic factory to produce a variety of intermediate goods — coal, steel, flour, lumber, and the like — which are further processed by other branches of the SPE into other products, until at the end of the chain there emerge "final" goods and services. These final goods and services are usually divided into three main categories. One is consumer goods — food, clothing, health care, and the like — that can be used to satisfy the needs of households. A second is investment goods, such as tractors and factory buildings, that can increase the productive capacity of the economy. The third is government purchases, understood here as goods that can be used by the leaders of the system to further goals of primary importance to them. These might include armaments for military power and security, research and development for scientific progress, or foreign aid for enhancing their power and prestige in the world.

The consumption goods are returned to households to complete that cycle of exchange. But one of the distinctive aspects of the Soviet-type system is that the SPE has been able to retain a very large share of the total output to be used for investment. Indeed, the unusual power of the system to impose this pattern is important in explaining its rapid growth. Also, the leaders can choose to devote an unusually large share of the total output to the power and security objectives they consider important.

One should note that this arrangement implies unequal exchange between the SPE and households. A considerable part of the output produced with their labor is not returned to the households, but is diverted to the ends the leaders think important. To put it in Marxian terms, there is embodied in the consumption goods and in the agricultural production inputs returned to households a considerably smaller labor input than the labor they have supplied through their work and in the form of agricultural produce delivered to the SPE. This is possible because the SPE occupies a uniquely powerful bargaining position in its transactions with households. It is a monopolist — the only source from which the population can obtain the goods necessary for survival — and a monopsonist — the only buyer of their labor services. The only analogy familiar to us that illustrates the degree of this power in the Soviet system is the company town — where one company owns everything, is the only employer, and can force everyone to buy at the company store. And as an institution that integrates the political and economic structures, the SPE can back up its economic bargaining power with all the instruments of state power. To continue the analogy, USSR, Inc., owns the police department and the judges, the newspaper and the radio and television stations, and also runs the elections! Considerations of this kind lie behind the distinction made above between rural and urban households. The economic bargaining power of the SPE versus *rural* households is somewhat attenuated by the fact that the peasants do have alternatives. Much of what they need for survival — especially food — they produce themselves, and so they have an alternative to dealing with the company on the terms it offers. The response of the SPE to this situation historically was to employ with added force the noneconomic forms of power at its disposal — that is, political power — up to and including what can only be called war against peasant households.

This sketch of the basic sectoring and classes of transactions suggests that we might profitably divide the discussion of how the Soviet-type economy operates into two divisions: the SPE's dealings with these external sectors, and the management of the SPE itself as it carries on its gigantic job of organizing most of the production activity of the society.

The State Production Establishment

To understand how the SPE is managed, it is helpful to recognize it as a special case of the very general phenomenon of administering any organization. All organizations have a great deal in common; they work according to a kind of standard paradigm that serves as a very convenient framework for thinking about the Soviet-type economy. First, organizations are created in order to accomplish goals that cannot be achieved by individuals acting alone. A corollary is that it is usually possible to think of *organizational goals* that differ from the goals of individuals participating in the organization. All organizations are engaged in harnessing the efforts of individuals to the goals of the organization; it is often said that administration involves working through people to achieve the goals of the organization, and this is an excellent description of what the SPE is doing.

The process of administration can usefully be thought of as comprising a number of rather abstract general "functions."

(1) One of these functions is the definition of organizational goals and strategies at the top. This involves both *what* is to be accomplished, and some guidance as to *how* the goals are to be achieved. A business firm has profits as its goal, but the corporate leaders may have to balance profits against such other goals as growth, the public image of the corporation, or the social goal of environmental protection. In addition, they have to make choices between alternative strategies for achieving the profit goal — by innovation, perhaps by developing a reputation for quality, or possibly by destroying the company's rivals to attain a position of monopoly power. In the Soviet system, as we have indicated, the choice of goals and the setting of priorities is the prerogative of the political leadership embodied in the Party. A special competence in this respect is claimed for the Party on the basis of its training in and adherence to Marxist doctrine.

(2) A second function is *coordination*. The rationale for the existence of organizations is a goal beyond the ability of individuals to achieve on their own, and one function of administration is to divide the job into smaller assignments for smaller units within the organization, and ultimately for each of the participants. The aim is to coordinate individual activities into a coherent effort to attain the overall goals. In an organization that undertakes to manage all the production activity of a national economy, the coordination job is staggeringly complex. A national economy is a highly integrated entity, and coordination in this context involves two quite distinct dimensions. First, it is necessary to ensure that all units and participants work in a way *consistent* with one another's actions. In assigning a unit responsibility for producing coal,

it is important to specify that it produce enough to meet the needs of those who will be consuming coal, but no more. Second, the various assignments must be formulated to ensure that all this effort is *effectively* directed to meeting the goals of the organization. It would be better that no one produce coal if there were some other way to meet the energy needs of the economy at a smaller cost in resources. This function of coordination in the Soviet-type economy is institutionalized in plans that specify how much and what every factory is to produce, how much each store is to sell, how many x-ray treatments a hospital is to give, and so on, during the coming year. Plans for longer periods, typically five years, are also formulated, though these are much less detailed and operational than the annual plans. In the context of national economic planning, this coordination aspect of the administrative process hypertrophies to a point that threatens to overwhelm the masters of the SPE.

(3) A plan is not enough; organizations typically operate elaborate *control mechanisms.* There must be a feedback process by which the units of the system account for performance on their assignments. Their supervisors evaluate that performance as a basis for invoking sanctions and conferring the rewards that serve as incentives to harness the actions of the individual units to the attainment of the organizational goals. In the administration of a national economy this function, also, hypertrophies.

(4) Another ingredient in organizational functioning is what is sometimes called *leadership,* or *command.* There must be some legitimation of the authority structure, some internalization of the goals of the organization that will ease the conflict between what is good for the organization and the personal interests of the participants. Some loyalty and involvement are required to make the participants more than mere automatons. The importance of this function in the Soviet system is reflected in the heavy emphasis on Marxian ideology that is used to legitimate the Party's power and argue the objective necessity of its decisions about economic policy.

(5) Finally, an organization has a *structure,* established lines of authority and responsibility and channels of communication.

In some organizations this structure may be rather informal; but the larger the organization, and the greater the disparity between the organizational goals and the individual goals of the participants, the more formal and elaborate it must be. In the spectrum of organizations, the SPE's administrative structure resembles that of a military establishment more than that of a PTA.

In its internal structure, the SPE is a multilevel hierachy. At the top there is a central executive authority in the Council of Ministers and the central planning machinery. At the bottom are the mills, warehouses, laboratories, shops, and the like, that carry on production. In many respects, these enterprises are not much different from capitalist corporations. The things they produce they sell for money, and the things they consume they pay for in money. They are expected to carry on accounting and to determine their own profit or loss. The director of an enterprise, like the officers of a corporation, is in effect a steward of someone else's property, and is held responsible for the management and conservation of that property. This stewardship, the responsibility of enterprise management to the state for managing the enterprise productively, the Russians call economic accountability, or *khozraschet*.

The hierachy of organs linking enterprises with the center is constantly changing, and hence difficult to describe. During most of Soviet history, however, the level immediately below the top consisted of ministries (originally called People's Commissariats) and analogous bodies responsible for branches of production and economic functions (such as the Ministry of Agricultural Machinery, the Ministry of Finance, and the Committee on Foreign Economic Relations). Between the ministry and the enterprise there is often another layer of units, such as trusts that combine similar plants in a given area (e.g., territorial trusts in the coal industry) or groups of functionally interdependent units (e.g., the integrated combines in the oil industry supervising all exploratory, production, and transport enterprises in a given area).

The principle to which this structure should conform is that, moving downward, it represent a successively finer subdivision of the big tasks the leaders set at the top into smaller and smaller areas of production responsibility. Moving upward, it should appear as an agglomeration into ever larger units of closely related activities. This principle is difficult to realize in practice, however. The designers of the system constantly face such dilemmas as whether to put the plants producing construction machinery under the Ministry of the Construction Industry or under some machine-building ministry. The former would help make them responsive to the needs of their customers, whereas the latter would improve their production efficiency through close technical cooperation with other machinery plants. Whichever choice they make, some important interaction will be stranded on departmental barriers and handled inadequately.

Let us turn now to a description of how these functions are performed in the classical Soviet model.

Goals and Strategies

Discussion of priorities and strategies by the leaders is largely concealed from public view, though the decisions reached are promulgated in such *fora* as Central Committee meetings and Party Congresses. The important documents for planning are the "limits and directives" approved by the Party as guidelines for formulating a detailed plan. The directives have traditionally been a short document setting targets for such indicators as growth of industrial and other sector outputs (with output targets separately specified for some particularly important commodities, such as grain, steel, and electric power), size of the labor force, volume of investment, and the like. The directives usually offer strategic guidance as well, indicating that the goals should be sought by improving labor discipline, say, or by focusing on technological change or emphasizing some technical principle like "electrification" to revolutionize productivity across the whole spectrum of activities.

The Interdependence of Economic Sectors

The job of the Gosplan is to translate these aggregative guidelines into a detailed plan that specifies how much of each good is to be produced and by whom, and how it will be used.

Table 2.1 Input-Output Table

UNIT OF MEASUREMENT	PRODUCING SECTOR	Electric Power	Coal	Oil and Gas	Iron and Steel	Machinery	Chemicals	Lumber and Wood Products	Construction Materials	Textiles and Apparel	Food Processing	Agriculture	Transport	Other	Households	Government	Investment	Total Output
BKWH	Electric power	24.7	21.0	29.9	27.9	51.0	29.5	13.7	36.2	24.4	16.8	15.7	30.6	51.5	26.9	1.9	10.7	412.4
MT	Coal	160.7	44.5	.8	123.3	8.1	3.7	3.6	14.8	3.3	8.6	5.6	48.1	75.4	25.8	3.4	2.0	531.7
10MB	Oil and gas	17.85	.35	35.00	7.14	12.81	9.73	16.73	10.43	1.89	11.34	42.00	54.60	59.01	11.20	10.26	7.00	307.30
$B	Iron and steel	.02	.04	.02	2.58	3.26	.15	.13	.29	.03	.08	.03	.12	.62	.08	.20	1.60	9.25
$B	Machinery	.03	.10	.05	.28	8.28	.03	.05	.03	.03	.07	.91	.10	.03	1.76	8.15	9.33	29.23
$B	Chemicals	.01	.03	.06	.10	1.19	2.21	.18	.05	.61	.08	.43	.42	.58	.60	1.23	.29	8.07
$B	Lumber and wood products	.03	.40	.01	.08	.44	.17	3.12	.18	.14	.36	.12	.17	1.16	2.20	.73	3.01	12.32
$B	Construction materials	.02	.01	—	.01	.13	.04	.06	1.29	.01	.07	.02	.06	.08	.56	.13	5.67	8.16
$B	Textiles and apparel	.01	.13	.01	.11	.38	.51	.37	.07	15.37	.01	—	.14	.91	23.68	.92	.57	43.19
$B	Food processing	.02	—	—	.01	.01	.43	.03	.01	.62	13.37	1.58	—	.85	32.37	8.43	.09	57.82
$B	Agriculture	—	—	—	—	—	.01	.03	—	4.47	16.47	12.44	.02	.21	18.54	1.49	.01	53.69
10BTM	Transport	—	59.0	26.8	24.7	2.9	4.0	33.9	17.6	1.8	9.8	13.9	.3	2.6	17.2	12.3	3.4	230.2
$B	Other	.23	.25	.46	.30	1.04	.81	.43	.43	.33	.53	.31	.58	.33	1.55	.58	.10	8.26
TMY	Labor	405	1,254	191	990	6,915	754	3,210	2,037	3,740	2,530	34,200	6,941	7,324	3,696	13,983	6,302	94,472

BKWH = billion kilowatt-hours   10BTM = ten billion ton-miles
MT = million tons   TMY = thousand man-years
10MB = 10 million barrels
$B = billion dollars

This is an extraordinarily complex task. A good way to gain an appreciation of the kinds of interrelationships that make practical planning so difficult is to look at the picture of an economy provided by an "input-output table." A highly schematic and oversimplified example is shown in Table 2.1, which merits some unhurried study. Some experimentation with it will help greatly in understanding the mutual interdependence of different parts of an economic system. Reading across any of the rows in Table 2.1, one can see the distribution of the output of any given industry among its various users. For instance, the first row shows that, of the total output of 412.4 billion kilowatt-hours of electric power produced during the year in this hypothetical economy, 24.7 billion kilowatt-hours were used by the electric power industry for its own needs; 21.0 billion kilowatt-hours went to the coal industry; 29.9 billion kilowatt-hours were used by producers of oil and gas; and various amounts went to other branches of industry, to agriculture, and to transport. Finally, some was left over for meeting the needs of households and other "final" consumers. Similarly, in each of the other rows, the disposition of the total output of some branch of the economy is shown. The bottom row of the table, below the heavy horizontal line, shows the distribution of the labor force among the various sectors. During the year a total of 94,472 thousand man-years were worked, and of this total 405 thousand were for the electric power industry, 1,254 thousand were in the coal industry, 191 thousand in the production of oil and gas, 990 thousand in the iron and steel industry, and so on.

Looked at in another way, Table 2.1 reveals other important relationships. Glancing down any column, one can see the amounts of various goods and services that each industry bought and used in the process of producing its own output during the year. For instance, in order to produce its 412.4 billion kilowatt-hours of electric power, the electric power industry had to consume 160.7 million tons of coal, oil and gas equivalent to 178.5 million barrels of oil, and the amounts shown of transportation, labor, and other inputs. For each industry, the column shows the inputs from all other industries required by the given industry for the production of its output.

Thus, all the numbers to the left of the last four columns and above the "labor" row characterize the mutual interdependence of the demand for the output of any industry with the demand for the output of all other industries. How much coal will be needed depends on the levels of output of all those industries that require coal for their operation.

These interrelationships are more or less stable, at least for periods of a few years, because they are based on certain technological facts. In the case of the electric power industry, for instance, the consumption of 160.7 million tons of coal and 178.5 million barrels of fuel oil to produce 412.4 billion kilowatt-hours of electricity reflects the fact that, given the efficiency of the equipment now in use, on the average a certain number of BTU, or calories, is required to produce one kilowatt-hour of electric power. Similarly, the input of iron and steel products required to produce the 29.2 billion dollars worth of machinery reflects the existing state of technology in the machinery industry, the kind of things that the machinery industry produces, and so on. Some of these interrelationships are more stable than others, and all can change over time as technology changes and with other factors. By and large, such shifts proceed fairly slowly, and the relationships shown in the operation of the economy in a given year can be expected to hold fairly steady for the near future.

An input-output table illustrates very neatly the task of the Soviet planners. In Table 2.1, everything just matches. Each industry has been able to sell all the output it produced, either to other producers or to meet household, investment, and government demands. But as the planners look forward to the task of drawing up the plan for the next year, there will obviously have to be some changes in output. Let us suppose, for example, that the planners want to increase the output of electric power used by households by 20 billion kilowatt-hours, an increase equal to about 5 percent of the total output of 412.4 billion kilowatt-hours shown in Table 2.1. What will be the impact of this single change on the work of other sectors of the economy? Clearly there will be some impact on all sectors, not just on the electric power industry alone. In order to produce this extra power, the electric power industry will have to consume more coal, more labor, more transportation, and so on. If it took a certain number of tons of coal to produce the 412.4 billion kilowatt-hours in the previous year, it will take about 5 percent more to increase output by 5 percent, and so on. The electric power industry will require larger inputs from all the industries that supply it, and this, of course, means that the output of every other industry will have to increase. But this is far from the end of the story. If each of the industries that supplies inputs to the electric power industry must increase its output, each will in turn require larger inputs from other industries. Thus there must be another round of adjustments, which will have to be followed by another, and so on in endless repercussion. Moreover, these kinds of interrelationships involve wheels within wheels. For instance, the electric power industry will have to have more coal, but since considerable amounts of electric power are used in coal mining, the coal industry will have to be supplied with more electric power in order to meet the increased demand. So the electric power industry in turn will have to consume still more coal.

This example assumes that there is no bottleneck in the capacity of each sector of the economy to produce the output required if it receives enough current inputs. We have assumed that once the planners determine how much each industry should produce and insure that there will be available to it the required amounts of power, fuel, and materials, each industry will be able to produce its assigned output. In fact, however, this is not always the case, since the production capacity of the industry — that is, the number of plants and the amount of equipment it has for turning out its product — may be inadequate to handle the assigned production program. In such a case it will be necessary to construct new capacity. In the case of the electric power industry, for instance, it may turn out that the assigned output of electric power cannot be produced without construction of new power stations. If this happens, there will be an induced need for more investment, and the amounts of goods available for investment — namely, the amounts listed in the next-to-last column of Table 2.1 — will have to be increased over whatever initial levels were previously planned. To build this electric power station will require some output from the machinery industry, from the iron and steel industry, from the construction materials industry, and so on. This in turn will generate a new chain reaction of demands on all sectors of the economy. Whatever scheme the planners finally arrive at, it must not require more capacity in any industry than is at hand or can be added in the period in question. The labor supply also sets a limit to total output — a production program that required a labor input for all industries in excess of the labor force would not be feasible. Obviously, Table 2.1 represents a highly oversimplified picture of the interrelationships in the economy. In a real economy, there are not just thirteen branches but several hundred; moreover, the final claimants on output are not only households, investment, and government, but also exports, increases in inventory, the military, and others. But even this simplified table illustrates clearly our main point; namely, that it is impossible to plan the activity of any one sector of the economy in isolation from the rest. The decisions of people in charge of planning any one aspect of the economy have an impact on the decisions of those planning the activities of all other sectors of the economy, and there must be some mechanism for coordination.

The kind of input-output table illustrated in Table 2.1 can be recast in a way that makes it possible to express the problem of balance in the form of a mathematical problem, amenable to handling by computer. But, paradoxically, the input-output approach was developed in the United States, rather than in the Soviet Union where it would seem to be so much more useful. Following Stalin's death, when Soviet economists became freer to follow the development of economics in other countries, they became intrigued with input-output analysis and have been experimenting intensively with it as an aid to planning. More will be said about these efforts in a later chapter; here we will limit the discussion to how the planners have coped with the balancing problem in the traditional Stalinist model.

Balancing in the Standard Soviet-type Model

The traditional way of handling coordination was the "method of material balances," which is essentially a trial-and-error method of equating supply and demand. An idealized description goes as follows: Gosplan develops some more or less feasible, consistent, and highly aggregated targets for the economy as a whole and for its main branches — output, labor force, investment, and so on. The ministerial planners give the limits and directives for their branches a more detailed and specific definition as they disaggregate them and pass them down to the enterprises. Enterprises respond, registering objections and counterproposals concerning output assignments, and their needs for materials to carry out the programs. These more detailed output plans and requisitions for inputs are channeled to the Gosplan, where they are sorted out and entered in a material balance, a record listing on one side the sources of supply of each commodity (classified in various ways — by region, by ministry, domestic production versus imports, and so on) and on the other the needs for that commodity, again appropriately classified. Of course, there is no assurance that the needs and availability for any commodity will balance, and there then ensues a messy process of juggling — switching users from deficit materials to substitutes in surplus, raising the production assignments for deficit commodities, or cutting the requests of some users for those commodities. The latter may be done with various degrees of realism. That is, orders to increase the output of some commodity in short supply may or may not allow for the allocation of more inputs to its producers; in either case, the planners' judgment as to whether more output could be squeezed out may be reasoned and based on real possibilities or purely arbitrary. Once the balances are reconciled to the extent the planners can manage, final output targets and purchase authorizations are issued to higher-level bodies, which once again pass them down to the enterprises. In the process, contracts are drawn up between specific suppliers and consumers within the framework of the output assignments and purchase authorizations.

Even this schematic description suggests numerous ambiguities and perplexities as to how this process might operate. A concrete and detailed explanation of how it works in all its real-life complexity is a task for a full-length book, and the reader is referred to some of the works listed in the bibliography. We will here offer only a few suggestions as to how it can work at all. First, the balancing at the center is aggregative and selective. Some commodities are not covered by the system at all — there is no material balance for dill pickles. The center treats some industries in rather aggregative value terms, and even for those commodities in which it is more interested — things like steel, coal, diesel fuel, cotton, and lathes, that are produced in many regions and used by many industries — it uses fairly aggregative classes. Even so, there are some thousand to fifteen hundred commodities for which material balances are made at the center. Many commodities' balances are made at lower levels; the oil refining industry makes the allocations of specialized products like transformer oil and additives, such as tetraethyl lead and some regional planning agency draws up the plan for locally produced building materials. Perhaps the most important thing to emphasize is that the plan never does get balanced in reality, even if it is forced into balance on paper, and during the year supply and demand are equated by very considerable changes in the plan targets, and by the operation of a priority system that sacrifices the output targets for "buffer sectors," such as housing or consumer goods, to divert the materials promised them to other producers so the latter can meet their targets. It is also important to recognize that the process does not operate just from the top down, but rather that there is a constant interaction between the higher and lower levels of the hierarchy in the formulation of the plan.

This balancing process is a tremendous job, imperfectly done. Moreover, it generates such perverse behavior as that of enterprises, which knowing that their requests are likely to be arbitrarily cut, request more inputs than they really need; higher levels, in turn, feel justified in cutting what they know are padded requests! The same distortion operates with respect to output targets. It is thus an expensive system to operate, both in terms of the time and resources required to carry on the planning procedures themselves, and in the distortions and irrationalities in resource use which it breeds. It is important to point out that some of these costs were smaller and easier to justify when the Soviet economy was less developed, with a smaller number of commodities and enterprises and a more stark set of priorities to guide the adjustments the balancers had to make. The factor of size also explains a differential dissatisfaction that the smaller countries of Eastern Europe have felt with the system, both among countries and within each country as output has grown.

Optimality of the Plan

Balancing supply and demand, as we observed earlier, is not enough — plans should also be "efficient" in the sense that they ensure the largest possible output from the limited resources available. This involves many subquestions. The mix of consumption goods should match what people really want. The goods exported should be those that will produce the most foreign exchange for a given amount of domestic resources used to produce exports. Every input should be used where it makes the biggest possible contribution, or, from another point of view, every output ought to be produced with the combination of inputs that places the least burden on society's resources. That we have said nothing about this in the discussion of Soviet balancing is not accidental; Soviet plan making has never given these issues the attention they deserve. As one writer has said, the Soviet planners for a long time did not even conceive of planning as an optimizing process.

Obviously, decisions on all these matters do get made, but at many different points in the system, and often without anyone ever having considering them explicitly. Some are partly foreclosed by the kind of strategic choices that the top leadership makes. Khrushchev decided that the output mix of agriculture would be better if it included more corn, and its input mix better if it included more fertilizer; he was no doubt right and was able to impose these views from the top. But the details — which farms shifted from wheat to corn, what kind of fertilizer was produced, what crops it was used on — were often settled without careful consideration. Some decisions get made in the execution of plans (discussed in the next section). If an enterprise is unable to fulfill the production plan targeted for it, management must somehow decide what part of the program to abandon or whether to fulfill the quantity indices by lowering quality. It is thus difficult to discuss this aspect of planning in an integrated way; but one aspect that has a certain coherence in planning procedures and that we can appropriately discuss is what the Russians call *project making,* which is essentially the design of productive facilities and equipment. In the process of working out the plan for the power industry, for instance, there comes a point at which someone must design the new generating facilities that will make possible an expansion of electric power output. Once an effort to expand agricultural output by a big increase in fertilizer supply has been decided upon, chemical engineers will have to choose and design a complex of raw-material sources, producing and transforming technologies, and equipment and procedures for using the fertilizer. The institutions that make these decisions in the Soviet Union take many forms — some are research organizations in the Academy of Sciences, some are attached to the central organs of administration, and some are located closer to the bottom of the administrative pyramid. Large projects usually involve the cooperation of a number of such organizations.

In defining the task of the project maker, the planners specify a few main variables. They may fix the location or specify the level of output of the new facility. But even within the limitations imposed by such directives, the project-making planners have a great deal of latitude in choosing among technological alternatives. In designing new electric power plants, for example, the temperature and pressure at which steam is circulated in the system are important technical parameters that the engineer can manipulate. The choices he makes will have important implications for the specifications of the materials used in constructing the equipment and for the thermal efficiency of the station. Technology offers such a range of choice that a mere specification of the general characteristics of a project leaves many questions unanswered. The designers who finally turn out blueprints and specifications must themselves make many decisions, and these decisions affect importantly the allocation of resources. Whether these decisions about resource allocation are made correctly turns mainly on whether the Russians understand the economic issues involved in a given problem and have the information needed to make correct decisions. It is to Marxism, of course, that the Russians have usually turned for guidance on economic issues, and their commitment to this body of doctrine may interfere with their understanding of important issues involved in economizing. Even when their theoretical analysis of an economic problem is correct, the planners may still be unable to make correct decisions because they lack the necessary information. These points can be illustrated with two typical project-making issues – the design of the turbodrill and the location, specialization, and scale of new plants. Other illustrations appear in later chapters.

The Turbodrill. Equipment such as lathes and rockets must be designed. Soviet project makers have often simply copied western equipment designs and followed western patterns in designing whole factories. But there are cases in which they have developed technologies on their own. One of the most interesting examples is the turbodrill. In most of the world, oil wells are drilled by the rotary method, in which a rock-cutting bit attached to the bottom of a long string of steel pipe is rotated in the hole by rotating the pipe. Drilling mud is forced down the pipe string, and flows through and around the bit and back to the surface through the space between the pipe wall and the side of the hole. This circulating mud cools the bit, flushes the crushed rock out of the hole, and counteracts the pressures encountered in the well. Rotary-drilling technology is very demanding in its requirements for quality in the steel pipe and for precision in the machining of the tool joints by which the lengths of pipe are screwed together. Soviet drilling performance has in the past been quite unsatisfactory, partly because the Russians were never able to cope very effectively with these quality problems. The low quality of their pipe and bits meant a large amount of time lost in breakdowns due to broken pipe, lost tools, and the like. The Russians sought to bypass these difficulties by a radical change in the technology, i.e., by developing the turbodrill. In the turbodrill, the bit is powered by a long slim turbine placed at the bottom of the string of drill pipe. The mud that is pumped down the drill string serves as the working fluid to operate the turbine. Thus the turbodrill can be thought of as a kind of hydraulic system for transmitting power to the bottom of the hole, in place of the mechanical transmission principle used in traditional rotary drilling. The turbodrill has, in fact, enabled the Russians to make considerable progress in improving productivity in drilling; but we are interested here in the turbodrill as an illustration of Soviet errors in making design decisions.

In the design of a hydraulic system like that of the turbodrill, there are many choices to be made concerning pressures, the rate of flow of the working fluid, the shape of the turbine vanes, and the diameter of the drill pipe. In choosing values for these parameters, the engineers who designed the turbodrill settled them on the basis of the only criterion they knew — mechanical efficiency. They chose values for the design parameters with an eye to minimizing the amount of power lost through friction and maximizing the power delivered to the bit at the bottom of the hole, thereby speeding up the rate at which the bit cut through the rock. Most of the costs of drilling a well are proportional to time, so that by drilling the hole in a shorter period of time its cost can be reduced. But despite this general economic rationale justifying their goal of engineering efficiency, the designers of the turbodrill technology overlooked some important considerations relevant to economic efficiency. Mechanical efficiency required that the turbine and bit rotate at a high speed, and this shortened the life of bits. The number of feet drilled by a bit before it wore out and had to be replaced was drastically reduced. Shorter bit life means a larger number of bits required to drill a hole to a given depth and an increase in the number of times the drill string must be pulled out of the hole to replace the bit. Such a round trip is a time-consuming operation since it involves raising the string the length of one joint, unscrewing the joint and stacking it in the derrick, and repeating the process until the whole string is dismantled. A new bit is then lowered to the bottom by repeating the whole process in reverse. During the time the bit is being replaced, the hole is not getting any deeper, of course. Thus while the design engineers were pursuing their goal of maximizing the mechanical efficiency of the process and the rate at which the bit penetrated the rock while actually drilling, the economic goal was being undermined by the loss in time from extra round trips, which more than offset the time gained from pushing the bit through the rock more rapidly. The Russians have now recognized that they made a serious mistake here and are seeking to correct it; this will take considerable time, however, since their preoccupation with the turbodrill kept them from doing research and development work on rotary methods. This situation, in which design decisions are in the hands of engineers who do not fully understand or appreciate the *economic* issues involved, is common in the Soviet Union, and the sacrifice of economic efficiency to some engineering prejudice is a characteristic weakness in this sphere of decision making.

Scale, Specialization, and Location of Plants.   Project makers must deal with an extremely complicated group of questions in deciding where to locate industrial plants and how large and specialized to make them. The optimum size of plant in a given industry is determined by such considerations as the savings that result from large-scale production, the transportation costs of shipping the product to the customers in a market area of a given size, and flexibility in service to customers. In most kinds of industrial processes, enlarging the plant, up to a certain point, brings reductions in costs because of the possibilities of better organization and other "economies of scale." There is, however, a point beyond which further expansion brings no economies in production costs but requires that the plant must serve a larger and larger market area. The resulting increase in transport charges will affect delivery cost adversely. The best size for a plant for any given industry is determined by balancing all these factors against one another.

The Soviet system seems to have made some expensive errors in this area of decision making. For example, policies of plant size and location in one important branch of the economy — the iron and steel industry — have been carefully analyzed in one study with the following conclusions: In the

Thirties, the designers of iron and steel plants strove to make them as large and as specialized as possible in order to cut production costs to the minimum. In doing this, however, they more or less ignored a number of important factors that should have been taken into account in deciding the best size of plants from the overall national economic point of view. Rolling mills, for instance, were designed to be so big and so specialized that a single rolling mill could produce the entire output of a particular item for the whole country. This meant very low production costs for that output, of course, but by the time the item was delivered to customers all over the Soviet Union the delivered cost was excessively high. That this could happen was partly the result of the institutional structure of the Soviet economy. The operative goals for the Steel Ministry were cost and volume of output; project makers within the Ministry were instructed to make decisions that would improve these indicators as much as possible. It made no difference to the designers of iron and steel mills that their decisions would involve extra work for the railroad system or that customers would be inconvenienced. That was the worry of the customers and of the railroads. Toward the end of the Thirties, the folly of this approach to planning became obvious. It was found that in a number of areas of the economy the emphasis on large-scale plants and neglect of transportation costs and customer service were wholly undesirable. There followed official condemnation and a campaign against "gigantomania" — a bias in favor of giant plants — and planners were instructed in the future to design smaller plants scattered throughout the Soviet Union. Two other interesting studies of the cement and lumber industry showed that, although transport of output between existing plants and customers has been quite effectively routed, the original decisions about location and capacity meant that more haulage than necessary was being done.

Execution of Plans

No matter how carefully plans and assignments are formulated, administration cannot work without some control over execution. How, in the administrative economy, has it been possible to induce bureaucrats to exert themselves to carry out the plan as formulated? The basic incentive in the management of the SPE is large material rewards for good performance. Successful managers in Soviet-type economies who fulfill and overfulfill plans are well rewarded through bonuses. Bonuses have usually been tied to rather simple aspects of performance (mostly output, with some allowance for cost targets), structured to make it important to fulfill plans in terms of those indicators, and set at a level constituting a significant element in managerial income. A typical scheme might involve bonus payments for fulfilling the output plan equal to 15 percent of the base salary, with an additional 1.5 percent of base salary for each tenth of a percentage point by which costs are reduced compared to plan, and 3 to 5 percent of base salary per percent of overfulfillment of output goals. It is probably these material rewards that work most powerfully to assure dedicated managerial effort, though other motivations, such as a desire to serve society, to exercise power, and to use one's initiative and energy in some creative way, are also operative. Soviet officials have also had to keep in mind some extremely harsh negative sanctions for poor performance, particularly during the Stalin years. Failure to fulfill plans might bring accusations of criminal negligence or economic crimes against the state, and the responsible persons could be imprisoned or shot. Negative sanctions work best if they lurk more or less in the background. Making managers excessively insecure defeats the objective of keeping them productive, and terror as a sanction was probably an aberration of the Stalin period rather than an inherent feature of the system.

Problems in the Administration of Incentives

Cheating. Thus, there are strong incentives to show good performance, but Soviet experience has revealed two important problems. The first is simulation or outright cheating. When the pressures to fulfill the plan are so strong, managers are tempted to comply by "simulation" — achieving the appearance, rather than the substance, of good performance. One of the easiest methods is to arrange beforehand for an easy plan.

In the process of planning, enterprises propose plan targets, and smart management bargains for a small output goal, a generous allocation of materials, and as large a labor force as possible. It is possible to engage in such bargaining because it is very difficult for people at higher levels to know what the performance of an enterprise really should be.

A more blatant form of cheating is to falsify reports of plan fulfillment. To forestall this, the Soviet system maintains an elaborate system of auditing and multiple lines of communication into the enterprise. The principle of multiple lines of communication is illustrated by the position of the chief bookkeeper in the enterprise. In many respects he is not subject to the authority of the manager of the enterprise but to the superior organ, which must approve him and can remove him. The description of his functions and responsibilities makes it clear that his job is to insure accurate reporting to his boss, the bookkeeping department of the superior organ. Another channel of information is the *Gosbank,* the "one big bank," which serves the whole Soviet economy. It is in a particularly strategic position to check on and control an enterprise's actions, since all the monetary transactions of the enterprise pass through its hands. The bank is supposed to check the legality of all the firms' transactions to ensure that prices are in accordance with those fixed by the government, payments are for purposes specified in the plan, and so on.

The Ministry of Finance and the Central Statistical Administration also have some responsibility for checking on the reports of enterprises, and all of them have auditing staffs that have access to the books of an individual enterprise. Finally, two very important channels of communication and agencies for control are the Communist Party and the secret police. In every unit of the economy there are representatives, and perhaps an organization, of the Communist Party, and in many plants of strategic importance the secret police have offices located on the premises.

This may seem an excessively complicated set of controllers to post as watchdogs over the activities of economic units, but in a system like the Soviet economy there is always a danger that people at the lower level, *including the controllers,* will form a coalition against pressure from above. For instance, life is much easier for a Minister if he can report that all the plants for which he is responsible are increasing output and cutting costs. And if enterprises propose relatively easy plans, it may be to his interest not to act the relentless taskmaster but to approve the easy plans and defend them as they pass on up the hierarchy. Similarly, if the Party group within a plant knows that there are unexploited possibilities for increasing output, or even that certain illegal operations are being carried out, it may prefer to remain quiet about such deficiencies so long as every one else thinks the plant is doing a good job. The Russians have a special term — "familyness" ('semeistvennost') — for this phenomenon of collusion among the controllers and the controlled. It constitutes a potential weakness in any bureaucratic structure, and multiple lines of communication widen the circle of persons who would have to be drawn into such a coalition.

The Measurement of Success.   The most serious problem in operating the system of incentives is the choice of appropriate indicators of plan fulfillment. The Russians explicitly rejected profit as a synthesizing indicator of the quality of performance. The whole rationale of the Soviet command system is a belief that the central planners could make better decisions for enterprises than they would make for themselves in the pursuit of profit.

But the fact that so many details are specified complicates the job of the superior organ when it comes to evaluate plan fulfillment. Plans are never so accurate, or the manager's control over his operations so complete, that he will simply fulfill all the indicators exactly. He will do better than the plan on some of the targets but underfulfill some others, or at least meet different targets in varying degrees. A perplexing problem of evaluation arises for the authorities. What should their reaction be if the output plan has been overfulfilled by 10 percent but the planned wages expenditure has been exceeded by 5 percent, or if the plant has produced 20 percent more of one commodity than the plan specified but 10 percent less than the planned amount of another? How can these various indexes of performance be balanced against one another so that it is possible to decide whether or not the plan has been fulfilled and whether or not to hand out rewards or to employ sanctions for failure? Sooner or later there must emerge a set of priorities to guide the controllers in making their evaluations of plan fulfillment. And once the managers have learned what the trade-off between the relative importance of different indicators is, they will adjust their behavior accordingly.

The establishment of the correct system of priorities is a tricky business, however. Whenever controllers give high priority to one particular goal in their evaluation of plan fulfillment, and make that priority effective through bonuses, enterprise managers will violate other parts of the plan in order to fulfill the high-priority indicator.

Bonuses have usually been tied almost exclusively to quantity of output, and enterprise managers have had no incentive to economize on labor, little concern with cost, and little incentive to maintain quality or to innovate. If they could increase output by letting performance on any of these goals deteriorate, the crudity of the payoff system made this their best course.

There is a difficult problem even in measuring output, and the ambiguities inherent in measuring output frequently lead to thoroughly irrational behavior. The total output of any enterprise is likely to consist of many different kinds of output. Even if its output seems to be essentially one kind of product — steel, for example — a simple physical measure of its volume is likely to ignore important economic dimensions of the product, such as quality or degree of fabrication. Thus, to define output in any one way means that the other dimensions can be neglected by the enterprise in its drive to fulfill the output target. When windowglass output was measured in tons, it was advantageous for the enterprise to make glass extra-thick — which meant saving on processing and handling. But from the point of view of the national economy, of course, this meant a reduction in the area that could be covered with a given tonnage of glass. When the measure of output was redefined in areal terms, i.e., square meters of glass produced, the enterprise found it advantageous to make glass extra-thin. The enterprise's effort to do what seemed advantageous to itself meant a waste of resources for the economy as a whole – a Soviet discussion of the problem reported that one-fourth of all glass arriving at construction sites was broken, which the author blamed on the excessive thinness of the glass.

The most widely used measure of output in Soviet industry has always been value of gross output *(valovaia produktsiia).* Since the controllers are especially interested in growth, this indicator has been defined in terms of constant prices so that it can measure increases in physical volume from period to period. Because the measure is gross output, there is a temptation for the manager to fulfill his output plan by emphasizing those products that are "material intensive," that is, products that have large inputs of purchased materials and parts per unit of output. The main bottleneck that the manager faces in achieving the output goal is his limited labor supply and the limited processing capacity of his enterprise. If he spreads this labor and processing capacity over a larger volume of raw materials, he naturally achieves a larger gross output, although the net value his enterprise has added is no greater.

The use of constant prices to measure output frequently stimulates the enterprise to violate the assigned assortment of output. If actual costs change unevenly, some goods become disadvantageous since they take more resources per ruble of payoff. The manager finds it easier to fulfill his output plan by producing large amounts of the high-value commodities that take relatively small amounts of inputs. The others he neglects. Thus there may arise consistent shortages of some goods and excesses of others.

This description of problems in the control function could be greatly expanded, but we will conclude with only two more. The first is the shortness of the control cycle. The most intensive cycle in the Soviet system is the annual one, but the process of checking up and imposing sanctions and rewards is operated at the quarterly and monthly level as well. This leads to the phenomenon of "storming" – a pattern in which most of the work is concentrated in a paroxysm of effort during the last ten days of the month, followed by collapse in the first part of the following month. In oil-well drilling, it is said, the pressure to fulfill monthly footage targets leads drilling outfits to such irrational actions as failing to stop drilling to case a well, as called for in the specifications, and shifting crews and rigs to newly started wells to get the easy footage at the shallower depths. This, of course, imposes heavy burdens on future operations. The short time horizon is one of the important disincentives to innovation. The introduction of new technologies and products is likely to cause short-run disruptions, which management feels it cannot risk.

The other problem concerns the nature of the "payoff functions," i.e., the formulas used for relating performance to bonuses. One difficulty is discontinuities; there is an all-or-nothing quality to the measurement of success. If the plan is fulfilled by only 99.7 percent, no bonus is forthcoming; but if the magic number of 100 percent can be reached, there is a big bonus. One writer describes a taxi driver's reaction to this situation. Toward the end of the month, it begins to look as if he will not meet his output target, expressed in kilometers of paid travel, and will not get a bonus. So he turns on the meter, drives aimlessly about, paying out of his own pocket the fare the meter rolls up. The bonus is large enough so that he will still be ahead. From society's point of view, of course, he is being induced to waste gasoline and other resources and is rewarded for doing so! The example is trivial, but the phenomenon is widespread and extremely disruptive. An analogous problem arises when the payoff function includes several performance indicators, say both cost and output. If the coefficients for each aspect are not set right relative to each other, or if the tradeoff between them is constant, it may work out that only one of them will be operative.

It is difficult to put these aberrations into perspective and judge how serious they are, say, in terms of the loss of potential GNP they impose on the Soviet economy. After all, the U.S. economy is not free of similar problems, since we have large areas of administrative resource management, both within corporations and in the large public sector. Consider the case of the New York City Sanitation Department, which exhibits derangements of a painful similarity to Soviet examples. Its operations are oriented to a simple success indicator — the tonnage of refuse removed from the streets of New York. This is the measure in which the leadership conceives its mission and around which the incentive structure is built, right down to the crews on the streets. There then emerge problems of "advantageous" and "disadvantageous" garbage, with crews poaching on each other's territories to get the advantageous refuse and leaving other areas without attention. The crews have their loads weighed as they drive into the dumps, and a standard form of simulation is to dump their loads incompletely. Driving out with the truck still half full makes the next truckload much easier to gather. Anyone who has worked in a corporate or government bureaucracy can point to examples of these kinds of perverse behavior.

My judgment is that these problems have posed an extraordinarily large burden on Soviet-type economies, much greater than in ours. The phenomenon is much more pervasive there, simply because the administrative system controls so much higher a share of the resource allocation process. But I also believe that the *quality* of administration has been bad in these economies. These difficulties are inherent in any administrative process, but their seriousness can be ameliorated by adaptive response, by internalizing the organizational goals in lower-level decision makers, and by creative effort to generate improvements. The Russians are badly handicapped for creative effort by their general backwardness and by the alienation of the population from the regime. I have been much impressed by the handbook that the U.S. National Aeronautics and Space Administration uses as a guide in its performance contracting, dealing with the problem of multiple performance criteria in the payoff function mentioned above. NASA has multiple objectives for the work its contractors do — early delivery, weight savings, improved reliability, lower cost — and may want to offer bonuses for good performance on more than one. Nothing I had seen in thirty years of reading Soviet discussions of controlling plan fulfillment remotely approached the straightforward analysis of how to deal with this problem that NASA personnel had evolved in a few years.

Also, a secular change in the seriousness of the problem should not be forgotten. It may be that, in the USSR and some of its emulators in Eastern Europe, the wastes and inefficiencies arising from imperfections in the control system were out-weighed until recently by the kind of pressure for growth that this system of crude commands and evaluations enabled the leaders to exert on production enterprises. Whether this judgment can remain valid for the future is more problematical. We will return to this issue in Chapter 6.

3

Basic Institutions of the Soviet-type Economy: (II)
Relations with Households and Agriculture, Money,
and Prices

The relationship of the SPE to the population, we have suggested, is similar to that of the single employer in a company town.
In this relationship there is an illuminating contrast with the
methods used for allocating resources and making decisions
within the production establishment discussed in Chapter 2.
The difficulty of trying to apply the command principle used
within the SPE to the approximately 100 million persons in
the Soviet labor force is obvious. It is as if each person in
a company town were told what occupation to enter, what
skills to acquire, and where to work, and allocated a set of
supporting inputs – a specified ration of consumption items.
Any attempt to do this would be impossibly cumbersome and
inefficient. There are simply too many people involved, and
they are too differentiated from each other in the relevant
respects, i.e., their tastes and talents. Given the tremendous
variations in human personality and the requirements of different jobs, one important element in getting the most out of
the labor force is to match the right person with the right job.

Another is to suit the reward (primarily material) that he earns to his special tastes and circumstances. Because people's tastes are so different, the amount of effort that can be extracted from the labor force will be much less if each worker is simply paid a standard ration than if each is allowed to choose the particular market basket of goods and services that he considers best. The best approach to both these problems would seem to be to let households make their own choices, guiding and controlling them through the use of a price system. A price system has been defined as "the terms on which alternatives are offered." By setting prices on consumer goods and on various kinds and grades of labor, the Soviet regime is telling households the terms on which it will deal with them: "If you want to be a janitor, you can expect X rubles of income; but if you have the talent and are willing to make the effort and acquire the training to become an engineer, and thereby make a bigger contribution to productivity, we are prepared to pay you a much bigger income." At the same time, it is communicating to them by the prices it has set on consumer goods the manifold combinations of goods into which they can translate that ruble income. This approach will secure much more effort from the labor force than the system applied in a military organization or on a slave plantation, which simply assigns a person to a job and doles out the standard ration. Thus even under socialist planning it has been found expedient to organize the link with households in two more-or-less free markets — a consumer goods market and a labor market. Reliance on the market and on the price system to guide decisions in this area imposes a certain discipline, however. The terms offered, i.e., the relative prices on consumer goods and the wage structure, must satisfy certain conditions if the method is to be effective and if the resulting allocation is to be rational.

Financial Equilibrium

The first condition is that the general level of prices in these two markets be set relative to each other so as to achieve macro-balance. The total amount paid out as wages through the labor market must be just sufficient to buy back the consumer goods offered in the other market. Consider the following simplified model of an economy: Suppose that it is planned that the SPE will produce 100 billion rubles' worth of output, of which it is proposed to allocate 60 billion rubles for household consumption, with the other 40 billion to be used for such state objectives as investment or military spending. The creation of 100 billion rubles' worth of goods means paying out to workers money incomes of 100 billion rubles. What makes the aggregate output worth 100 billion rubles is the fact that it has cost 100 billion rubles to produce it, and in the Soviet economy, until recently, the only primary resource for which compensation is paid is labor.[1] Obviously, there is going to be something wrong in this situation. The population will have 100 billion rubles with which to buy 60 billion rubles' worth of goods, and the state will have nothing with which to pay for the 40 billion rubles' worth of investment goods that the planners have caused to be produced for it.

The state could simply create additional money to pay for the investment goods, leaving the population with the 100 billion rubles to spend on 60 billion rubles' worth of goods. But that would be a highly unsatisfactory solution. It is true that, under the system of physical plans, consumers could not divert additional resources into consumer goods production by bidding up consumer-goods prices and making them more profitable. But the excess purchasing power would have a disastrous effect on incentives. There would be no point in going back to the factory to earn more money if one already had money that could not be spent for anything. Thus the physical division of the output of the economy into consumption goods and investment goods must be reinforced by a system of financial controls that absorbs the excess purchasing power and assures financial equilibrium. Somehow 40 billion rubles of the income received by the population will have to be taken away from them and given to the state to use in paying

---

[1] It is true that any production enterprise will have as one of its costs payments to other enterprises for materials. But eventually this outlay ends up as wages to the workers of the supplying enterprises or other workers still further back in the chain of suppliers.

enterprises for the 40 billion rubles' worth of investment goods. The answer, obviously, is some kind of tax. An income tax would have adverse effects on morale. Marginal rates of taxation would have to be so high that people might be discouraged from making the extra effort to produce more or to improve their skills. The regime has worked hard to create the incentive system, and it would not make sense to dilute it by too obvious a tax bite. An income tax would be an obvious kind of exploitation that people would resent.

The technique that Soviet planners have found most satisfactory for mopping up the excess purchasing power is an indirect, invisible tax — the famous "turnover tax." The price that the producer of consumer goods receives is sufficient only to cover his costs and to give him a small profit. In the wholesale distribution network, however, a heavy tax is placed on consumer goods, so that when these goods reach the retailers they are priced at levels far above their costs. The price paid by the consumer has usually been in Soviet-type economies nearly twice the cost of producing and distributing the goods, with the difference accounted for by the turnover tax. Only about half the money paid by the population for consumer goods goes to pay the costs of producing and distributing them — the rest is tax.

Micro-balance — Clearing Individual Markets

Effective use of markets in dealing with households also imposes a necessity for "micro-balance." Relative prices must be set to clear individual markets — they must be juggled to ensure equality of supply and demand for each consumer good and for all the different categories of labor. It would be undesirable for the prices of shoes to be so low that there was a shortage of shoes and the prices of television sets so high that the available supply could not be sold. Such disequilibria in the consumer-goods markets are wasteful of people's time, produce frustration, and, even worse, create the conditions for speculation and black markets. When there are shortages, people spend too much time standing in line and they cannot find the goods they want, and a person who succeeds in acquiring scarce goods can resell them at a large profit to someone else who did not. Such uncontrolled activities, and the incomes to which they give rise, have always been regarded by the Soviet regime as very threatening. Surpluses, also, are an obvious waste from the point of view of the regime — resources tied up in unsalable television sets are not making any contribution toward extracting effort from the population (or in generating satisfaction, if we attribute some altruistic motives to the regime). The same desiderata apply in the labor market — the planners would not want to find that the existing wage pattern failed to attract enough people into some occupation, such as that of bookkeeper, foreman, or nurse, or that it offered insufficient incentive to move people into whatever new projects or new regions they were trying to open up.

Consumer Sovereignty

The requirement of clearing the market is obvious and easy enough to understand — whenever it is not met, shortages and surpluses develop immediately. This is not to say that the planners of the Russian and other Soviet-type economies have usually succeeded in achieving micro-balance, but failure to do so leads to obviously undesirable results that the planners can appreciate. It takes no great sophistication to sense that shortages call for raising prices, and excesses for lowering them. But if the resulting allocation is to satisfy the requirements of rational resource use from the point of view of the socialist planners, another more subtle and less obvious condition must also be satisfied.

Price relationships among consumer goods should be the same as their cost relationships. If a suit costs three times as much to produce as a pair of shoes, the prices at which they are sold to the population should be in the same ratio. This rule suggests that the rate at which turnover tax is charged on consumer goods should be the same for every good. Prices on goods sold to the population will be considerably above what it actually costs to produce them (to solve the macro-balance problem), but the ratio of price to cost should be the same for each good. In the example given above, in which goods costing 60 billion rubles are to be sold at 100 billion rubles, each good should be priced at 1⅔ its cost. The reasoning behind this principle can be understood from the figures in Table 3.1. Imagine that these are the only consumer goods there

Table 3.1   Equilibrium Conditions in Consumer Goods Market

	SHOES	PEANUT BUTTER	SHOES AND PEANUT BUTTER
Number of units sold	2,000 pairs	4,000 kilos	
Actual cost per unit	15 rubles/pair	5 rubles/kilo	
Turnover tax	15 rubles/pair	10 rubles/kilo	
Selling price per unit	30 rubles/pair	15 rubles/kilo	
Aggregate value	30 x 2,000 = 60,000	15 x 4,000 = 60,000	120,000

are, and that both macro-balance and micro-balance have been achieved. That is, at these prices, demand just equals supply for each good, and the aggregate value of the goods of 120,000 rubles just exhausts the purchasing power that has been handed out in wages. The resulting allocation would still be wasteful. Consider the effect of reducing the production of shoes and increasing the production of peanut butter. Given the relative prices, decreasing shoe production and sales by one pair would mean a loss of revenue of 30 rubles. To maintain macro-balance, that 30 rubles would have to be made up by producing and selling more peanut butter to the population — 2 kilos more, to be precise. But a look at the cost figures shows that this shift has saved the regime some resources. The cost of the extra peanut butter (resources worth 10 rubles) was more than covered by the saving of resources in shoe production (15 rubles' worth) and the regime has saved itself 5 rubles' worth of resources, which can now be devoted to some goal such as investment or military spending. And the important point is that this gain was made without diminishing the welfare of the population. Their behavior shows that they are just as well satisfied as before. They were perfectly willing to give up one pair of shoes to get two kilos of peanut butter. As this shift continues, of course, the "market clearing price" for peanut butter would have to come down and that for shoes to rise, by lowering the rate of turnover tax in the one case and raising it in the other. The advantage of further shifts would vanish just at the point we have suggested, i.e., where the ratio of price to cost is just equal for both goods. This conclusion can also be stated in terms of the concept of consumers' sovereignty. We take for granted that in general the choice of how resources ought to be used is in the Soviet-type economy the prerogative of the regime, not of the population. But the example shows that within the limits of the resources allocated for the satisfaction of consumer wants, consumer sovereignty should prevail. This is necessary in order to minimize the volume of resources devoted to consumption, and hence to permit the regime to maximize the attainment of its own goals.

The analogue of this principle in the labor market is that prices must not only equate the supply of each category of labor with the requirement for that kind of labor, but must also be proportional to the productivity of different workers. Raising pay to whatever level is required to attract enough workers to man the coal mines of Vorkuta does not by itself guarantee efficiency — it might turn out that the necessary wage rate is so high that the cost of the coal would be excessive compared to other ways of meeting fuel needs. Just as in the case of the consumer goods market, rationality in the market approach requires adjustment in the quantities of different categories of labor demanded until the market clearing prices are proportional to the contribution each worker makes toward production, as well as to the relative attractiveness to him of different jobs.

The foregoing is essentially theoretical — an exercise in the application of the theory of markets. The question naturally arises of how well the Soviet-type approach to the labor market and the consumer goods market conforms in practice to these requirements for rationality. The answer is complex. In the first two decades of their history, the Russians did a very poor job of achieving macro-balance and suffered from inflation as a consequence. Money incomes of the population always exceeded planned amounts, and this surplus purchasing power was not immediately extracted. The regime, therefore, had constantly to be raising prices of consumer goods to eradicate the unplanned increases in purchasing power. At the same time, the rise in wage payments forced up costs in most enterprises, and the government had to increase wholesale prices on producers' goods as well so that enterprises could cover their costs. This inflation led to many difficulties in the planning and administration of the economy. Changing price levels and changing relationships between physical goods and value magnitudes are bound to complicate planning and control. More recently, since about 1950, financial planning and financial controls have greatly improved and the Soviet economy has managed to prevent inflation and even to achieve some deflation of the general price level. But the most interesting thing about the experience of the Thirties is that slackness in financial controls did not frustrate the channeling of a large portion of the national income into investment. The system of physical controls described earlier made that possible even when financial equilibrium was not attained. The experience of other Eastern European countries has been more or less the same.

Nor have the socialist policy makers honored the micro-balance requirements very consistently. At various times they have introduced a considerable degree of administrative interference into both the consumer goods market and the labor market. They have resorted to rationing in the consumer goods market over an appreciable part of their history, and have used administrative controls and criminal sanctions as a substitute for wage incentives in the labor market. Beginning in the late Thirties, the Russians tried increasingly to make people work at designated jobs by means of coercive labor controls in lieu of wage incentives. Workers were more or less tied to their jobs by means of labor books. The labor book was a permanent work record that the worker had to surrender to his employer on getting a job and unless his employer was willing to release him by returning it he could not move to another job. During this period the law also provided severe punishments for workers who were late for work, came to work drunk, or were absent from work. At one point a worker who was twenty minutes late for work might end up with a prison sentence of two to four months.

Over time the Russians have generally moved toward reliance on market principles and away from administrative direction in both these markets. In the labor market, especially after 1956, there has been a big effort to dismantle the coercive labor controls instituted during the war and to reform the wage system so as to satisfy the micro-balance requirements described above. In the consumer goods market, the Russians have generally preferred to avoid the clumsiness and costs of rationing, though their pricing has never been flexible enough to keep supply and demand in tidy equilibrium. The consequences of this failure — shortages and surpluses — are there for all to see, and the remedy is not hard to figure out.

On the other hand, in none of the Soviet-type economies have the planners been perceptive enough economists to see that it is in the interests of the regime to honor consumers' sovereignty within the limits of resources allocated to consumption. As a matter of fact, they have been much more likely to seek micro-balance in consumer goods markets by juggling turnover tax rates and prices on consumer goods than by adjusting quantities to conform to consumer preferences. This is understandable, in terms both of their failure to grasp the issue at stake and of the way production decisions get made. It will be remembered from Chapter 2 that determination of the mix of consumer goods is made in response to the exigencies of balancing and the pressures of *khozraschet* expediencies. The producers' motivation is to satisfy their bosses, rather than their customers.

How well the wage structure conforms to the relative productivity of different kinds of labor is hard to say. But one would guess that it is easier for decision makers to be nudged in the right direction here by administrative considerations than it is in the area of consumer goods. Soviet and East European discussions of wage setting show a considerable awareness of the importance of productivity considerations in setting relative wages; and, in general, enterprise management is freer to adjust the quantities of labor hired to minimize costs under a given wage structure than are consumer goods producers to alter the mix or quality of consumer goods to produce what people want.

Agriculture

Since agriculture is an important sector in its own right, it will be useful to make a detour here to describe some of the features that distinguish it from the nonagricultural sectors. Along the way we can say something about how the policies of other Eastern European countries have differed from the Russian model. As the discussion in Chapter 1 indicated, the relationship with the peasants was a crucial issue for the designers of the Soviet planning model and development strategy. A large share of all economic activity was in agriculture, so that if incomes were to be diverted to investment, agricultural incomes would have to be restricted. With the possible exceptions of East Germany and Czechoslovakia, the emulators of the Soviet model have resembled the USSR in this respect, and their aspirations for growth have also been based on a hope of extracting a surplus from agriculture. As was suggested in Chapter 2, agriculture is managed differently from the other sectors, being much less fully integrated into the administrative machinery of the SPE.

The story of the controversy over this problem was left in Chapter 1 at the point when Stalin had pushed through a special kind of "solution." It is commonly held that the treatment of agriculture in the classic Stalinist model is an essential feature of the Soviet strategy and one of the ingredients required for Soviet-type growth to take place. But there has been great variability in the way different Soviet-type economies have treated agriculture, implying that the Stalinist approach is not necessarily the best. Also, it is far from certain that Stalin's collectivization solution was really necessary, or actually contributed importantly to Soviet growth. Let us first consider how agriculture has been treated in the classic Soviet model, and then offer an interpretation of the problem that may help in evaluating the rationality of this feature of the Soviet-type model and in offering some guidance for reorganizing it.

Agricultural Organization. Since collectivization, there have existed three rather distinct economies in the Soviet agricultural sector — state farms (*sovkhozy*), collective farms (*kolkhozy*), and private production on the small plots that collective farm members and some other members of the population are permitted to farm. State farms are operated like any other firm in the SPE, and their output is intended primarily for sale to state procurement agencies. There is a relatively small number of them (about 15,000 in 1970); they are worked by a hired labor force; and they are fairly well controlled by the mechanisms of planning and administration used in the SPE generally. State farms are usually rather specialized in certain lines of agricultural production, such as dairying, wheat farming, or ranching.

Collective farms are theoretically cooperative enterprises operated by, and for the benefit of, their members. In fact, central planning has placed many constraints on their autonomy, and they have been exploited by the general techniques suggested in Chapter 2 to provide resources for accumulation. A very large portion of their output is required to be sold to the state. The money income thus earned, together with whatever output has not been sold, is distributed among the members in accordance with their productive contribution as measured in "labor-days." The various jobs are rated, and the collective farmers' work recorded in this unit of account. A labor-day is not literally a day's labor — a day's labor at the more skilled or responsible jobs may be rated at more than one labor-day; for other jobs, it may be less. Until the reforms of the mid-Fifties, the incentive effect of renumeration in labor-days was undermined by the fact that the collective farmer worked for an uncertain share in a future pot of unknown size. More important, because the state has required so much of collective farm output and has paid so low a price for it, the reward to collective farm members has generally been too low even to guarantee subsistence. Thus, for a large part of their income, collective farm members have had to rely on the output of the small private plot permitted each collective farm household. These plots are small (usually somewhat over half an acre) but, by being cultivated intensively, they yield a considerable output, which is either consumed as output in kind or turned into money income by sale on the collective farm market. The collective farm market is the essentially free market described in Chapter 2, in which collective farmers sell surplus produce to the urban population at prices fixed by supply and demand. Workers on the state farms also have private garden plots, though these plots are of much smaller importance in the total. Collective farmers and other citizens are also permitted to own specified numbers of livestock, and in fact a large share of the farm animals in the USSR has always been owned privately. This share has fluctuated and slowly declined, but until quite recently nearly half the milk cows, over a quarter of the pigs, and most of the goats were owned privately. Well over half the chickens are still privately owned. Thus, the collective farm member is typically engaged in two kinds of activity at once — as a generally reluctant participant in collective farm production proper and as a private farmer on his own account. Approximately 40 percent of all Soviet agricultural output originates in the operations of the collective farms, 32 percent on private plots. The remaining quarter is the output of state farms. These general proportions are of long standing. Thus, one of the anomalies of Soviet agriculture is that a third of it was never collectivized!

Agriculture is a hybrid sector in terms of decision making and control in the Soviet economy. The three economies comprising it form a kind of continuum. At one end of the continuum are state farms, whose relatively small number of units, use of traditional incentives, and specialized character make the command principle characteristic of the rest of the economy more or less effective. At the other end of the continuum, the central planners have scarcely attempted to influence decision making in private production. Though they have always tried to restrict and limit its interaction with the rest of the economy, the planners have left this activity almost completely outside the control of the command system. Its purpose is to enable the peasants to take care of their own subsistence and to provide a significant flow of food supplies for urban dwellers. The planners have often tried to levy fairly heavy tribute on this production in the form of taxes and compulsory deliveries but, generally speaking, they do not try to impose their ideas about resource allocation in this area of production.

In the middle of the spectrum is collective production in the *kolkhozy,* which has been the dominant source for supplies of what the SPE requires as inputs of food and agricultural raw materials to be processed. Here the situation is ambiguous — the planners have aspired to impose on collective farm production the kind of central direction they use in the SPE. They issue commands about crop patterns and output goals; they allocate inputs; they try to centralize decision making. In the past, the agencies for transmitting these commands were primarily the machine-tractor stations and the procurement agencies. More recently they have been regional production boards. Also, throughout the period since collectivization, one of the main functions of the local party apparatus has been to see that agricultural plans were carried out. Unfortunately, because of the large number of units, the variety of conditions in which they find themselves, the distance from the controllers, and the disruptive effect of weather on fixed routine, agriculture is just not a very promising sector for control by administrative techniques. It shares with household behavior some of the traits that make it desirable to rely on price to guide behavior.

Agricultural Performance. Performance in agriculture, and especially in this crucial middle sector, has always been very poor. Collective farm agriculture is unreliable, irrational, wasteful, unprogressive — almost any pejorative adjective one can call to mind would be appropriate here. Much data to support this generalization will be considered in Chapter 4. The explanation lies in the inability of the Russians to cope with the basic dilemma described above. The objective conditions would seem to call for a kind of market approach toward agricultural production. The administrative approach has been economic only in certain specialized kinds of agricultural production, such as dairying, truck farms, and the like. Usually when the regime tried to organize agriculture in the form of state farms, they found the result was high costs, partly because they had to pay labor a living wage. On the other hand, the Soviet leaders, pushed by Stalin, decided in the late Twenties that it was not really possible to handle this link by a market approach. The idea was that the regime would have to be exploitative — indeed, confiscatory — toward the population to accumulate resources for industrialization. However, it was much harder to do this in relation to rural households than to urban households. The administrators had a monopoly-monopsony position in relation to urban households — to turn Marxist jargon against its users, the urban worker was alienated from the means of production, which were monopolized by the state.

But the peasants were not equally dependent on the state, and were harder to exploit by paying them lower prices and charging them higher prices. The peasants had the land, the rain, and the sun, and were more nearly able to exist apart from the regime. The Stalinist answer to this dilemma was to use the administrative approach in a most coercive way, forcing the peasants into collective farms and imposing on the collective farms an administrative apparatus made up of the Party, the machine-tractor stations, and procurement officials. But this solution did not work very well, and led to an unstable situation. The failure of coercive administrative techniques called for more coercive methods — attacking the private plots, giving the machine-tractor station power to dictate production decisions, and arbitrarily forcing each region and each farm to deliver its share of the tribute required to meet the overall quotas. The latter disrupted proper regional specialization — everything had to be grown everywhere at whatever cost. Members' unwillingness to work in collective farm production was met with arbitrary requirements about the number of days to be worked by each member. Collective farm management in effect faced a fixed labor supply, which in the accounting of the collective farm cost nothing except the meaningless labor-days, and so management had no incentive to economize on labor. It appears that, toward the end of Stalin's reign, the administration of agriculture simply followed the formula of making the pressure greater as things got worse.

A Model of SPE-Agriculture Relations.   Because of the crucial role collectivization has played in Soviet development, it is worth examining this aspect of the model a bit more carefully. Granted that a Soviet-type SPE finds it necessary to exploit the peasants, how best might it do so, and what factors condition the results? The SPE is going to trade nonagricultural output to the peasants for agricultural output, and would like to get as much as possible while giving up as little as possible. This is almost like two sovereign nations dealing with each other, and we can analyze the situation with the apparatus of offer curves used in international trade discussions. Figure 3.1(a) presents the situation in somewhat oversimplified form, assuming that there is only one agricultural good the SPE is buying (grain), and one nonagricultural good being offered in exchange (fertilizer). We will consider more complications later. Prices are represented in Figure 3.1(a) by a straight line (P_1) through the origin. Any point on this line demarcates on the two axes how much of one good is required to be equal in value to the other, and hence shows the relative value of a ton of grain and a ton of fertilizer. Line P_1 represents a price ratio such that a ton of fertilizer has a price fifteen times that of a ton of grain. A line with a different slope would represent a different relative price, or different terms of trade between grain and fertilizer.

Curve A is the peasants' "offer curve"; that is, it represents their response to all possible prices. For instance, point M is their response to the relative price for grain and fertilizer indicated by line P_1, i.e., a ton of fertilizer priced at fifteen times a ton of grain. Offered that relative price, they would be willing to sell in the aggregate 60 million tons of grain, and would buy 4 million tons of fertilizer. Behind the offer curve lies some kind of calculus on the part of each peasant producer that he would be willing to trade a certain amount of grain for fertilizer at a given price because at that price he can use the fertilizer to produce more grain and still come out marginally ahead. The curve has the shape it does because at the unfavorable (for agriculture) terms of trade represented by a steep price line, there are only limited instances when this exchange is advantageous for some grain producer; as the

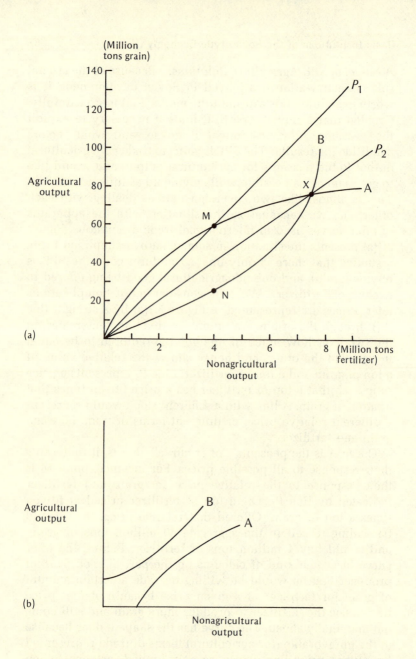

Figure 3.1 Offer Curves and Trade Potential between Agricultural and Nonagricultural Economies

terms of trade become more favorable, the bargain becomes advantageous in more cases. The curve is concave downward because as more fertilizer is used, the effectiveness of additional amounts in increasing grain production decreases, and the trade will be accepted only if the terms are made more advantageous.

Curve B represents the bargaining stance of the nonagricultural economy, the hardest terms that could be driven with producers of fertilizer. It says, for example, that they would be willing to receive as little as 25 million tons of grain for 4 million tons of fertilizer (point N) because in the light of the transformations the nonagricultural economy can make — turning grain into labor, which can be turned into such things as electricity and minerals, which can be turned into fertilizer — 25 million tons of grain is equivalent to 4 million tons of fertilizer. So the offer curves can be thought of as representing the cost of turning fertilizer into grain (agriculture's offer curve) and grain into fertilizer (nonagriculture's offer curve). The relative shape and position of nonagriculture's offer curve are determined by the same kinds of considerations as are those of the peasant's offer curve, and the reader will find it useful to spell out the argument himself. In this situation, in which the farmers can turn fertilizer into grain at a ratio different from that at which nonagriculture can turn grain into fertilizer, there is a great gain to be made by engaging in trade, and either side is prepared to give the other a better trade than is really necessary, considering how badly the other side wants what is offered.

If there were many competing producers of fertilizer and of grain on the respective sides, and free trade prevailed, we would arrive at point X, with about 75 million tons of grain being exchanged for 7.3 million tons of fertilizer. The prices would be the reciprocal of this ratio, i.e., the price of fertilizer per ton would be 75/7.3 times the price of grain per ton. If we started with any other ratio of prices, supply and demand would not be matched. For example, at the price represented by price line P_1 there would be many fertilizer producers who could not sell the fertilizer they would find it advantageous to produce, and they would undercut each other on the price of fertilizer until the terms of trade reached P_2.

The Soviet model differs from this one in that the nonagricultural economy is organized as the SPE, and so has the power of a monopolist-monopsonist in relation to the peasants. The SPE can offer any terms it chooses; that is, it can set the price line at whatever level it chooses, and the individual peasant producer can take it or leave it. The offer curve shows the extent to which the peasant producers as a group will take it. The best outcome for the SPE would seem to be where the gap between the two offer curves is greatest, a point approximated in Figure 3.1(a) by point M on the peasants' offer curve. If the SPE offered the price represented by line P_1, it would get 60 million tons of grain and have to deliver 4 million tons of fertilizer. The amount of grain represented by the gap between the two lines, i.e., about 35 million tons, would be a surplus in the sense that the 4 million tons of fertilizer delivered by the SPE really cost it only 25 million tons of grain to produce. This surplus could be turned into investment goods, foreign exchange, bureaucratic salaries, or any other good the leaders wanted.

Now we come to an interesting question: is it possible that the SPE could do better than this? Suppose the bosses of the SPE told the peasants, "We are requiring you to deliver 70 million tons of grain, and to assist you in doing so we are delivering you 4 million tons of fertilizer." Of course, this implies — in line with the macro-balance problem discussed earlier — that they would be setting the price of fertilizer at 70/4 times the price of grain. The discussion so far suggests that such a trade can be effectuated only if the state is willing to engage in coercion of some sort. The only way to enforce such an ultimatum is to force the peasants to plant the required acreage, make them harvest it, take away the 70 tons of grain demanded, and insist that they use the fertilizer offered. We will return in a moment to the question of whether or not that is feasible.

An Evaluation of Collectivization.   We have a framework for interpreting collectivization. When Stalin said that collectivization was necessary to support the goals of the First Five-Year Plan, and when it is said today that Stalin had no choice but to collectivize, this implies either that there was something anomalous about the position of those offer curves, or that coercion was possible and effective. For instance, it was often argued that the peasants were withholding grain as a political tactic against the Bolsheviks, or that the regime had to procure a minimum ration of grain from the countryside to meet the caloric needs of the urban population, if it was not to place itself in jeopardy. These arguments are akin to saying that the offer curves resembled those in Figure 3.1(b). But that assertion is hard to accept, implying as it does that there was no price that would have been advantageous to both sides. That might make sense for the peasants if they really thought they could topple the regime, in which case their offer curve is no longer an economic-behavioral pattern, but a political bargaining stance. But that this was their position is hard to believe. The position implied for the regime's offer curve seems internally inconsistent — saying that the state needed grain very badly, but contradicting that assertion with another that the need was not so great that the state could afford to give advantageous terms to the peasants to induce them to part with it. Recent research has suggested that the reason for the difficulties in grain collections in the late Twenties — difficulties which were the pretext for collectivization — was not a peasant bargaining stance like the offer curve in Figure 3.1(b) but inept procurement policy. To fully appreciate this argument, we must amend our simple model somewhat to point out that the SPE buys from and sells to the agricultural producers not just one good, but a variety of goods; this makes us realize that, as in the dealings with households discussed above, the problem is not just to set the overall terms of trade correctly, but also to attain the correct price relationships *within* the bundles of goods being bought and sold. There is sound evidence that the difficulty in grain collections was due to the state's procurement organs not only having tried to keep agricultural prices too low, but also having set the procurement prices for meat too high relative to those for grain, so that it became advantageous to agricultural producers to convert grain to meat before responding to the regime's offers of trade.

Another possible view of collectivization and of the regime's relationship to agriculture is that the regime was greedy or overambitious — the Party leadership wanted to grow fast and thought that they could consistently coerce out of the peasants more than the surplus we have described, i.e., the maximum gap between the offer curves, and thus grow faster. This is the kind of interpretation that is sometimes offered when people try to rationalize collectivization as part of a strategy to make a Soviet-type economy grow unusually rapidly. But it is abundantly clear that such a policy is not in fact very effective. Coercion is costly in the resources required to administer it, and in the Soviet case there was a special cost — the heavy losses of livestock. Peasants killed and ate a large part of the animals they owned rather than handing them over to the collective farm. Livestock numbers dropped catastrophically at the time of collectivization, and reached precollectivization levels again only in the Fifties. There was widespread slaughter of horses also, so that most of the expensive investment the regime made in machine-tractor stations as part of its collectivization policy went to make up for the lost draft power of the horses that had been sacrificed. Much of the increase in grain procurements was accounted for by the reduction in the amount of output previously fed to animals, which could now be used to feed humans instead. Thus the surplus that the regime seemed to be extracting from agriculture as a result of collectivization was in part illusory — it was offset by a big flow of investment goods to replace horses, and was in part due to a reduction in the quality of the diet. In addition, after collectivization the SPE was no longer getting grain converted into animal products but grain itself, and so the "surplus" was not extracted from agriculture, but from the whole population. That looked like a gain, since grain consumed by humans as bread provides more calories per ton of grain than if it is processed into meat.

But the more serious consequences of the collectivization decision were long-range ones. Economic development should cause an outward movement of the offer curves, as illustrated in Figure 3.2. Remember that each of these curves is based partly on the technology of turning one product into the other, and that economic development should result in technical change that reduces most of the related technical input coefficients. It is a regularity of modern economic development that the amount of fertilizer, energy, and capital inputs required to produce a ton of grain falls. In the nonagricultural economy, as productivity rises, it takes less grain to feed the workers who produce the inputs that go into producing the fertilizer, energy, and capital inputs that are exchanged with agriculture. The present model is based on the idea that the SPE appropriates all the surplus, but to the extent the SPE allows incomes

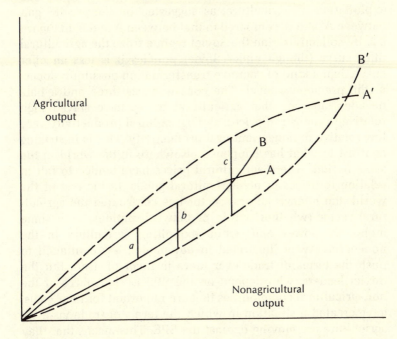

Figure 3.2 Presumed Shift in Offer Curves Due to Economic Development

Curves A and B represent the offer curves at the beginning of the development drive. Because of growth and technical progress, the SPE's offer curve moves outward towards B'. But if coercion and administrative interference operate to stultify progress in agriculture, and prevent its offer curve from moving out to A', the potential surplus that the SPE could extract will increase only from a to b, rather than from a to c.

to rise, among either urban or rural households, the low-income elasticity for food should also have the same effect. For example, as peasants' real incomes rise, their basic preferences are likely to incline them to exchange grain they would otherwise consume for industrial consumer goods on terms ever more favorable for the producer of nonagricultural consumer goods. A similar inclination on the part of urban households means that the SPE will find it increasingly cheaper to turn grain into fertilizer.[2]

The consequence of such a dynamic would have been to increase the surplus that could have been generated by the exploitation of agriculture, as suggested by the greater gap between A′ and B′ compared to that between A and B′ in Figure 3.2. By collectivization the Soviet regime froze the agricultural offer curve (though under Soviet policies it is less an offer curve than a kind of coercive transformation possibility locus) at the premodern level. The consequences three and a half decades later are that agricultural prices have stayed high relative to industrial prices, and agricultural productivity very low relative to nonagricultural productivity. This is in striking contrast to what has happened elsewhere in the world in the same period, where agricultural prices have tended to fall in relation to prices of nonagricultural goods. In the rest of the world, the nonagricultural sector has confronted the agricultural sector (whether within or between nations) with some monopoly power and, while exploiting agriculture in the noncoercive way illustrated in our model, has continued to push the terms of trade ever more in favor of itself. But the Soviet leaders, who depend on the SPE as the source of the nonagricultural commodities that are important for their goals, have created a situation in which the terms of trade vis-à-vis agriculture are moving *against* the SPE. This means that they have had to hand back to agriculture an astonishingly large share of the output of the SPE to obtain agricultural goods

---

[2] The main threat to this happy trend would be a population dynamic in which population grew faster than food supply. How serious a danger that was is a difficult question to answer — actual Soviet population growth was very small, as we will see, but that was partly a consequence of the package of repressive measures of which collectivization was an integral and perhaps causal part.

and to achieve even modest increases in their amounts. One of the contradictions in western thought about the Soviet economy has been to say that the bosses of the SPE have stinted agriculture for resources, while the figures show that they have steadily devoted to agriculture (except during World War Two) about 15 to 20 percent of investment, compared to the 3 to 5 percent of American investment that goes to agriculture. And, as will be seen, the investment share of which this is a fraction is much larger in Soviet than in U.S. national product.

An interesting study by a Soviet writer shows that during the First Five-Year Plan the flow of goods from the SPE to agriculture grew more rapidly than the flow from agriculture to the SPE. And there are interesting conclusions to be drawn from a more disaggregated look: The SPE did succeed in turning the terms of trade sharply against collective farms proper, but lost much of this gain in the heavy investment it had to make in state farms and in machine-tractor stations; the peasants regained much of the loss by selling produce from their private plots at very high prices on the collective farm market. The levy on peasants was in part shifted to urban households.

It is difficult to escape the conclusion that collectivization was a colossal policy blunder that did little to enhance growth. And one of the most tragic and ironic things about it is that because it was such a blunder, with such painful consequences, it is a kind of sacred cow. As we will see in Chapter 8, there have been important changes in agricultural policy since Stalin's death, but the basic institution of the collective farm seems inviolable.

How to handle the relationship with a small-scale peasant agriculture has been a central issue for all Soviet-type economies, because they are all relatively underdeveloped and because the Soviet experience looms so large in the thinking of their leaders. Most of them have thought they had to socialize and exploit agriculture, and most of them have made some use of the main Soviet institutions — the state farm, the collective farm, and the machine-tractor station — while leaving some room for private production. More will be said about this subject in Chapter 5. Here let us simply point out that, in general, the borrowers of the Soviet model have treated agriculture more cautiously and pushed collectivization more slowly than the Russians did. Two countries, Yugoslavia and Poland, have managed without collectivizing agriculture, and all have been content to exploit agriculture more along the lines described above than in a frontally coercive way.

Prices and Money in the Soviet Model

The foregoing discussion of the relations of the SPE to households and agriculture has contained many references to prices and financial aggregates. Aggregate household incomes and outlays, relative prices of the various agricultural commodities, and relative level of prices on the goods sold to agriculture and the goods purchased from agriculture have all been mentioned. The importance of these prices has been made clear, as have the principles that ought to guide planners in setting them. In recapitulating, we need only emphasize that in these transactions between the SPE and other sectors, prices are important, since the actions of the people in those sectors will be guided by them. Thus an arbitrary approach to setting prices may cause great difficulties in operating the economy. What has not been mentioned, however, is the role of prices and money *within* the SPE. How are they set? Do they matter?

Briefly, the answer is that prices and money play a much more limited role within the SPE, where the behavior of decision makers is guided more by commands and plans sent down from above than by prices and such monetary indicators as profit. Administration is mostly conducted in the language not of money and prices, but of commands, physical allocations, policies, and success indicators expressed in physical or quasi-physical form. But under the principle of *khozraschet,* enterprises do use money in their transactions with each other, the things they buy and sell have prices, and the physical targets and physical allocations that constitute their plans are converted through prices into financial plans for cost and value of output, profit, investment, and so on. What, if any, consequences do these prices have for the behavior of the decision makers within the SPE, and are prices set with an eye to guiding this behavior in the right direction?

These prices certainly have consequences for the behavior of administrators. We have already mentioned that prices are used in aggregating the various outputs of an enterprise to determine its gross value of output, or *valovaia produktsiia,* and that to the extent that the manager can control the composition of his output, he will be sensitive to and will react to the relative prices on the alternative things he might produce. Note that what matters here is not the actual transaction prices but the constant prices in which *valovaia produktsiia* is measured. Another area where prices play an important role is that of project making, described earlier. These decisions always involve weighing one set of considerations against another. The questions take the forms "Is the extra output worth the extra cost?" "Is the saving in the future worth the extra cost right now?" "Is the cost of this way of doing something more or less than the cost of doing it some other way?" The function of prices is to reduce all the considerations on each side of such questions to a single number, representing the cost or value, so that one can determine which way is cheapest or whether the value of the output equals or exceeds the cost. In deciding whether it is best to dieselize or electrify a given section of railway line, for example, the alternatives involve very different combinations of inputs and, in order to see which is cheapest, each of these combinations must be aggregated by means of prices. If prices are not a fairly accurate reflection of the real burden to the economy of producing these alternative combinations, there is a danger that decision makers will choose the alternatives that look cheapest on paper but are not cheapest in reality. Similarly, if the prices to which the *khozraschet* decision maker refers, in deciding what is most advantageous for him in terms of the established success indicators, depart very far from the real value of output or the real costs of inputs, the pursuit of his local interest will be wasteful of resources from society's point of view.

The kind of prices the Soviet-type system has operated with, both in the USSR and in other communist countries, does indeed seem to be a very imperfect measure of the real costs of resources. In the Soviet-type economy, prices are set not by supply and demand but by administrative order. Most prices are set by fairly high-level organs of government, others by price-setting organs in the ministries or economic councils, and some by local authorities. The point of departure for setting most prices is supposed to be the reported cost of production but, in practice, prices usually depart considerably from the actual costs of production. The prices of some goods reflect large subsidies, while others have been set high enough to return very high rates of profit. Moreover, prices customarily do not include any charges for rent or capital and seldom reflect the use value to the customer. Once set, prices have remained fixed for long periods of time. This is an important administrative convenience for the planners in making their calculations and drawing up plans, but it means that, as costs change with the passage of time, prices get out of line with costs. As a result of these peculiarities in the planners' accounting and pricing system, the price placed on a good has often been an inaccurate measure of what it really cost to produce or what it was worth.

The current interest in externalities, and the many ways in which social cost may diverge from private cost in a market economy, also prompts one to ask how well Soviet prices allow for such social costs as water pollution, and other such indirect effects. A great deal of research has been done on this question in the last few years, demonstrating emphatically that the Soviet model seems to have no special virtues here. The prices to which decision makers in the SPE react do not assess environmental costs, and the Soviet system has compiled a very poor record of environmental disruption to date. The social costs of air and water pollution, natural resource depletion, and the like are not communicated to decision makers via either prices or nonprice signals, and under the pressure to expand output and fulfill plans, planners and producers generally ignore environmental costs. Indeed, because the Soviet-type price system has omitted on principle any charges even for such appropriable natural resources as minerals and land, socialist producers have not felt the pressure that capitalist firms feel to use such resources economically.

With such distortions in the price system, it is very difficult for planners and decision makers to know whether their choice of the cheapest way of doing something is realistic. Soviet planners themselves have frequently expressed doubts about the validity of calculations based on existing prices. In many cases they have tried to make unofficial corrections of existing prices to render them more nearly accurate measures of real cost to the national economy, but such guesswork corrections are likely to be arbitrary and inaccurate. Because the Russians, as Marxists, did not appreciate the function of prices or understand the principles of price determination, they never took them very seriously or quite understood how to set them properly. The meaning and usefulness of prices has been one of the revelations they have had to cope with in their efforts to reform the economy; we will return in Chapter 7 to a discussion of the recent revolution in economic thought in the socialist world, which has led to a better understanding of the concept of value and the proper principles of price formation. Chapter 8 will explain how prices have been improved in the reforms of the Sixties.

II

The Economic Performance of
Soviet-type Economies

4

The Soviet Economic Growth Record

This chapter will discuss how well the distinctive set of institutions we have described has performed in achieving the various objectives one might postulate for any economic system. In particular, how well has it fulfilled the special goal the Soviet leadership posed for it of "overtaking and surpassing the advanced capitalist nations"? Success on this score might be evaluated in terms of two more specific questions: How fast has the Soviet economy grown, and how big is its output today compared to U.S. output? We might also ask about efficiency and productivity; these are important factors in interpreting past growth, in evaluating performance, and in judging the reserves for future growth.

The Measurement of Output and Growth

Thinking about economic growth requires that one master a primer of three basic economic ideas: (1) the notion of the gross national product (usually abbreviated as GNP) and its components, (2) the rate of growth of these magnitudes, and (3) the notion of an index. The gross national product can be described simply enough as the total output of a country's economy. The practice of national income accounting embraces a whole family of related concepts, differing in their precise definitions but all intended to measure the total output of an economy during a given period such as a year. Thus when the United States Department of Commerce reports that the GNP of the United States in 1971 was 1,050 billion dollars, this means that the total amount of automobiles, new highways, clothing, and all the diverse outputs produced in that year was 1,050 billion dollars' worth. This total includes not only the concrete physical objects produced but also such intangible "goods" as the services of doctors, teachers, and basketball players.

The "gross" in GNP refers to the fact that no allowance has been made for capital consumption — the wear and tear on capital stock — that the year's production activity involved. When this allowance has been made, we speak of net national product, or NNP.

It is useful for many purposes to know not only the total amount of output but also something about its composition. The total GNP can be broken down in various ways, of which two are important for our purposes here. (1) The first is according to end use — that is, how much of the total went for current satisfaction of people's wants, how much was invested in the creation of capital assets such as machines and factories, how much was used by the government for military and other purposes, and so on. (2) The second breakdown is according to the sector of origin — that is, how much of the total consisted of goods manufactured in factories, how much of agricultural output, and how much of services. Both these analyses can be undertaken with various degrees of fineness.

The absolute size of GNP tells little about economic performance or about efficiency. But the study of a nation's GNP over time gives us a useful measure of its economic performance and, indeed, the growth of GNP is one of the most commonplace measures of the progress of an economy.

Comparisons of economic magnitudes such as GNP or industrial output are often expressed by means of *indexes*. A series of annual GNP figures, expressed in terms of dollars, can be translated into an index in the following way: A value of 100

Table 4.1   United States GNP, Measured in 1958 Prices

YEAR	IN BILLION DOLLARS	AS AN INDEX
1929	203.6	100
1933	141.5	69
1939	223.2	103
1944	361.3	177
1950	355.3	174
1971	739.5	363

is assigned to the figure for one of the years, called the base year, and all the other figures in the series are assigned values on this scale representing their size relative to the base year figure. (See Table 4.1.) For instance, if GNP in 1929 is assigned a value of 100, then the index for GNP in 1971 would be 363 (i.e., 739.5 divided by 203.6 times 100) and so on for the other years. Use of indexes also makes it possible to express diverse time series, such as GNP measured in dollars, employment measured in man-hours, or Soviet GNP measured in rubles, in terms of the same units.

How fast an economy grows is usually expressed in terms of the *percentage rate of growth* of GNP, industrial production, or other aggregates. The total output of the American economy in 1971 was 740 billion dollars, as against 720 billion dollars the year before, an increase of 2.7 percent. (The index would be 102.7.) When we consider a longer period of time, say from 1950 to 1971, we speak of the *average annual rate of growth,* also expressed as a percentage. Gross national product in 1950 was 355 billion dollars, and in 1971, 740 billion dollars. On the average, if one starts with an output of 355 billion dollars in 1950, by what percentage would output have to be raised each successive year in order to end up with 740 billion dollars by 1971? The answer is 3.7 percent per year.[1] Output did not

---

[1] The formula for this and similar calculations is very simple, i.e., $355(x)^{21} = 740$. It simply recapitulates in the form of an equation the question we asked above; namely, what number applied to the preceding year's output for 21 successive years will get us from an output of 355 billion dollars to one of 740 billion? The solution of the equation, $x = 1.037$, means that the multiplier would have to be 1.037—an increase of 3.7 percent. Other ways of conceptualizing the average annual rate of growth are possible, and perhaps preferable, but for simplicity we will use this one throughout.

actually rise by that exact percentage each year but, taking the period as a whole, this was the average percentage growth from year to year.

How fast the Soviet national product and its components have grown turns out to be a very difficult question to deal with, because of the peculiarities of Soviet economic statistics and certain difficulties inherent in trying to measure the growth of aggregative economic magnitudes. Because the question of the Soviet rate of growth is a controversial one, concerning which there are widely divergent opinions among the general public and even among economists working on the problem, it is desirable to explain the essence of the problem as carefully as possible.

Peculiarities of Soviet Statistics

There is a very large literature on the problems of using Soviet economic statistics (and those of other socialist countries, where the problems are identical), but we can summarize the main difficulties under three headings.

First, socialist statistics often employ concepts recommended more by ideology than by usefulness in measuring economic performance. The most important of these distortions is the idea that what should be measured as the output of the economy is "material production." As indicated earlier, the western concept of GNP includes the output of both *goods* and *services*, since both place a drain on society's resources and both contribute to welfare. But following a Marxian distinction, socialist statisticians generally consider the production of services a "nonproductive" activity, in contrast to the "productive" activity of producing material goods, and hence exclude nonproductive activities from their aggregate measures of the economy's output. Industry, agriculture, and construction are examples of material production, while education, housing, and the services of soldiers and scientists are examples of nonproductive activity. This ill-conceived distinction is difficult to apply consistently. Faced with what to do about transport and communication, the theoreticians decided that since freight transportation "serves" material production, it should be considered material production, though passenger transport is not. Trade, though it is really a service, is thought of as an "extension" of material production, with its output included in the national product, though here the distinction between serving households and serving producers is ignored. There are some differences among socialist countries on these matters (the Eastern Europeans usually define all transport and communication as productive, for instance). Also, there is now a growing recognition that it may be useful to compile a broader measure of the economy's output that includes services. As output per capita rises, so that these countries can afford to devote an increasing share of their resources to providing services rather than material goods, the present measure is likely to understate actual growth. But for the present, the national income and output figures compiled and reported in these countries refer only to material production; to obtain a comprehensive picture of how they use their resources and how total output of the economy has grown, it is necessary to make our own calculations of their GNP.

A second reason for caution in accepting official statistics is that there are very strong pressures in the administratively organized economy to produce statistics that exaggerate output. The statistics are reported by people with an important stake in what they show, since they are the measures on which rewards are based. Two illustrations will suffice to explain the problem.

1. There has always been a problem with pricing new products. Many measures of output are calculated in "constant prices," i.e., the output of a Soviet industrial firm in 1975 is reported both in actual prices and in the prices of 1973, so that it is possible to compare 1975 output with that of 1973 without having the issue confused by the effect of price changes. But new products are continually being introduced for which no price existed in the base year. There is thus a certain latitude in establishing a hypothetical "constant price" for such a product, and this latitude is likely to be used to exaggerate the growth in output. Indeed, it may be to the interest of the enterprise to create such situations. It has a motive to modify slightly some item it is presently producing,

say a machine, and to get it designated a new product for which it may be possible to get an inflated "temporary" price established, which will then serve as the constant price for that new product. In this way a firm could show an increase in output in constant prices even if it were producing about the same number and kind of machines as before.

2. One of the most serious distortions involves the switch the Russians made in the Thirties from barn yield to biological yield in the measurement of crop output. In the Thirties grain output came to be reported in terms of biological yield — i.e., an estimate prepared before harvest by sampling in selected areas to estimate the weight of grain per unit area when mature, and then extrapolating this to an estimate for the whole country. This process contains numerous elastic linkages (in the representativeness of the sample, the projection to maturity, adjustment for harvest losses, and so on) and eventually, under the pressure to present a favorable picture of the grain situation, the grain crop as reported exceeded by one third that actually harvested and delivered into storage. Because of the political importance of this indicator, the connivance at distortion extended to the very top levels of the hierarchy, and the system became a victim of its own deceptions, until Khrushchev finally eliminated this scandal in the Fifties. Ironically, he later fostered an analogous situation when his pledge to catch up with America in meat, milk, and butter output led to purchase quotas that the hardpressed procurement officials could meet only by selling back to the farms some of the output they had already purchased so that they could buy it a second time.

Such outright falsifications are corrected eventually, but a more subtle kind of degradation of the data under the stress of the success indicator system never gets corrected. Since output indicators are likely to cover only some dimensions of output, managers respond by making any adjustments they can in other dimensions to improve their showing on the measured dimensions, say by reducing quality to enhance quantity. In the Soviet cement industry, where the producers lowered the average quality to meet the quantity goals, the quantity increase was exaggerated, since more of the lower-strength cement was needed to meet strength specifications in constructing a building. In fact, a real measure of the cement output increase, would have necessitated adjustments for all the extra aggregate, extra transport, and the like, that the use of lower-quality cement imposed on the economy.

Our quarrel is thus not solely with the aggregations that Soviet statisticians have made; we also need to treat with some caution the raw material out of which we fashion our own aggregate indicators of output and growth. Much of the work of the specialist on the Soviet and East European economies lies in determining the meaning of published statistics.

The Index Number Problem

Finally, in evaluating either the progress of the system over time or its performance compared to that of another country, there is a problem of pricing — finding common denominators for the collections of goods and services being compared. In measuring growth, we are trying to answer the question, "How big is the collection of goods the economy produced in 1970 compared to the collection it produced in 1928?" In trying to determine how far the Soviet Union has come in catching up to us, we want to know how big the collection of goods and services the Soviet economy produces in a given year is compared to the collection the U.S. economy produced in the same year. In assessing priorities and policies, we are determining such things as the volume of resources the Russians channel into investment in a given year compared to all the resources they disposed of, i.e., GNP, in that year.

Consider first comparisons over time and comparisons between the U.S. and the Soviet output. There is no *conceptual* difficulty in individual elements of these comparisons. We could easily determine how many locomotives or pairs of shoes were in one collection compared to the other, though there would be problems of adjusting for differences in quality and of goods unique to one collection.

But these individual answers concerning relative output are not unanimous. The collections compare in locomotives differently than they do in peanut butter, and an overall measure of increase in output or comparative size requires that we combine these separate answers into a single answer, giving each partial answer an appropriate weight in synthesizing the whole.

The common-sense answer to how important a place should be given the locomotive comparison relative to the shoe comparison should be how important locomotives are in the collection compared to shoes. In trying to decide how close the Chinese have come to catching up to the Russians, no one would give much weight to the fact that the Chinese outproduce the Russians in soy sauce. That activity takes so little of either society's resources that it shouldn't be given much weight in the overall evaluations. The best measure of the importance of a pair of shoes relative to a locomotive would seem to be

Table 4-2. Data for the Computation of an Industrial Output Index

	1926 output	1926 prices	Value in 1926 prices	1939 output	1939 prices	Value in 1939 prices
Tractors	500	3,000 R	1.5 MR	2,000	9,000 R	18 MR
Shoes	20,000	50 R	1 MR	20,000	300 R	6 MR
Total	—	—	2.5 MR	—	—	24 MR

Table 4.3. Computation of Industrial Output Index Using 1926 Prices

	1926 output	1926 prices	Value in 1926 prices	1939 output	1926 prices	Value in 1926 prices
Tractors	500	3,000 R	1.5 MR	2,000	3,000 R	6 MR
Shoes	20,000 prs.	50 R	1 MR	20,000 prs.	50 R	1 MR
Total	—	—	2.5 MR	—	—	7 MR
Index			100			280

Table 4.4. Computation of Industrial Output Index Using 1939 Prices

	1926 output	1939 prices	Value in 1939 prices	1939 output	1939 prices	Value in 1939 prices
Tractors	500	9,000 R	4.5 MR	2,000	9,000 R	18 MR
Shoes	20,000 prs.	300 R	6 MR	20,000 prs.	300 R	6 MR
Total	—	—	10.5 MR	—	—	24 MR
Index			100			229

price, and the usual practice in these comparisons is to add up the value of each collection by using the same set of prices for each. This will perhaps be more easily understood through use of a concrete example. Imagine a hypothetical economy with a very simple industry sector that produces only two industrial products, tractors and shoes. Assume that the output and prices of these products in two different years are those given in Table 4.2. The question to be answered is, "How much has total industrial output grown between the two years?"

Clearly it is improper just to compare the rubles' worth of output in the two years, since much of the increase from 2.5 million rubles to 24 million rubles has been caused by the rise in prices rather than by a real growth in physical output.

← *Note to tables:* The formula for the weighted index, starting from the information on outputs and prices given to Table 4.2, can be spelled out as follows, where T stands for tractors and S for shoes:

$$\frac{\dfrac{\text{1939 output of T}}{\text{1926 output of T}} \times \dfrac{\text{1926 price of T}}{} \times \dfrac{\text{1926 output of T}}{}}{\dfrac{\text{1926 output of T}}{} \times \dfrac{\text{1926 price of T}}{} + \dfrac{\text{1926 output of S}}{} \times \dfrac{\text{1926 price of S}}{}} + \frac{\dfrac{\text{1939 output of S}}{\text{1926 output of S}} \times \dfrac{\text{1926 price of S}}{} \times \dfrac{\text{1926 output of S}}{}}{\dfrac{\text{1926 output of T}}{} \times \dfrac{\text{1926 price of T}}{} + \dfrac{\text{1926 output of S}}{} \times \dfrac{\text{1926 price of S}}{}}$$

The reader can easily satisfy himself that this expression reduces to

$$\begin{array}{c}\text{Index of output} \\ \text{of T}\end{array} \times \begin{array}{c}\text{T as percent} \\ \text{of total output in 1926}\end{array} + \begin{array}{c}\text{Index of output} \\ \text{of S}\end{array} \times \begin{array}{c}\text{S as percent} \\ \text{of total output in 1926}\end{array}$$

Looking back at the longer formula, the numerator can be simplified by cancelling out the terms denoting output in 1926. When this is done, the formula becomes

$$\frac{\dfrac{\text{1939 output of T}}{} \times \dfrac{\text{1926 price of T}}{} + \dfrac{\text{1939 output of S}}{} \times \dfrac{\text{1926 price of S}}{}}{\dfrac{\text{1926 output of T}}{} \times \dfrac{\text{1926 price of T}}{} + \dfrac{\text{1926 output of S}}{} \times \dfrac{\text{1926 price of S}}{}}$$

which is identical with the computation carried out in Table 4.3. Thus a procedure in which we weight indexes for individual commodities is formally identical with one in which we compute value of output in constant prices. We can use or think in terms of whichever one is more convenient.

To make a valid comparison, it is necessary to measure the output of both years in identical prices. One possible approach would be to calculate what the value of output in 1939 *would have been if prices had not risen since 1926* and then compare this with the actual value of output in 1926, which, of course, is already measured in 1926 prices. This is done in Table 4.3. Total output in 1939, measured in 1926 prices, is 7 million rubles (MR), as compared to 2.5 MR in 1926. If these figures are converted to index form, the index of output in 1939 would be 280.

This index number will acquire some additional meaning if it is explained that it can be determined by a somewhat different computational route, as follows: If the outputs of shoes and tractors are considered separately, an index of output can be determined for each, without using any prices at all, by comparing the physical amounts in the two years. Thus in 1939 the index for tractors is 400 and that for shoes is 100. Those are partial answers to the question posed earlier. The index for all industry is obviously some sort of an average of the two. But if one examines the situation in 1926, it appears that tractors made up more than half of total industrial output, and shoes less than half. Since the two commodities are not of equal importance, we do not want a simple average of the two indexes, in which we would just add them and divide by two. Instead, we want an average that gives the separate indexes their proper weight in the average index. Such an index is called a "weighted" index. Since tractors make up 60 percent of total output and shoes 40 percent, we make up the weighted average by adding together 60 percent of the tractor index and 40 percent of the shoe index, as follows:

$$400 \times .60 + 100 \times .40 = 240 + 40 = 280$$

This approach gives the same index as before, i.e., 280, because arithmetically it actually amounts to the same computation as was performed in Table 4.3.

Here we come to a major problem. Instead of using 1926 prices, we might alternatively add up the value of each year's output *in the prices of 1939*. But if this is done, a different answer is obtained, as may be seen by looking at the calculation carried out in Table 4.4. In 1939 prices, total output of industry rose from 10.5 MR in 1926 to 24 MR in 1939, which gives an index of 229. But the index in 1926 prices was 280. Why is the answer different when 1939 prices are used as the constant prices?

Essentially, the answer is that the prices of tractors and shoes relative to each other were different in 1939 and in 1926. The influence of this change in relative prices can be most easily comprehended by thinking in terms of the weighted index approach to the overall index. It will be remembered that using the 1926 prices was equivalent to calculating a weighted average for all industry by taking 60 percent of the tractor index and 40 percent of the shoe index. These were the respective percentages of the two commodities in total output in 1926, in 1926 prices. But if the 1926 output is valued in 1939 prices, it turns out that tractors were only 43 percent of total output, rather than 60 percent, and that shoes were 57 percent, rather than only 40 percent. The relative share of tractors and shoes in total output in 1926 is different in 1939 prices than in 1926 prices because tractors were less valuable relative to shoes in the 1939 price structure than in the 1926 price structure. If these percentages are inserted in the formula for the weighted index approach, the result is

$$400 \times .43 + 100 \times .57 = 229$$

Using 1939 prices gives more emphasis in our average to the growth of the shoe industry, which is low (in fact, nonexistent), and less to the growth of the tractor industry, which is quite high. The result, naturally, is a lower average index for industry as a whole.

The situation illustrated by this example has been very common in the Soviet economy. Those commodities that have grown the most have also experienced declines in their prices relative to other, slower-growing commodities. This is typical of the early industrialization experience of most countries. In such a period, those outputs that grow fastest are generally the ones that experience the greatest increases in efficiency of production, and therefore also experience reductions in costs and prices relative to other goods. As the Soviet Union industrialized, the output of "traditional" commodities like shoes did not increase much, and no great gains were made in the productivity of the shoe industry. But the output of such goods as tractors increased very rapidly and, because these were new branches of production, they experienced great gains in efficiency and a lowering of costs and prices relative to other goods. The long-continued use of the prices of early years (i.e., 1926/27) in the calculation of the official Soviet index of industrial output made it show much higher growth than an index based on the prices of some later year. Eventually, the Russians shifted to the use of prices from later years, and it is thought the index number effect is less important in their measures of growth since World War Two. But the index for earlier years is still based on the 1926/27 prices, so that Soviet claims about growth for the whole period of their growth must still be discounted.

This issue of what prices are used, known as "the index number problem," also arises in comparisons of U.S. and Soviet output, as can easily be understood if one thinks of the 1939 situation in the above example as representing the U.S. economy in a given year and the 1926 situation as representing the Soviet economy in the same year. In this interpretation, adding up each country's output of shoes and tractors in 1926 prices is to compare the two outputs valued in rubles, while using 1939 prices is like valuing each country's output in U.S. dollars. The result in this case — that comparison of the two GNPs in dollars makes the Soviet output look closer to U.S. output than does valuation of both in rubles — does in fact emerge when we try to compare the Soviet and the U.S. GNP.

Since we can always get two answers, we need to think hard about which is preferable. An answer requires that we first specify more exactly what we are trying to measure. What should be the meaning of a statement that output has doubled? One possibility would be that the output of each and every commodity doubled but, since in real life the output of different commodities grows at different rates, such a conception would be too confining. Actually, we want a statement that output has doubled to mean a doubling of something more abstract than actual output — i.e., the capacity to produce goods in

general (what economists call "production potential"). In the
light of this definition of the growth concept, the index number
problem exists because the relative burden that different goods
put on production potential changes with industrialization.
During growth, some goods become cheaper relative to others,
so that an economy's capacity to produce an assortment in
which goods with falling costs predominate increases faster
than its capacity to produce an assortment with a higher
proportion of relatively more costly goods. Without going into
the complex details of the argument, we may simply assert
that measurements using early-year weights are likely to be
a better measure of change in capacity to produce the late-year
mixes. Subject to some reservations, the index of 290 measures
the changing capacity to produce the 1939 mix of shoes and
tractors, while the 229 index measures the changing capacity
to produce the 1926 mix. Seen in this way, the index of 290
is probably preferable as a measure of growth. After all, one
of the main objectives of the industrialization effort was to
move from the mixes characteristic of a relatively unindustrial-
ized country to a more modern and industrialized mix. Hence,
the changing capacity to produce late-year mixes is the most
relevant to an evaluation of growth.

Resolution of the index-number ambiguity in comparisons
of the total output of two countries involves a somewhat similar
approach, i.e., asking what we would like to be the meaning
of a statement that one output is twice as big as the other.
But the problem is more complex in this situation, and we
will defer discussion of it until later.

Beyond the index-number ambiguity that arises when there
is a choice of prices, measurement in Soviet-type economies
is complicated by the fact that the prevailing prices tend not
to be very good measures of the relative worth of different
kinds of commodities in any year, either in terms of their drain
on production potential, or in terms of welfare to consumers.
Thus, even if one were content to accept the relative resource
outlays for different industrial goods in 1950 as weights for
combining them into an index, the actual prices that existed
in 1950 might be very poor measures of real resource costs,
since the planners (in both the Soviet and other socialist

countries) have never been especially concerned with making prices accurate measures of cost or value. For example, industrial prices tend to be set above cost, and agricultural prices below cost. Thus, in combining indexes of industrial and agricultural output to get an index of their combined growth, weighting them according to the value of each sector's output at prevailing prices would be to give the high industrial growth a greater prominence in the overall growth rate than it deserves. These prices may also mislead when one wants to assess how big a share of GNP one of these countries allocates to military uses, or to investment. If we add up both total GNP and its constituent elements of consumption, investment, military expenditure, and the like, in the prices at which these goods are bought and sold in the economy, we get a misleading picture of the structure of the total, since a ruble's worth of consumption goods stands for 50 kopecks' worth of resources and 50 kopecks of tax, whereas a ruble's worth of investment or defense goods stands essentially for a ruble's worth of resources.

For all these reasons, western researchers have felt it important to make independent calculations of Soviet and East European growth, and the following discussion is based on these research studies.

Growth of Soviet Output

Estimates of growth in the early stages of the Soviet development push depend on the weighting system used. Evaluated in 1928 prices, Soviet GNP grew between 1928 and 1940 at about 10.5 percent per year. When 1937 prices are used, the rate is 5.8 percent per year, which is still quite a high rate of growth compared with other historical examples of industrialization. This performance was in startling contrast to the relative stagnation of output in the developed capitalist countries in those years. World War Two stopped growth; output actually declined, though ultimately there was some offset through expansion of territory. But after the war there was a period of rapid growth during recovery and, taking the first three decades of the Soviet effort at growth as a whole, output by 1958 was about seven times as large as it had been in 1928, for an average annual growth rate of about 6.7 percent. This is an impressive record.

Growth has continued to the present at high rates, but the most striking feature of the postwar period is that there has been a decline in growth rates. The period 1950–1955 (the first quinquennium not strongly affected by the exceptional growth of a recovery period) shows slower growth than the prewar period. Moreover, there seems to have been quite a significant break in growth rates some time in the mid-Fifties — the period 1950–1958 had an average rate of about 7.5 percent, while the years from 1958 into the Seventies have had growth at a rate between 5 and 6 percent per year. This is still a good record, but an undeniable deceleration; in a period when numerous nonsocialist countries are growing rapidly (unlike in the Thirties) it represents a much less distinctive accomplishment.

Within this overall picture of growth, there has been sharply differentiated growth among sectors and uses. The highest rates have been achieved in industry and construction. Within industry, considerable differentials among branches reflect a distinctive Soviet pattern. Producer goods have grown very much more rapidly than consumer goods and, within the producer goods group, machinery has far outstripped the other sectors in growth. The direction of these differentials is the same in all modernizing economies, but the magnitude of the differentials in the Soviet case has been quite extraordinary. Producer goods have grown more than twice as fast as consumer goods, and machinery output has grown twice as fast as producer goods in general. Several factors play a role in the explanation for this phenomenon. The rapid growth of machinery is due largely to the high share of investment and military end uses, both voracious users of machinery, in the Soviet GNP. In addition, the high share of producer goods generally is connected to the wasteful use of intermediate output that the system engenders, and to the growth in specialization that growth and modernization has brought.

At the other extreme of the performance spectrum is agriculture. Farm output actually declined during the early years of the Soviet growth effort and two decades later, by 1950, had barely surpassed the level already achieved in 1928. After Stalin's death in 1953, agriculture began to grow fairly rapidly in response to some radical changes in agricultural policy, and by the beginning of the Seventies gross output of agriculture was a little more than double what it had been in 1928. Considering that the population has grown by one half in these years, it is easy to understand why the problem of agriculture remains a crucial one for Soviet policy makers.

The transportation sector also experienced a high rate of growth, but more so in freight traffic than in passenger traffic. In developing economies the transport job grows rapidly compared with other kinds of output, as the mix of productive activities shifts in the direction of more bulky commodities (such as fuels, heavy raw materials, lumber, and construction materials) and as regional specialization proceeds.

A large part of the national income in modern economies originates in the production of various services — education and research, health care, wholesale and retail trade, housing, government administration, and others. Growth in this part of the economy has been heterogeneous. Some of these activities, such as research, education, and health care, are important for the attainment of state objectives, and have experienced rapid growth in the USSR. Others catering more exclusively to consumer goals, such as housing, utilities, and municipal services, have grown relatively slowly.

Looked at in terms of end use, the fastest-growing parts of the Soviet economy have been the military program, investment, and such state-provided services as health and education. The use of resources for military purposes has grown faster than any other major use — i.e., about 12–15 percent per year over the whole period. In 1937 prices, investment grew at almost 8 percent per year, compared with the average GNP growth of a little less than 5 percent. Consumption, on the other hand, actually declined in the early years of industrialization, then rose slowly, and met a second setback in World War Two. As late as 1950, per capita consumption had advanced little, if at all, beyond the level Soviet citizens had enjoyed in 1928. Thus, until about 1950 the Soviet regime employed the increments of output made available by growth almost exclusively for state ends. Apart from allocating enough of the additional output to provide the traditional ration of consumption goods and services to the added population, it employed all the gains from economic development for such state goals as investment and military strength. Since Stalin's death, however, the consumer has been treated somewhat more generously. There have been important variations from year to year but, taking the period since 1950 as a whole, the consumption share of GNP has grown more or less *pari passu* with other uses. This means that it has also grown faster than the Soviet population, with the result that per capita consumption has increased considerably. With the Ninth Five-Year Plan, covering the years 1971–1975, consumer wants seem for the first time to have become a strong influence on the priorities of the Soviet planners. The Plan acknowledged consumption as a high-priority use, and made the rate of growth of consumption somewhat higher than the growth of GNP. Also, the very costly purchases of foreign grain in the early Seventies indicate that the time has passed when the Soviet regime can let the consumer bear the burden of production shortfalls.

Size and Allocation of GNP – U.S. and USSR Compared

Let us look a little more closely at Soviet output – how it is used and how big it is compared to U.S. output, both overall and for individual components.

GNP by End Use. Table 4.5 shows the percentage distribution of Soviet and U.S. GNP among major end uses at the beginning of the Seventies. The U.S. distribution has been derived by the author from the U.S. national income statistics; that for the USSR is based on extrapolations and adjustments of the detailed studies of Soviet GNP in the Sixties produced by researchers at the Rand Corporation and other studies by U.S. scholars. In both cases the figures are designed to show output at "factor cost" – i.e., to reflect the actual burden that each of the uses places on the economy's production potential, rather than at prevailing prices which, especially in the Soviet Union, contain very large tax markups for consumption goods. For the Soviet Union, the figures involve numerous approximations, but the general pattern they reveal is undoubtedly correct.

Table 4.5 Distribution of U.S. and Soviet GNP by End Use

| | SHARE IN TOTAL GNP (IN PERCENTAGES) | |
	U.S.	USSR
Consumption	72	56
Defense	7.2	10
Investment	17.8	33
Government administration	3.0	1

The most striking difference between Soviet and American distributions is the very high share of investment and low share of consumption in the Soviet economy. The high rate of investment in the Soviet Union is all the more remarkable in view of the relatively smaller output of the Soviet economy and the many other demands on it. In the years since World War Two, a number of developed countries have devoted to investment nearly as high a share of GNP as the USSR, and in some cases an even higher share. But in most of these countries the competing claim of military expenditures has been kept to a figure far below the 10 percent of GNP allocated by the Russians.

The internal composition of Soviet investment is also markedly different from that of more wealthy advanced countries such as the United States. The general patterns indicated in Table 4.6 are of long standing, though there have been some changes over time. The difference in the two countries is most strikingly seen between the top and the bottom half of the table. In 1970, the Russians directed 57 percent of all fixed investment into industry and agriculture, compared to only 34 percent in the United States. This was made possible by their restraint in investing in housing, facilities to provide such services as health and education, and urban amenities. They have also directed a substantially smaller share into transportation and communication, primarily by avoiding the construc-

Table 4.6 Structure of Fixed Investment, U.S. and USSR, 1970 (percentages of total)

	U.S.	USSR
Industry	29.6	39.7
Agriculture	4.7	17.2
Housing	20.3	16.4
Trade, education, and other services*	28.3	17.2
Transportation and communication	17.2	9.5

*Includes municipal economy.

tion of the elaborate kind of highway system that has required such large resources in the United States, and by contenting themselves with a primitive communications network. The high share of investment that the Russians devote to agriculture is somewhat surprising, considering that they have consistently tried to limit the claims of agriculture in order to conserve resources for high-priority industrial investment. But the agricultural sector is so large, and the productivity of its resources so low, that they have still had to allocate a much larger share of the total to agriculture than does the United States.

Origin by Sector. It is also instructive to look at output by sector of origin, and to ask what portion of it was generated in industry, in agriculture, and so on. A comparison of the United States and USSR in this respect is shown in Table 4.7, which is based on U.S. official national income statistics and western studies of Soviet national income. One remarkable

Table 4.7 National Income by Sector of Origin (percentages of total)

	U.S. 1970	USSR 1969
Industry and mining	29	37
Construction	5	9
Agriculture	3	21
Transportation and communications	6	11
Domestic trade	17	6
Other services	40	16

difference between the USSR and more advanced countries in this respect is agriculture's high share in the total output of the USSR. Although the Russians have come a long way in the effort to industrialize, a very large share of the total population is still engaged in agriculture, and agriculture still accounts for 21 percent of the total output of the economy, compared with only 3 percent in the United States. There are two separate reasons for this difference. In the United States, high productivity in agriculture has made it possible to divert the preponderance of American resources into activities other than the primary one of feeding the populace. Second, high productivity in American farm operations makes the relative cost of agricultural products quite low, so that even though our agricultural output is large in physical volume, its value in relation to the total output of the economy is further depressed. That so high a share of Soviet product should be generated by agriculture reflects the inability of the Soviet system thus far to realize analogous gains in agricultural productivity.

Paradoxically, considering how much of its resources the USSR must allocate to feed itself, the share of income created in industry is also higher than is the comparable share of United States income. The explanation of this paradox is an extension of the argument already cited. In the United States, high productivity in industry and agriculture means that our requirements for the outputs of these activities can be met with far less than all our resources, and we can afford to devote the rest to providing a varied multitude of services. The service sector of the economy, producing such items as education, health, conveniences to the consumer, recreation, and so on, is where the much poorer Russians have had to skimp in comparison with our pattern of resource use.

Another remarkable difference is the relatively low share in the total output of "other services" — a category covering a great variety of personal, business, and social services — in the Soviet Union.

Relative Size of Soviet and U.S. GNP.   In trying to determine how big Soviet GNP is, the figures in rubles produced by U.S.

scholars are no help: one inevitably asks, "How much is that in dollars?" for comparison with U.S. GNP. To get an answer, we might follow the procedure described in our discussion of the index-number problem and ask how much Soviet GNP would be if each item comprising it were given a dollar price tag and the total summed. When this has been attempted, the result shows Soviet output well over half, and, by the early Seventies perhaps as much as two thirds, of U.S. GNP. We might equally well calculate how much U.S. GNP would be if all its components were valued in rubles, and compare that with Soviet GNP. Soviet output looks considerably smaller in the ruble comparison than in the dollar comparison. A computation made for 1965, for example, showed Soviet GNP as 35 percent as large as American when the comparison was in rubles, and as 57.5 percent as large when the comparison was in dollars.

As the difference in the end-use pattern implies, the Russians are much closer to us in their production of military goods and investment goods than of consumer goods. Since the former are more expensive compared to consumer goods in the dollar price system than in the ruble price system, the dollar comparison emphasizes the defense and investment aspect of the Russians' comparative standing more heavily and the consumption aspect less heavily than does the ruble price system. This index-number problem shows up within each major end-use as well.

Which of these alternative answers we should accept depends on what we have in mind in asking how close the USSR has come to catching up with us. If we are interested in comparative welfare, the dollar comparison is far from persuasive. It gives much more emphasis to the relative standing in investment goods and defense goods than is proper in thinking about welfare. Nor is this just a projection of our own views — Soviet citizens themselves would not have chosen a mix so lopsidedly devoted to investment and defense goods if they had had any say in the matter. It may stir their national pride to see how closely they rival the United States in this regard, but that can hardly make up for the limited ration of consumer goods they receive as a by-product.

But we may prefer to skirt this issue, eschewing judgment on the allocation choices the regime has made, and ask rather how big Soviet "production potential" is. That is, how does the Soviet economy compare in a kind of abstract capacity to produce any mix of goods, whether the one it actually produces or one more like ours? In this case, there is more to be said for the dollar comparison, but it still overstates considerably Soviet comparative production potential. The reasoning behind this conclusion can become quite complex, but one simple element in it is that a very large portion of the total at dollar prices is not final product, but intermediate goods and primary resources. The calculation measures the resources expended for education and health care, not the output of these activities. New textile plants and other additions to capital stock included in the investment component are only a token of future output. We have added up the dollar value of the resources devoted to research and development, and made a dollar budget for the manpower, tanks, and missiles bought for the Soviet military program. Remember that for the USSR nearly half of the total is made up of such items. We know that in the Soviet system the transformation of inputs into outputs is generally less efficient than in ours, and it seems a mistake not to make some allowance for the putative lower productivity of those elements of GNP that are actually intermediate rather than final goods.

Moreover, in those cases in which the Russians use these intermediate goods in very different proportions from ours — as in research, where they use much more labor, in contrast to computers and copying machines, than we do — it is a mistake to give their high relative standing in research-and-development manpower the heavy weight inherent in the dollar price system. Considering how many researchers they have thrown into the breach to make up for the smaller supplies of other inputs to research and development, the manpower probably brings diminishing returns; dollar valuation of the services of all those research-and-development personnel exaggerates the contribution they make to producing actual research results.

The best way to reduce the index-number problem in international comparisons is to focus on more precise questions. When one asks about the relative size of Soviet GNP, he usually has in the back of his mind some narrower question, such as how well Soviet consumers fare compared to Americans, or how formidable the Soviet military effort is. Looked at in this way, the answers turn out more or less as follows: the Soviet Union is very, very far behind the United States in the amount of consumption goods produced and, because of their larger population, still farther behind in per capita consumption. Per capita consumption is on the order of one fifth the U.S. level. In other uses, however — uses that are highly relevant to international image-making and military rivalry — the Soviet Union is a great deal closer. They devote as considerable resources as we do to creating and maintaining their military strength. They have a bigger investment program than we do, and investment, of course, is a crucial determinant of future growth prospects. One still faces the problem of averaging these separate estimates into an overall evaluation of the competitive position of the Russians in the struggle for international prestige and power. But for this purpose one can probably find better weighting criteria than relative prices.

Productivity as an Aspect of Growth and Comparative Performance

So far we have gauged the performance of the Soviet economy by examining various dimensions of its output, but another useful perspective on performance can be gained by comparing outputs with inputs.

First, it is instructive to relate the growth of Soviet output to the growth in the flow of inputs — the rising volume of labor services from a growing population and the great increase in the productive services of capital that big investments have made possible. It appears that much of Soviet growth can be accounted for by this factor. The Russians claim that their stock of fixed capital has grown by about 14 times between 1928 and 1970, i.e., faster than output and much faster than any of the other important inputs. One form of capital not included in this measure is investment in human resources. A comparison of the amount of investment embodied in the present population (i.e., the amount of resources that have gone into their education and training) with the situation three and a half decades ago shows a tremendous growth in this input also. Labor input has grown considerably, and it is significant that it has grown faster than the population. This was made possible by favorable changes in the age structure of the population, which increased the share of the population in the main working ages, and by favorable changes in participation rates (i.e., the percentage of people of working ages who actually work), especially on the part of women. Also, the average number of hours worked per person probably increased somewhat. Between 1928 and 1970 the labor input rose by about two and a half times.

This disparity in expansion of the capital stock and the labor force was no doubt a highly favorable circumstance for growth. It meant that, rather than scrambling to keep new entrants into the labor force supplied with the same amount of capital as existing workers had, it was possible to raise the ratio of capital to labor and to provide more modern technology in the newly created production facilities.

When we consider all inputs together, their supply has not grown as rapidly as has output, leaving a portion of growth to be accounted for by increases in productivity. One would expect the Russians to have made extraordinary gains in productivity. They were in a position to borrow technological improvements from more advanced countries without themselves having to make large investments in research and development or in the long process of experimentation that characterizes the emergence of important innovations. Technological borrowing is an advantage available to any underdeveloped country, and the Russians resorted to it on a grand scale. They took as models the most advanced machinery designs, plants, and processes they could find in developed countries, and created fairly modern industries by replicating these units over and over again. But the interesting thing is that, despite this advantage, Soviet productivity gains seem not to have been exceptional. The rate of increase in resource productivity differs little from that achieved in other countries. This obviously implies that exceptional growth should be attributed more to the ability of Soviet command planning to mobilize resources – to accumulate capital, to educate on a mass scale, to move people from low productivity occupations such as agriculture to high productivity ones such as industry, and to force increases in participation rates – than to any special ability to use resources efficiently and increase their productivity.

International productivity comparisons are much more difficult, but even a rather crude effort is justified in order to put Soviet production into perspective. The Soviet Union's resource supplies put it, along with the United States, in the select company of superpowers. In 1972 the labor force in the United States comprised 86.9 million persons (81.9 million in the nonfarm sector and 5 million in agriculture). Soviet employment in the nonfarm economy was larger than ours (89 million persons), and there were an additional 37 million persons engaged in agriculture, putting the Russians far ahead in total labor force. With respect to capital stock, the Russians' relative position is much less advantageous. Capital is probably the most difficult of all resources to measure, but if we simply take the ruble value of the Soviet national wealth and convert it at a ruble/dollar ratio reflecting the relative ruble and dollar prices of capital goods, the Soviet capital stock appears to be approximately one half as large as ours. Economists sometimes try to aggregate all of these kinds of inputs to derive an overall measure of resource input in the two countries. But this is an exercise full of ambiguities, and quite different conclusions have been drawn by different writers. We will be content to assert that the relatively high standing of the USSR on all these comparisons of resource input, when their output is only about half ours, obviously implies a very much lower productivity for resources in the Soviet economy.

This difference in productivity strongly suggests that there are great inefficiencies in the way the Soviet system utilizes the resources available to it. There is another point of view, however, which holds that this difference in productivity is inconclusive as a judgment on Soviet-type institutions and planning as such; after all, there are many other countries which are indubitably market-organized, but which lag behind U.S.

productivity levels to virtually the same degree. In these cases, we are likely to explain their low productivity in terms of level of development, interferences with competitive forces, cultural impediments to change, and so on. A choice between these two interpretations is not really necessary here; the fact remains that the Soviet Union has a long way to go to catch up with the advanced capitalist countries in this regard, and has great unutilized potential for getting more output from the tremendous flow of inputs available for production if they can somehow develop a strategy for releasing it.

Productivity comparisons at the macro level are not very helpful in understanding *why* the Russians don't get more output from the resources used. That question can be better examined by looking at concrete linkages in the web of relationships through which the Soviet economy transforms primary resources into final output. This will help reveal what factors lie behind the global differences, and may also provide clues to the weight that should be assigned to the systemic inefficiencies of Soviet-style planning compared to other possible explanations of its low productivity. It is a fascinating exercise to pursue this question sector by sector, but we will here limit ourselves to only two cases — not necessarily representative, but useful in demonstrating the variety of influences on the low Soviet productivity levels.

Productivity in Fuel and Energy. Nature has provided the Russians with very large primary energy resources, which they extract, transport, and transform into other energy forms and which ultimately contribute to the production of various final goods and services. At every point along the way, they employ some of their huge labor force and use some of the large stock of capital, the two other primary resources that produce the national product.

First, for a broad picture of Soviet effectiveness in the fuel sector, let us compare Soviet and U.S. output per worker. In 1970 the United States produced 59,568 trillion BTUs of primary fuel, an enterprise that required the efforts of less than 200,000 production workers. In the same year, the USSR produced appreciably less — 34,678 trillion BTUs of primary fuel — but the number of production workers engaged in doing so was 1,285,000 more than six times the number required in the United States. Labor productivity was thus eleven times higher in the United States than in the USSR.

To understand why this is so, let us consider the two main subbranches of the fuel sector — coal, on the one hand, and oil and gas on the other — separately. This will also make it possible to make some judgments about how effectively capital is being used. In 1970 output per man per day in Soviet coal mines was less than 3 metric tons, compared with over 18 metric tons in American mines. Several possible explanations come to mind. Knowing from our own experience how much higher productivity is in strip mines than in underground mines, one wonders if the Russians are disadvantaged in having few strip mines. This is indeed part of the story — 35 percent of American coal, but only 27 percent of Soviet, is extracted from strip mines. But it is interesting to note that the Soviet share has been falling while ours is rising, which raises a question about the choices they are making. In underground mines, the Russians face a handicap in geological conditions, a considerably larger share of their output being derived from relatively thin seams, and at lower depths.

Perhaps the Russians, with their limited supplies of capital, have not yet been able to achieve American levels of mechanization — the rise in output per miner in the United States in the last several decades owes much to increases in the capital equipment that supplements the miner's power. To pursue that argument reveals a paradox. Horsepower of equipment per miner does turn out to be much less for Soviet than for American coal miners, but in relation to output the Russians have as much horsepower as we do! One might ask what would happen if enough Soviet miners were eliminated to bring their horsepower-per-worker ratio up to the American level? We may properly be suspicious of the argument that since each miner would have as much power to work with as his American counterpart he would display the same productivity. The suspicion rests on the probability that the horsepower in Soviet coal mining is scattered over a stock of equipment that requires a large labor force to operate. In other words, the explanation

for low labor productivity is the inefficient and obsolete technology embodied in the capital stock, a situation probably very
common in the Soviet economy. Even with all these explanations for low labor productivity in coal mining, the poor
Russian showing must also reflect poor organization, planning,
and motivation.

A look at the oil-and-gas branch reveals a much more
respectable performance, with labor productivity not far from
U.S. output per man. This is partly because the Russians face
better geological conditions than we do in the United States —
they are producing most of their output from very large fields,
with favorable production characteristics and a relatively
advanced technology. These conditions also enable them to
make big capital savings. They produce their output with not
many more than 50,000 gas and oil wells, whereas in the United
States we have over half a million producing wells (though
most of the output comes from a relatively small fraction of
these). It is a little misleading, of course, to measure capital
by numbers of wells, since those wells are extremely expensive
for them to drill and equip. The Russians drill wells very
ineffectively, drilling only a third to a half as much with a
drilling rig in a given amount of time and using much more
labor. They also use all the other inputs that go into constructing
a well — steel, cement, and the like — much more extravagantly
than we do.

Since productivity is much better in oil and gas than in
coal, one wonders why the Russians were so slow, compared
to other countries, to shift from coal to gas and oil. The answer
is basically that the planners were very slow to realize what
large resources of oil and gas the USSR possessed and to
appreciate the productivity gains that a shift in the fuel balance
would bring. One of the difficulties with the high-level strategic
decision making so prominent in the Soviet-type system is that
when those who think big make mistakes, they are big mistakes,
wasting resources on a massive scale. It is thus presumed that
defects in the decision-making system play a large role in the
comparatively low productivity of the USSR in this sector.

Fuel is for the most part not a final product, and it is
interesting to ask what happens to it as it continues through

the production process. A very large portion of the total is consumed in the generation of electric power. One of the most important technical indicators in electric power generation is the amount of energy consumed to produce a kilowatt-hour of electric power. In the early Seventies the Soviet rate closely approached the 10,580 BTUs per kilowatt hour achieved by the U.S. electric-power industry. Only ten years before the Soviet rate was 10 percent higher than in the United States. This situation lends support to the view that low Soviet productivity is largely a matter of level of development, and that as time passes Soviet productivity will move much closer to ours.

To follow the story another step, we might ask about the expenditure of electric power per unit of output. Comparisons here are treacherous, since electric power can be substituted for other kinds of input, so that a high ratio of electricity use per unit of output may be an indicator of modernity and productivity rather than the reverse. But, to take only one example, consider all the horsepower used in the coal-mining industry (mostly in the form of electric motors). Taking the capacity of electric motors as a surrogate for consumption, one of the implications of the previous discussion is that they are using electric power wastefully in producing coal. A recent study of Soviet electric locomotives (which now do nearly half of all railroad transport work) shows that the Russians have been very slow to introduce a series of innovations achieved in world technology that would economize on electric power. The decision makers who control the pace of technological change in the Soviet Union appear to lack incentives for quick adaptive behavior.

Productivity in Agriculture. Agriculture is a special case, probably the most inefficient branch of the Soviet economy. As we have said, the Soviet agricultural labor force is almost eight times that of the United States. Soviet agriculture also employs much more land — in recent years, total crop land harvested in the United States has been about 290 million acres, compared to about 510–520 million acres in the Soviet Union. However, the USSR is much less well supplied with pasture and grazing land than the United States — about 500 million acres compared with our nearly 700 million acres. The stock of farm animals in the Soviet Union nearly equals that of the United States. The Russians have fewer head of cattle (and these are predominantly milk animals, rather than beef cattle), but they have more than four times as many sheep and goats. The Soviet swine population has fluctuated widely, but in recent years has exceeded ours. With these resources, however, the Soviet Union produces a considerably smaller agricultural output, perhaps 80 percent as large as ours.

The contrast between the relative standings in output and resource input obviously implies very low comparative productivity of resources in Soviet agriculture, and examination of detailed productivity ratios bears this out. Crop yields per unit of land in Soviet agriculture are very low — for all grains taken together, less than half the United States figures; for potatoes, one third. The overall yield for cotton is about the same, but the Russians produce almost exclusively irrigated cotton, which shows appreciably higher yields than cotton grown without irrigation. Compared with irrigated areas in the United States, Soviet output per acre is only half as large.

Yields in animal husbandry (which represent a kind of capital-output ratio) are equally low. Soviet cows produce only a little over half as much milk per year as American cows, and the number of eggs produced per chicken is much lower. The USSR has a very small meat production, considering the size of its animal herds. Soviet animals are of poor quality, are not fed adequately for rapid weight gain, and are slaughtered at low weights.

The explanation for the low productivity of resources in agriculture is complicated. Unfavorable natural conditions are an important factor. In terms of growing season, rainfall, temperatures, and soil fertility, the Russians are at a serious disadvantage compared with American farmers. One reason for the high American grain yield is that corn is an important element in the grain economy, and corn has a yield per acre several times that of wheat. The Russians have a very limited area where they can grow corn to maturity. Soviet wheat yields are low because, throughout much of their wheat area, a short growing season interferes with both planting and harvesting and there is insufficient moisture. Low labor productivity can be explained partly by the fact that Russian agriculture has always been stinted on mechanical equipment and other capital. In 1970 the Russians had about 1.2 million trucks on farms, compared to over 3 million on American farms. They have a little less than 2 million tractors, compared to our 5 million.

But low productivity must be explained primarily as a result of the system. Soviet agricultural policies and institutions have been a serious obstacle to improvements in productivity. In most of the rest of the world, and especially in the United States, truly spectacular rises in productivity have been achieved in agriculture in the last two decades. Yields per acre, per animal, and per man-hour have risen dramatically. The present high productivity of resources in American farming is due to rapid technological progress of diverse forms — better equipment, better seed varieties and animal breeds, more efficient ways of organizing agricultural production, fertilizer, chemical means for pest control, and so on. These innovations are the result of an elaborate system of government-sponsored agricultural research; a system for disseminating knowledge of new techniques, crops, and methods; and a motivation at the working level to adopt these improvements. The Soviet collective farm system and central planning of agriculture has seemed constitutionally incapable of effecting rapid technical progress.

At the time of Stalin's death, the Russians had come to a real impasse in agriculture — the technique of exploitation could not well be pushed further, and any increases in agricultural output demanded improvements in agricultural productivity. The next five years or so, to about 1958, was a period of considerable improvement. Present productivity performance, bad as it seems, represents a great improvement over the situation fifteen years earlier. The core of the reforms made in the years under Khrushchev was to give collective farmers more incentive by raising prices, to give them more control over farm operations by dissolving the machine-tractor stations, to make studies of costs as a guide to better regional specialization, and to increase investment in agriculture. This attack on some of the basic difficulties was accompanied by a crash program to break the output bottleneck by an expansion of sown acreage in the virgin lands program. Between 1954 and 1961 the Russians plowed up around 100 million acres of land in Kazakstan and Western Siberia not formerly cropped and planted it to wheat. (This is double the United States wheat acreage, and represents an expansion in Soviet acreage of about one fourth.) This was something of a gamble, since the area is characterized by a deficiency of moisture and dustbowl tendencies, but it succeeded as a short-run measure to cope with the grain crisis while allowing a breathing space for a more fundamental attack on the problem of farm efficiency. In the years since 1958, there have been frequent ups and downs. After the success of 1958, attention to agriculture was reduced, but after Khrushchev was replaced in 1965 by Brezhnev and Kosygin, a rather sustained effort to increase the flow of inputs to agriculture was made. This has achieved a fairly consistent advance in output, though there have been weather-related setbacks at fairly frequent intervals such as the crop failure in 1972 that forced the Russians to import large amounts of grain from the U.S. But output in 1970 was half again as big as it had been in 1958.

Conclusion

The general answer to the question with which we opened this chapter — how well have the Russians done on their goal of catching up with the United States? — would seem to be as follows:

Considering the whole history of its development effort, the Soviet Union has achieved under planning a remarkably high average rate of growth. It has been a highly variegated record. Impressive growth and modernization in some sectors have been accompanied by virtual stagnation in others. But these failures are partly the result of conscious choices, rather than of inadequate planning. The leaders chose deliberately to assign consumption to a subordinate place in their hierarchy of values, and as a consequence were reluctant to make a big effort to increase agricultural output. There has also been considerable variation in performance when shorter time periods are distinguished. In particular, the last few years have witnessed an appreciable deceleration of the rate of growth. The first few years of the Ninth Five-Year Plan have seen the lowest rates of growth yet experienced by the USSR in peace-time years. In total output the Russians are far behind the United States, though their allocational choices have permitted them to nearly equal us in such areas as investment, military expenditures, and research and development. The productivity of resources is still far below that which we have achieved, a situation which can be interpreted either as a demonstration of the inefficiency of the system, or as an indication of potential for further gain relative to the United States.

5

The Soviet Model in Eastern Europe

In the years since World War Two, the Soviet system has spread to a large number of other countries — the countries of Eastern Europe, China and North Korea, and later to North Vietnam and Cuba. The process is still continuing, with Chile as a possible second case in the Western Hemisphere. Many of these countries have experienced considerable growth success under the institutions of the Soviet command-economy model and the Soviet strategy of development. But one of the most remarkable aspects of this diffusion process is that even when the system was borrowed originally in its Stalinist form, experience soon led to some disillusionment with it, and a process of adaptation to local conditions has taken place. The result has been a process of reform and adaptation of the original model which, together with the Russians' own modifications, has led to extensive differentiation. There are now numerous versions of socialist planning and socialist development strategy in operation in the world. This process of differentiation has been interesting as a possible harbinger of what the Russians themselves may do, but it has also been instructive as a demonstration that the Soviet model as it originally developed in the USSR is not a universally applicable approach to the problem of economic development. Its inappropriateness to the differing contexts of other countries prompts us to abandon the idea of a well-defined and consistent "Soviet-type" strategy of development, and enables us to see better that each socialist country must tailor its development model to the special conditions it faces, and to the stage of development it has reached. It also makes us realize that Soviet strategy is not necessarily universally successful, and we must think of communist regimes as facing a variety of situations that defy this easy panacea. Even if they are socialist, and decide to copy most of the Soviet institutional features, this does not necessarily assure them a solution to the problem of economic development.

We will develop this complex theme in two stages. The present chapter discusses the experience of the small countries of Eastern Europe in borrowing the Soviet model, and their growth under it. One of the special problems they face is that as small countries they are much more dependent than the Soviet Union has ever been on foreign trade, an activity that the system handles very poorly, and foreign trade problems have played an important role in their reaction to the Soviet model. Also, the creation of additional Soviet-type economies meant that the earlier situation was complicated by the introduction of trade between socialist countries, as well as between a socialist country and the capitalist world. One task of this chapter will be to deal with foreign trade as an aspect of Soviet-style planning and development strategy.

Chapter 6 will examine the Soviet and Eastern European approach to development as a "strategy," and analyze how these institutions and policies deal with the problems of development. That will provide a useful base for looking at two additional countries, China and Cuba, analyzing their experience in the light of the Soviet strategy, looking for differences and similarities.

Eastern European Growth Experience

In the first few years after World War Two, the countries of Eastern Europe — Hungary, Poland, Czechoslovakia, Yugoslavia, Bulgaria, Rumania, East Germany, and Albania – underwent a socialist revolution that converted them to Soviet-type societies, and established for them in almost carbon-copy form the goals, institutions, and growth strategy that we have described for the USSR. By the early Fifties, the reconstruction period was generally completed, and these countries had started on a course of economic development like that of the USSR. Our general purpose here is to describe the experience of Eastern Europe with this Soviet growth strategy. We might add that one of the countries, Yugoslavia, soon departed from this approach to follow its own "road to socialism." A political dispute with the Russians prompted Yugoslavia to reject Soviet experience as a model, to develop a distinct institutional framework, and even to reject central planning. This situation offers an interesting experiment in comparative performance under alternative strategies, to which we will devote some attention.

It should be understood that this group of countries was heterogeneous with respect to economic characteristics. Czechoslovakia and Eastern Germany were relatively advanced and industrialized countries. Hungary and Poland were at an intermediate level of development, and the others were quite underdeveloped, as demonstrated by all the standard indicators of economic development. In Bulgaria, Rumania, and Yugoslavia, about 80 percent of the labor force was employed in agriculture. In Czechoslovakia and East Germany before World War Two, the fraction of the labor force engaged in agriculture (about one fourth) was already less than that of the USSR in 1970. There was also considerable heterogeneity in the resource base of the Eastern European countries. Some had the mineral and fuel resources needed for industrialization, others did not. Poland had coal, but most of the others had relatively modest coal resources. Only Rumania had significant resources of oil and gas. The ores for metallurgical branches were absent in several.

Moreover, several of the Eastern European countries worked under considerable handicaps in mobilizing resources for investment. In the first years after World War Two, it was Soviet policy to exploit them in a variety of ways. Those that had been allies of Germany were subject to the payment of war booty and reparations, and in this way lost a significant part of their physical capital and suffered a continuing drain on current output. Also, in most of those countries, joint companies were established, the output and income from which were shared with the Russians. Because the joint companies were accorded a number of special preferences, they drained off resources to the Russians and constituted a burden on domestic development. Only in 1953, after the labor disturbances in East Germany, were the burdens of reparations and joint companies finally lifted by the Russians.

Despite these differences, however, each member of the group followed an essentially identical pattern. They set up the same institutions the Russians had established, usually with the direct assistance of the Russians. Soviet advisers arrived to advise them on how to organize and staff the various offices, how to set up the planning and reporting forms, what the statistical definitions and concepts should be, and so on. In addition to this institutional copying, the new socialist systems embarked on plans embodying the development strategy the Russians had evolved. They raised the rate of investment and constrained the growth of consumption, and redirected investment to shift emphasis from agriculture to industry and, within industry, to favor the growth of producer goods branches at the expense of consumer goods branches. They embarked on numerous big, high-priority projects embodying these decisions in dramatic ways — steel works, machinery plants, and power-generating facilities.

Growth of Total Output. In general, the adoption of this strategy led to appreciable growth, although there was a great deal of variation between countries and between different periods in each country's progress. Table 5.1 lists both official claims for growth of national income and the findings of one of the more extensive studies of Eastern European growth in the postwar period, involving independent recalculations by a group of western researchers. Note the sharp difference between the growth rates of the two least developed countries — Bulgaria and Rumania — and the others. Only in Bulgaria

Table 5.1   Growth Rates for Eastern European Countries in the Fifties and Sixties (in percentages)

COUNTRY	GNP WESTERN CALCULATIONS		OFFICIAL NATIONAL INCOME	
	1950–1968	*Major variations*	*1950–1960*	*1960–1970*
Bulgaria	6.8	None	10.9	7.8
Czechoslovakia	4.2	4.9–1960–3.3	7.5	4.4
East Germany	4.4	5.7–1960–2.9	10.4	4.4
Hungary	4.6	Dip in 1956	5.9	5.4
Poland	4.8	None	7.6	6.0
Rumania	6.2	5.8–1960–6.3	10.3	8.3
Yugoslavia	5.4	4.2–1956–6.5	6.6	6.5

Source: Western calculations from Thad P. Alton and J. T. Crawford in U. S. Congress, Joint Economic Committee, *Economic Developments in Countries of Eastern Europe* (Washington, D. C.: Government Printing Office, 1970).

and Rumania did output grow at a rate like that calculated by Bergson for the comparable period of the Soviet industrialization drive, say 1928–1958. This may suggest that the Soviet model is more suited to underdeveloped countries than to more advanced countries, though it is possible that the least developed countries underwent the most marked structural change and that the use of early-year weights in these indexes exaggerates their growth somewhat compared to the others. Note that the record does not reveal much about the comparative effectiveness of the variant path chosen by Yugoslavia. The growth rate shown for Yugoslavia is less than the highest, but greater than the lowest of the rates achieved by the countries that remained true to Stalinist-style planning and growth strategy. This may imply that there is something less efficient about the Yugoslav model, since it began from a level of development like that of Bulgaria and Rumania. But many special circumstances confuse the issue here — the dislocation that resulted when Yugoslavia ruptured ties with the bloc and turned westward in its trade orientation, American aid, and other factors.

Allocation Patterns.   In the allocations these countries made of national resources, they clearly followed the same pattern

of priorities as had the USSR. Looking at the differentials in
the rate of growth of various end uses, growth was most striking
in investment and least impressive in household consumption.
There was some variation among the different countries, but
investment generally increased in the range of one and a half
to nearly two times as fast as household consumption.

The main exception is East Germany, where in 1950–1955
consumption rose faster than investment, a circumstance connected with the need to compete with West Germany and with
the existence of large amounts of excess capacity in industry.
The high rate of investment is characteristic of Yugoslavia as
well, even after the Yugoslavs abandoned the command economy institutions that enforced a high rate of investment in
the other countries. A high rate of investment in Yugoslavia
was achieved by a quite different set of instruments, especially
taxes, a banking system that gave credit freely, and the motivations of enterprise and local government decision makers.

When investment grows faster than other end uses, the share
of the GNP devoted to investment must rise. Investment's share
did indeed show a remarkable rise, from something like 15–20
percent at the beginning of the growth drive to something like
30 percent and more at the end. It seems, however, that this
rise should be understood as a consequence of devoting most
of the increment in output to investment, rather than as a
consequence of cutting consumption. These countries never
experienced the actual decline in per capita consumption that
the Russians suffered because of the ambitiousness of their
plans (and World War Two). Eastern European rates of growth
of consumption were generally below the GNP rates of growth,
but appreciably outpaced the growth of the population. There
was, however, considerable fluctuation in the relative emphasis
given to consumption and investment. In particular, most of
the countries started out in the early years with ambitious
growth plans and rapidly rising investment rates but, with the
death of Stalin and in response to internal pressures, most of
them embarked on a "New Course" in the several years after
1953, involving a slackening of the big investment effort and
more attention to raising consumption levels. The early plans
caused a variety of bottlenecks and incentive problems, and

the planners had to ease off the pressure to cope with these problems. But by the end of the Fifties, most of them resumed the push to raise investment, develop heavy industry, collectivize agriculture, and increase exports to pay off indebtedness. They also all had a very large diversion of resources into inventories. By the Sixties they were investing 30–35 percent of GNP.

Careful detailed studies of the status of military expenditures as an end use of GNP are lacking, but it seems likely that they grew, as in the Soviet Union, somewhat faster than GNP as a whole. Data compiled by the Arms Control and Disarmament Agency show them growing at 5.1 percent in 1964–1968, for instance, which is higher than the area GNP growth. Some more exact data on the personnel of the armed forces, which we can compare with the size of the labor force, show that, in this respect at least, these countries have made a significant military effort, with an appreciable percentage of the labor force tied up in military service. The percentage of the population in military service is similar to that of the USSR in the period since World War Two, but the demands of military programs have put a lesser strain on the Eastern European economies overall because they have not had to bear the cost of strategic forces and development of new weapons systems. For the three countries for which more detailed GNP calculations are available — Czechoslovakia, Poland, and Hungary — the explicit defense figure is around 5–7 percent of GNP at factor cost, compared to something more like 10 percent for the USSR. In this respect, then, the situation of the Eastern European countries has been more like that of Japan and Western Germany than like the U.S. or the USSR, and this is an important part of the explanation of their ability to achieve high rates of capital accumulation without such drastic efforts to constrain consumption.

Growth by Sector of Origin.   Examination of growth by sector of origin corroborates the assertion that the Eastern European planners were copying Soviet strategy. In general, the fastest-growing sectors were industry, mining, construction, and transportation, with agriculture growing much less rapidly, though there seem to have been quite variegated emphases placed on agriculture. The picture for services is complex, but it is reasonably accurate to say that the citizens of these countries benefited from a fairly rapid growth of education, health, research, and — with less benefit — the services of bureaucrats; housing services grew much less rapidly, and well below household consumption generally, so that in an important respect the mix of goods and services for the consumer probably worsened compared to what he would have chosen himself.

The pattern of intraindustrial differentials in growth rates familiar from the Soviet case is very evident in Eastern European growth. Producer goods branches grew rapidly, especially those producing investment goods such as machinery; consumer goods branches grew more slowly. For example, between 1950 and 1970 for the area as a whole, the output of trucks and buses rose 16 times, electric power 5.59 times, ingot steel 4.68 times, tractors 3.68 times, cement 5.04 times, and machine tools 3.1 times, while the output of soap increased 1.52 times, fabrics 2.14 times, sewing machines 2.35 times, butter 2.52 times, industrially processed meat 3.07 times, and shoes 3.75 times. One unusual feature of Eastern European industrial growth is that the output of manufactured consumer goods, especially consumer durables, grew much more rapidly than one might expect in light of the relatively slow growth of consumption. The explanation is that Eastern Europe has worked as a specialized supplier of such goods to the USSR. Eastern Europe's net exports of manufactured consumer goods, mostly to the USSR, grew at about 10 percent per year between 1950 and 1970, far above the rate of growth of consumption. Much of the increased output of consumer goods had to be sent to the Soviet Union to pay for the raw materials and fuels that were not available domestically but were indispensable for output growth, and for the investment goods that were needed for the investment programs.

Inputs, Outputs, and Productivity. Finally, of course, we want to relate the growth in output to growth in inputs. Comparison of the two underlines very clearly that these countries were following the same mobilization strategy that we have described for the USSR, with much of the growth of output accounted for by the growth of inputs rather than by increased productivity.

Let us consider labor first. Growth in this input was relatively small, compared to the rates of growth of output just discussed. For the area as a whole, the average annual rate of growth of the labor force was a little less than 1 percent per year. This growth in the labor force can be thought of as the result of two other factors, growth of the population of working age and an increase in participation rates — i.e., the fraction of people of working age that actually participates in the labor force. But the growth of the labor force is an incomplete measure of these countries' success in mobilizing labor. In most of them the labor force in 1950 included a large number of agricultural workers, many of whom were only partially employed. Providing them with full employment in other kinds of jobs thus represented another possible way of increasing the labor input.

Hence, an equally important measure of the growth of labor inputs is employment in the nonagricultural labor force. This grew at an average annual rate of about 2.5 percent per year, far higher than the 1 percent annual rate for the labor force as a whole. Some combination of these three factors, differing greatly from country to country, permitted nearly every one of them to increase greatly the labor input into production. The countries that were initially mostly agricultural were not very successful in increasing participation rates, since in the villages everyone was already in the labor force. But Poland and Rumania had a considerable growth in population, as well as large transfers from agriculture. The Bulgarian labor force experienced virtually no increase because Bulgaria had no population growth and was not able to increase participation rates. But Bulgaria was able to transfer some 1.2 million people out of agricultural employment, even while agricultural output was growing rapidly. Czechoslovakia had a low rate of population growth, but because the country was already heavily industrialized in 1950, the participation rate for women and young people was relatively low, and the Czechs were able to expand the labor force at almost one percent per year by mobilizing them. The country that fared least well was East Germany, where numerous factors combined to keep the rate of growth of the nonagricultural labor force at about one half of one percent per year. Yugoslavia is an interesting illustration of the great potential of all these factors in conjunction. High population growth, a large agricultural sector, and low initial participation rates, provided a reserve of labor so abundant that even a rate of growth of the nonagricultural labor force of 4.5 percent per year could not absorb it, and Yugoslavia, under a policy unique in the socialist world, has been able to send half a million people to work in Western Europe.

So we may generalize that the Eastern European countries were able to keep increasing the amount of labor devoted to producing the nation's output, though the rate of increase in this output was considerably less than the growth of output itself.

On the other hand, another important input — the services of capital goods — was growing at a rate much faster than labor, and indeed even faster than total output. This matter has been as systematically studied for these countries as for the USSR, but what information there is suggests the following generalization: Overall, capital has far outrun the labor force in its growth, though the relationship to the growth of output is more complicated. Until the early Sixties, the growth of output somewhat exceeded the growth of the capital stock, but in the second decade, while the growth of capital stock continued unabated, output growth dropped off. The effectiveness of capital infusions in keeping the output growing lessened. Output per unit of capital was beginning to fall after 1960. This was particularly striking at the margin, i.e., the increment in output associated with a given increment to the capital stock dropped sharply from year to year.

In this situation, growth in output per worker was reasonably high, as workers were steadily being shifted out of low productivity sectors such as agriculture into those with higher productivity, and were being equipped with even more capital.

But the important issue is how much output per unit of input was growing, when both capital and labor are considered together. We can combine the growth of these two inputs into a single index by weighting them appropriately, and compare that with the growth of output. When we do this, we find that output rose more rapidly than the input of capital and labor, but the difference, which we may interpret as the contribution of productivity gains to growth, was not especially large. As in the Soviet case, the growth of output was attributable more to the mobilization of inputs, especially the accumulation of capital, than to exceptional increases in the productivity with which these inputs were being transformed into output.

For a number of years, this recipe for growth seemed quite acceptable to the Eastern European policy makers — they had a system that was good at getting big increments of capital. By the Sixties, however, it began to look less attractive; the recipe seemed to be changing so that the amounts of capital required for a given output were rising alarmingly. We will interpret this phenomenon, and describe its sequel, in Chapter 6. Before doing so, however, it will be helpful to give some explicit attention to the role of foreign trade in the growth performance and strategy of the Eastern European countries. It is particularly appropriate that we consider trade in conjunction with the growth of the Eastern European countries, since it was a much more important phenomenon for them than for the Soviet Union, and also because the extension of Soviet-type institutions and strategy to Eastern Europe, and the creation of a "socialist world market" made up of Soviet-type economies, raised a number of new problems and complications in foreign trade planning and policy.

Foreign Trade in Soviet-type Economies

Since we gave rather short shrift to questions of foreign trade in our description of planning and economic decision making in the Soviet-type economy, we must first describe some of the principal elements of foreign trade planning and policy as these developed in the Soviet economy. As a starting point, it should be explained that foreign trade is inherently a difficult kind of activity for the Soviet-type economy to cope with. Foreign trade can be thought of as a sector that takes a set of inputs from the rest of the economy, called exports, and turns them into a set of outputs, called imports. Recall the balancing procedure by which annual plans are drawn up, a dialogue between the center and each sector in which the center indicates a set of production targets and some limits on the resources that will be available to the sector. The sector then responds with a detailed request for the inputs needed to produce the assigned output. But when we try to translate this general balancing procedure into the concrete situation of the foreign trade sector, several distinctive difficulties appear. The foreign trade sector could turn a given set of exports into many alternative sets of imports, or could procure any given set of imports with a great variety of alternative export combinations. Foreign trade lacks the technological determinism that in electric power production, say, permits the planners to consider a manageable list of alternatives and so makes the annual balancing operation feasible. Also, the foreign trade sector has nothing analogous to the capacity limitation imposed on the iron-and-steel industry, say, by its plant, which also helps narrow choices by setting a range for the output targets. It would be possible to contemplate widely varying levels of foreign trade activity — from, say, 10 percent of output going abroad and 10 percent of products used in the economy coming from abroad, to some much higher figure, such as 20 or 30 percent. This is a choice that can be made only by appeal to some notion of optimizing, which is something the balancing procedure has generally eschewed. In short, the planners face communication and information handling costs in this interaction that are very high compared to what they are in interactions with internal sectors. Accordingly, the Soviet planners have generally tried to run the economy with as little recourse to foreign trade activity as they thought they could get away with. The main motives for the planners to engage in foreign trade under the Stalinist model were to relieve bottlenecks in the balancing process, to import technology embodied in capital goods, or to short-circuit the transformation of surplus into investment goods, rather than to increase GNP through the benefits of specialization and comparative advantage. The point of departure in foreign trade planning tended to be the shortages that turn up in the balancing process, which are posted to the foreign trade sector as its output targets. But these imports require foreign exchange, and the balancers then try to make available the requisite amount of goods for export, in the form of traditional export goods, goods that have turned up surplus in the balancing process, and output windfalls that come about because of errors in past decisions about the structure of productive capacity. Needless to say, this approach is not necessarily conducive to rational specialization — socialist countries often end up exporting things that take more resources to produce than would the goods imported in return if the latter were produced domestically. Or it may mean that the composition of exports is irrational, in the sense that the same amount of foreign exchange could be earned with a smaller drain on domestic resources if a different set of goods had been chosen for export. The whole foreign trade operation is undercut by the lack of price information to guide choice rationally, and by the lack of a discipline to force rational choice.

The Foreign-Trade Monopoly. In conducting foreign trade operations, one of the guiding principles has always been the foreign trade monopoly, the purpose of which is to shield the central planners' control of the economy from the influence of the world market. Things are arranged so that it is impossible for some firm to look at the foreign price, the exchange rate, and the domestic price and decide to export or import some good because that is cheaper or more profitable; that would interfere with the planners' prerogative of deciding how resources are to be used. All foreign trade operations are conducted by the Ministry of Foreign Trade, in accordance with the foreign trade plan. The Ministry conducts its foreign trade operations in a way that eliminates most of the equilibrating instruments and mechanisms familiar in trade between market economies. The ruble is not an internationally traded currency and, indeed, it is illegal to export or import it. An official exchange rate is fixed for it, but this exchange rate bears no relationship to purchasing power parities, as do exchange rates elsewhere. The Soviet Ministry of Foreign Trade conducts its foreign trade largely in foreign currencies. Exports are sold on the world market at prevailing prices in foreign currencies. The foreign exchange so earned is banked abroad and is drawn on to pay for imports contracted for in terms of world market prices expressed in foreign currencies. Balance must be achieved in these operations, of course — the USSR is able to buy only the amount of foreign goods that it can pay for with the foreign exchange it has earned, or can get credit for. There is no danger of foreigners increasing or decreasing their holdings of rubles, since foreigners are not allowed to own them.

The trading organizations deal with their domestic suppliers and customers in terms of internal ruble prices. An exporting organization thus pays rubles for the goods it exports and receives foreign exchange, which it turns over to the bank in exchange for rubles at the official exchange rate. It can accordingly make a profit or a loss in rubles. The situation for the importing organizations is the reverse. Because the foreign exchange rate is arbitrary, these profits or losses may be quite large, but to some extent offset each other. If the official exchange rate greatly overstated the value of the ruble (as, for example, if it were set at one ruble = five dollars), the exporting organization that sold a Soviet machine in the west would get so few rubles in return for its dollar earnings that it would not cover the domestic ruble purchase price of the machine. But at that overvalued rate, importing organizations selling at domestic ruble prices would need to use so few of the rubles they took in to buy the foreign exchange necessary to cover their purchases abroad that they would make big profits. Thus the Ministry as a whole would come out about even. But the insulation of the domestic market from the world market precludes the kind of equilibrium in quantities and relative prices that in a free market would cause the trade balance in foreign prices to be of the same magnitude as in domestic prices.

In the situation we have described, in which one socialist country is trading with a capitalist world market, the Ministry of Foreign Trade has relatively easy conditions for carrying out its responsibilities. Anything that it is instructed to buy can be bought somewhere in the world at some price; anything it is given to sell can be sold somewhere. It may be necessary to offer higher prices to win imports away from other prospective purchasers, or it may be necessary to shade export prices to break into new markets. Thus the Soviet economy may have a terms-of-trade problem and a balance-of-payments problem, but there is no problem caused by the composition of the list of exports and imports in the foreign trade plan. Also, because in much of the world market currencies are freely convertible, it is required to achieve balance only multilaterally, not bilaterally. The foreign trade organizations can sell in the most advantageous markets and buy in the cheapest, and if the foreign exchange earned by selling in a given country does not cover purchases from that country, the deficit can be covered by the surplus currency earned in dealings with other countries.

Trade among a Number of Soviet-type Economies.   This situation changed appreciably when a number of other countries remodeled themselves on the lines of Soviet-type planning, and the nations of the socialist world began to conduct a large share of their trade with each other. The Soviet Union has consistently tried to encourage this kind of preferential trade; during most of the postwar period, the socialist countries have conducted something like two thirds of their trade with other socialist countries and only one third with the rest of the world.

When a group of countries, all conducting their internal balancing operations as we have described, try to trade with each other, foreign trade becomes even more complicated to plan and manage than for a single socialist country. To visualize the essence of the problem in a stark if somewhat simplified way, imagine that the Ministry of Foreign Trade in each country, having received an approved foreign trade plan, sends out a representative to conclude the deals with other socialist countries that will fulfill the Ministry's trade plan. Each representative has two lists — one of the things he is to buy, and another of the things he is to sell — and he approaches each of the other representatives in turn. If when the Czech representative, say, gets to his first appointment (let us suppose it is with the Rumanian representative) he finds that his selling list exactly matches the Rumanian representative's buying list and his buying list exactly matches the Rumanian representative's selling list, they can draw up contracts and go home. But there is no reason to expect that the process will work out so expeditiously; instead, they will be looking for *portions* of their lists that coincide. When the Czech and Rumanian negotiators have exhausted their mutual possibilities, each will go on to another of his appointments to try to make deals for the remaining portions of his lists. Apart from the problem of scheduling all these appointments, there is one very important complication that may prevent the job from getting done at all. If one could collect all these lists and total the quantities of particular goods, like shoes or wheat, that people were trying to sell, and then compare these with the corresponding totals from the buying lists, there is no reason to expect the amounts to coincide. Each of the countries makes up its two lists as a by-product of internal balancing, independently of the balancing process going on in the other countries. This possibility has serious implications.

It would be possible to proceed through the round of appointments most quickly if at each session the two representatives could deal with their four lists piecemeal. That is, if wheat was on the Czech's selling list and the Rumanian's buying list, they would make a deal for whichever amount was the smaller, and so on through all the commodities that were common to the Czech's selling list and the Rumanian's buying list or to the Czech's buying list and the Rumanian's selling list. When the results were totaled, the value of goods sold by the Czech to the Rumanian might not just equal the value of those sold by the Rumanian to the Czech, but this problem might be handled if the one whose sales exceeded his purchases accepted the other's currency to make up the difference. He would then expect to offer this currency in a future deal with one of the other representatives when it turned out that he was buying more goods than he was selling. But in view of the possibility that for all the countries together there may be more of some commodities than buyers want, and less of others than they would like to buy, this would be an imprudent course of action. Anyone who gives up goods in exchange for currency may find that the particular goods on his buying list for which he expected to exchange that currency never materialize. He might have to return to his Gosplan and report that he had not fulfilled his plan. Given the situation we have described, in which supply and demand of each good traded is not necessarily equal, someone is going to have that experience. But to avoid this contretemps for himself, each representative is going to try to achieve balance between the value of goods sold and bought in his deal with each of the other countries' representatives. In short, there is great pressure for bilateral balancing of trade flows.

The general situation we have described is clearly discouraging to foreign trade. Even for a single country, working out a foreign trade plan is difficult, and this encourages autarchy. A group of such countries, in their mutual dealings with each other, find it hard to get even such minimal plans fulfilled. This reinforces aversion to trade and pressures them into bilateral balancing, which is still another obstacle to trading as much as is desirable, since it rules out a lot of potentially valuable deals. Finally, these factors also interfere with getting the right composition of trade.

This situation was not so much of a problem for the Soviet Union because of its large size. Big nations can afford to be more or less autarchic, in the sense that they have a large enough internal market to support domestic industry in most lines of production. Also, they tend to have enough variety of resource situations to get the benefits of territorial specialization within their own borders. The institutional indisposition to trade in the Soviet economy was closely mirrored in the development strategy as well. In the beginning of the industrialization drive, the USSR engaged in a considerable amount of trade, primarily to import technology and to skirt the bottleneck of an inadequate domestic capacity for producing the investment goods its growth required. Even so, in the entire period before World War Two, the Russians never reached the volume of trade attained in the prerevolutionary years. But the important thing is that once industrialization was underway, they moved quickly to reduce foreign trade. The bulk of the imports of the first few years were capital goods, invested to build the domestic capacities that would free them from the need to import. And while output grew rapidly under the first three five-year plans, trade, after reaching a peak in 1931, dropped precipitously for the rest of the period before World War Two.

But when the Eastern European countries started on this path to development, they were far different kinds of entities. They are in aggregate output only about two thirds as big as the USSR, and are individually much smaller. Their raw material sources are not varied enough to support the whole range of outputs unless supplemented by imports, and their individual markets are not large enough to permit an economical scale of production if they are limited to selling in their own markets. So their trade has been larger in relation to GNP, and all the interferences that Soviet-type planning imposes on it were more disastrous for their development than was true for the Russians.

Detailed study of these countries has shown that trade plays a crucial role in their growth. Much of the variation in growth between countries, and from year to year within any given country, has depended on success in getting the raw materials and investment goods needed for expansion and operation of the economy, and this in turn depended on the country's ability both to divert some output from domestic needs and to find a partner willing to buy them.

This is related to the problem of "hard goods" and "soft goods" — hard goods being those in short supply within the group, and soft goods those that are in plentiful supply and hence difficult to sell. These terms also refer to the relative ease or difficulty of selling such goods outside the bloc. One reason hard goods were in deficit and difficult to buy within the bloc was that they were saleable in western Europe to acquire convertible exchange or difficult to buy there because of the chronic shortage of convertible foreign exchange. Soft goods, on the other hand, were easy to buy within the bloc because their producers found it difficult to sell them outside the bloc for convertible currencies.

Countries with hard goods to offer in exchange for soft goods had no trouble finding willing trade partners, and so had the benefit of expanding trade as a stimulus to growth. The reverse was true for those that had mostly soft goods to offer.

The concrete manifestation of the hard-good–soft-good phenomenon changed over time, however. Most of these countries started with a foreign trade pattern in which exports of primary and lightly processed products (especially raw materials and agricultural outputs) were their major earner of foreign exchange. But an important concomitant of the industrialization program was that it changed the structure of domestic production in a way that did not expand these sectors much and greatly increased domestic requirements for these products. In the early stages, when most countries were trying to raise the level of investment and shift the structure of output, capital goods were hard goods and primary products and consumer goods played the role of soft goods. But as the structure of output changed in each country, it was able to produce its own capital goods and also found it harder to divert primary goods to export channels, since domestic demand for these goods was growing faster than their output. Thus East Germany and Czechoslovakia began with a big advantage, but toward the end of the Fifties found their emphasis on capital goods an inhibition to growth, since it became more difficult to sell their machinery and highly processed manufactured goods. The ability of Bulgaria and Rumania to expand exports of raw materials and agricultural products in the new situation that developed in the Sixties helped to sustain their high rates of growth after the other countries had suffered slowdowns in growth. Note than Bulgaria and Rumania, with expanding agricultural output to export have had the highest rates of growth of trade in the 1958–1967 period, and Czechoslovakia and East Germany the lowest.

The discussion thus far has treated foreign trade primarily in terms of comparative advantage and specialization. But there is another function served by foreign trade that is extremely important in relation to economic growth and development. International trade is an important transfer device for new technology, and a stimulus to technical progress. Foreign trade permits a technically backward country to bypass some of the problems of developing technology on its own by buying technical knowhow from the more advanced countries. One form of this transfer is the outright purchase of technology, in the form of licenses and technical assistance, from foreign companies that have already mastered it. Another is to buy technology embodied in modern capital goods. The technology of an entire industry might be modernized by re-equipping or reconstructing it with machines or whole factories designed and produced in technically more advanced countries. Throughout their industrialization drive, the Russian planners clearly appreciated and exploited these possibilities of foreign trade, even if they tended to write off the idea of comparative advantage. During most of their history, machinery and equipment has accounted for the bulk of their imports — in the early stages of the industrialization drive, it totaled nearly half; today it represents something over one third. And there is no doubt that the new technology embodied in this equipment made a very big contribution to their growth. The potential of technological borrowing for stimulating growth is surely far from exhausted. In an effort to counter the decline in growth rates that has taken place in the Sixties, the Brezhnev-Kosygin leadership has attempted in the Seventies a historic reversal in Soviet autarchy in an effort to increase trade and acquire technology from the United States and other advanced countries.

This aspect of the Soviet strategy was also copied by other socialist countries, but with an important difference. They borrowed technology almost exclusively from the Soviet Union, rather than from the capitalist west. The Soviet Union was technically more advanced than many of these countries; this was certainly true in the cases of China, Bulgaria, and Rumania, for example. It had mastered more lines of production, had introduced more modern methods, and so on. But for some other countries, notably Czechoslovakia and East Germany, this was not the case. Nevertheless, the Soviet Union took the position that, as a big brother, it should be the source of technology for the other socialist countries. It would provide the equipment and the technical knowhow. This transfer took a special form in the Soviet world. One of the principles agreed on when Comecon (the Council for Mutual Economic Assistance, also abbreviated as CEMA or SEV for its Russian initials) was formed was that each country would undertake to transmit technical documentation, drawings, and other technical information to the other countries without charge, in accordance with the notion of socialist brotherhood. The volume of such exchanges was very large. Eastern European countries setting out to produce a new line of production might just build a factory on the basis of the design for an analogous Soviet factory, and produce a machine on the basis of the working drawings the Russians had used in producing the same model. And they equipped their factories with the machines the Russians were producing for equipping their own.

This had several disadvantages for the other countries. First, they were copying from a country that was itself still backward technically, whereas the Russians had copied from the most advanced. Secondly, countries were often unable to obtain the most advanced technology this way. For all the talk about socialist brotherhood, the more advanced countries were not really willing to share technological knowledge in those areas where they actually were advanced. One of the most advanced pools of technical knowledge, involving electronics, computers, atomic power, metals, and the like, is in the modern armaments industries, which the Russians have kept as their own special province; they are not going to give away that technology to others. Indeed, they have been quite slow even in transferring the advanced technology developed in the military and space sectors to other sectors of their own economy! Nor was any country eager to share its technology where to do so would conflict with economic self-interest. They did not want to threaten their own export markets within the bloc, or to encourage the creation of competitors for third markets. On the receiving side, getting technology *gratis* removed the incentive to think hard about whether what was offered was actually the best technical process or model to adopt. The conclusion seems to be that the role of the Eastern European countries as members of a socialist world market made them less able to exploit technical borrowing to accelerate development than the Russians had been. It put them in a position of technological dependency and left them with a big technological gap, both relative to the Russians and to the western capitalist countries.

In recent years the Eastern European countries have reacted strongly against these adversities in their international economic relations. They are strongly aware of the need to reform the economic mechanism so that they will develop more, and more rational, trade. Moreover, they would like to loosen somewhat their dependence on other communist countries as primary trade partners. There are competing outlooks on what ought to be done to increase trade and enhance their benefits from international trade. The Russians want to strengthen CEMA as a device for imposing their views concerning the appropriate pattern of specialization and trade. Some see a move toward market methods as an alternative route. They do not consider it possible to improve foreign trade motivations and decision making except as part of a reform of the whole system — giving up the foreign trade monopoly, decentralizing incentives, making prices more meaningful, introducing a real exchange rate, and the like. So the experience with foreign trade has been a strong motivation for economic reform, to be discussed in Chapter 8. But the proponents of neither of these positions has so far been able to persuade the others to acquiesce. The smaller countries see in any attempt to strengthen CEMA a threat to their own sovereignty over their economic fate. Rumania has led the fight on this issue, and has so far been successful. The other alternative is not really feasible without radical internal reform in all the participating countries, and it is clear that the rather reactionary stance of the Soviet Union on this issue is going to prevent its happening for a long time to come.

Diffusion and Differentiation

Let us in closing attempt some rather gross generalizations about the experience of Eastern Europe with the borrowed Soviet model.

First, despite the fact that all the Eastern European countries started out by copying the Soviet model literally, it was quite quickly adapted and differentiated in important respects. This suggests that the Soviet system is far from universally applicable. It is not an obvious and reasonable arrangement that anyone planning an economy would necessarily choose, despite a commitment to Marxism or socialism. The Yugoslavs insist on their Marxian and socialist credentials, but have rejected most of the central elements of the Soviet model, from its ideology to the technical details of the allocation mechanism. In general, Eastern Europe avoided the collectivization debacle that the Russians bumbled into, and, indeed, the Poles have demonstrated that collectivization is not even a necessary aspect of a centrally planned economy. They have shown, in short, that you can buy the machine without that expensive attachment. The Yugoslavs have demonstrated that it is possible to secure a high rate of investment with policy instruments quite different from the complex of physical planning and allocation that is a central element of the Soviet strategy. In short, the Eastern European economies have shown that, despite the systemic character of an economy, socialist planning need not be identical with the Soviet model.

Secondly, their experience has shown how dependent the effectiveness of the Soviet model is on certain special circumstances and conditions. Especially important is the level of development. The Soviet approach to development was really a very simple-minded strategy in which the mobilization of resources played a key role. In a backward country with a large pool of underemployed labor, primitive technology, and a small capital stock to begin with, the energetic and compelling hand of the central planners can mobilize these resources and turn them into extra output. The Bulgarians and the Rumanians are the only countries in the Eastern European group that have achieved sustained growth at the rates the Russians did. But when a country already has a big capital stock, a large reservoir of human capital, and a reasonably high level of consumption, and has already moved away from heavy emphasis on agriculture, its potential for growth lies less in the further mobilization of resources than in finesse in motivating and guiding the use of these resources.

Growth can no longer be attained with a few simple formulas or directives. If in 1950 a Bulgarian bureaucrat in charge of planning for machine tools had declared, "We need to increase the output of everything by 10 percent," he would have been talking about 90 extra machine tools, whereas a Czech planner who did the same would have been talking about 1,291 machine tools. Such issues as whether that many machine tools are needed, whether they should all be of the same kind, whether some ought to be exported, and so on, seem a lot more complicated to the man who is thinking about 1,291 than the man who is thinking about 90.

And a country that is producing a good share of its textiles by handicraft methods on cottage looms is going to find it easier to get a 10 percent raise in productivity in the resources used in textiles — just by moving the process into a factory — than is a country already producing textiles in modern factories with highly skilled workers who have long been organized by capitalist masters. The most eloquent testimony to the greater difficulty of the more advanced countries is the fact that in some years Czechoslovakia's GNP actually fell, an unheard-of phenomenon for a communist country, and that East Germany has one of the lowest growth rates in the whole group.

Third, the usefulness of the Soviet model to other countries is considerably diluted if they are so small that trade is important for them. Growth successes and failures in Eastern Europe can be explained in many cases by the ability of a country to expand its trade — and, for a number of countries, the clumsiness of planning and adherence to the bloc market imposed severe limitations on their ability to look for export-led growth.

Finally, these countries did not, by adopting Soviet-style planning, achieve an outstanding rate of growth. In the period since World War Two, many nonsocialist countries, analogous to the Eastern European countries in size and level of development, have had growth rates as high or higher. And this has usually occurred with less consumer sacrifice and no more cyclical instability. The growth performance of the USSR in the Thirties was especially impressive since it was seen against the background of recession and stagnation in the nonsocialist world. But competition has been tougher in the period since World War Two, and it takes a better record to convince one that the Soviet model has unique capacities for achieving economic development.

In general, the Eastern European experience makes it hard

to sustain the belief that Soviet-style planning offers a magic answer to the problem of generating economic growth. We need not try to settle here whether it was the best way for the Russians — "whether Stalin was necessary," as the argument is usually posed — but there is no denying that the Soviet model developed in special circumstances, and that many of its features are an outgrowth of specific Soviet historical conditions. In Eastern Europe it was an alien import, a doctrinaire transfer. Political independence from Soviet control, whether only aspired to or actually accomplished, has always roused a desire to junk many of the Soviet economic institutions and policies. The Yugoslavs are the only Eastern Europeans who managed to attain real political independence, but the Hungarians in 1956 and the Czechs in 1968 were as eager as the Yugoslavs to modify the model, even while remaining Marxist and socialist.

6

Soviet-type Planning as a Development Strategy

In describing the Soviet-type economic organization, and the pattern of growth achieved in the USSR and Eastern Europe, we have already implied a kind of "strategy" of economic growth, i.e., the specification of the variables the policy makers consider important, and the kind of instruments they use to try to control them. But it is useful to consider this question of strategy explicitly. Economic development is a crucial aspect of public concern and public policy in the modern world, but it is a goal that is not achieved with ease. Economic history and the experience of the contemporary world show us that there are many obstacles to economic growth, and that nations that want to grow must find some strategy for overcoming them. It is interesting to ask how the Russians and other socialist countries dealt with these obstacles, and to consider to what extent the Soviet-type strategy, if we can identify one, may hold lessons for other countries trying to accelerate their economic growth. Trying to formulate this strategy explicitly will also provide a useful base from which to consider two other variants of the Soviet-type economy — the Chinese and the Cuban.

The Soviet Approach to Growth

A Mobilization Approach. The outstanding characteristic of the Soviet approach to development is that it is what might be called a "mobilization" technique. Output grew rapidly but, as we saw in Chapter 4, this was primarily due to rapid growth in the inputs to production. The increment in output arising through increased productivity of resource inputs was not at all impressive. The system was designed to accumulate large amounts of capital and to achieve intensive utilization of labor. It acquired capital by constraining consumption and got more labor into promotion by transferring people from sectors in which their labor was underutilized to those where it could be fully utilized, increasing participation rates in the labor force, and devoting large resources to training and education to build up a stock of modern skills in the population. Many features of the system, such as the passive character of money, the de-emphasis of market and price in favor of a system of physical allocation of material inputs, and so on, were intentionally designed to enforce these mobilization goals. One of the ironies of the situation, however, is that the institutions that were so successful in mobilization create serious obstacles to effective *utilization* of the resources so mobilized. High-level decisions on capital allocation channeling large amounts of capital into high-priority sectors almost inevitably meant the neglect of a multitude of small uses for capital that would have had very high potential productivity. Similarly, the lavish resources expended on creating an impressive research-and-development establishment have contributed much less to the growth of output than they might have, because the inflexibility of plans, the distortion of incentives, and the suppression of rational economic signals discourages putting the results of this research into production.

Thinking Big. Closely connected with this feature of the Soviet model is what might be called a "strategic" habit of thought; that is, the decision making of the Soviet leadership was based on a highly aggregated and oversimplified view of the mechanisms, alternatives, and behavior of the world with which they were dealing. The reality of production possibilities is heterogeneous and constantly changing, but the Soviet leaders tended to treat them as standard, fixed, and amenable to manipulation by means of relatively simple policies. They also tended to simplify goals into a scheme of relatively stark priorities. They have always focused on certain crucial sectors, tasks, or technological policies, and assumed that if these were successfully dealt with everything else would take care of itself. Every Soviet plan ever promulgated begins with a listing of "key tasks" for the given period and a designation of a few sectors that are to be "leading links." Lenin once said that Communism was "Soviets plus electrification," and this is a perfect example of their penchant for slogans and panaceas. In the Thirties Stalin declared that "the issue of personnel determines everything," and it was under the influence of this slogan that the excesses of the Stakhanovite movement were carried out. Benjamin Franklin gave us the slogan, "if one looks after the pennies, the nickels will take care of themselves." The Soviet decision makers have operated unabashedly with the opposite notion, i.e., that if they concentrated their attention on nickel-sized issues, the penny issues could be ignored.

In his fascinating study of Lysenko's influence on Soviet biology, David Joravsky provides an interesting review of Soviet policy toward potato culture. Potatoes are subject to a virus-caused blight, and because of the potato's vegetative method of reproduction, the virus may easily be passed from one generation to another. Virus-infected potatoes may lose their productivity and vigor from generation to generation. In most of the countries of the world, this problem has been dealt with through a system of careful growing and certification of seed potatoes. Seed potatoes are grown in northern areas, where climatic conditions are less favorable for the development of blight. During the growth period the plants are carefully monitored by government inspectors, and any plants showing signs of blight are eliminated, with perhaps even destruction of whole fields. The certified seed potatoes are then shipped to other growing areas of the country.

This is a rather demanding approach that requires high standards of administration, some talent for organization, and transport inputs – all of which were in short supply in the early years of the Soviet development experience. Respectable scientific opinion (especially that of the Vavilov brothers, famous Soviet biologists) recommended copying the complex certification system used elsewhere in Northern Europe. Lysenko claimed that this was unnecessary, and that seed potatoes could be grown on the farms where they were to be planted. If seed plantings were made in the summer, and seed harvested in the autumn rather than in the summer, there would be less chance for blight to develop. Such an approach would eliminate all the complexities of organizing a system of seed certification and transport between different regions. This was one of the grounds on which Lysenko succeeded in winning official backing for his position in biology. In practice, of course, his proposal turned out to be a disaster, but it illustrates the kind of panacea to which the Soviet system has been very susceptible – a bold flanking movement that sidesteps all the organizational and technical obstacles to solving a problem.

Stalin was inordinately partial to such schemes, and never more so than in his famous "plan for the transformation of nature." Poor agricultural performance in the USSR is explained partly by relatively poor natural conditions – low fertility, scanty rainfall, and dry winds. But these are not absolute obstacles to economic development. They simply require a great variety of adaptive measures – special seeds; proper regionalization; irrigation; rotation and tillage methods that destroy weeds, conserve moisture, and prevent erosion; and so on. This kind of locally differentiated adaptive behavior has always been weak under the collective farm system. To undertake such procedures requires tremendous administrative resources, and is perhaps impossible without remodeling the whole system. It is perhaps not surprising that Stalin thought it simpler to transform nature than the collective farm system. In the Forties he pushed ahead an elaborate plan for transforming nature by planting shelter belts, altering the direction of flow of Siberian rivers, and other such grandiose measures.

The most extreme examples of these distortions are found in agriculture, but they are by no means missing from industry. In the iron and steel industry, when the planners examined western developments, they thought they could see certain trends, such as growth in the scale of plants and specialization, that were crucial for growth in productivity and efficiency. They then took these ideas as the basis for their own technological policies, and set out to design their iron and steel industry on the basis of the most advanced western models — the largest plants, the most highly specialized production patterns, and so on. When implemented, however, these policies had serious drawbacks, such as a large amount of cross-hauling, unresponsiveness to consumer needs, and very long delays in getting plants into operation.

In the machinery industry, a decision was made to follow the American model of relatively specialized large-scale plants using relatively unskilled labor, and to limit very strictly the variety of models produced and the rate at which new models were introduced. The idea was that they would choose the very best models, as demonstrated by western experience, and specialize production on them. Also, their design philosophy was generally to develop simple, rugged, unsophisticated models — universal machine tools in preference to custom machine tools, a few simple standard models of railway steam locomotives, and so on. Indeed, this was thought to be an important advantage of the planning system. They felt it unnecessary to duplicate the "wasteful" variety engendered by the "chaos of competition" in the west.

A corollary of this approach — perhaps intended, perhaps not — was that these sweeping high-level decisions were rarely reviewed or changed. Once a standard design had been chosen for a steel mill or a petroleum refinery, the industry was expanded simply by replicating this same plant over and over. Tractor models, once mastered, continued to be produced without change for years. Once a plant was set up to turn out a certain kind of lathe, it simply continued to produce the same model year after year, rather than modernizing it or replacing it with a more advanced version. Soviet steam locomotives did not undergo the small yearly modifications that in the west generated great improvement in the productivity of steam locomotives until they were replaced with diesels.

Perhaps one of the most interesting illustrations is fuel policy. In the early Thirties a careful review was made of all aspects of fuel policy. The fuel-and-energy sector offers a tremendous variety of alternatives. The fuel needs of the economy can be met with numerous basic energy sources, such as oil, coal, gas, wood, peat, and shale. Each can be subjected to many alternative transformation processes. There are numerous locational alternatives, such as converting coal into electric power at the mine and transmitting the power to market or hauling the coal to market and transforming it to power there. There are many competing forms of transport available. In the Thirties all these choices were evaluated, and a policy developed. Two of its outstanding features were a relatively high degree of regional self-sufficiency and, as a corollary, an extremely heavy emphasis on coal (often low-grade varieties) and other inferior local resources, such as peat. Oil and natural gas were relatively downgraded. These decisions may well have made sense in the light of the cost relationships and technologies existing in the Thirties. At the same time, they were made in a context of ignorance about the real oil and gas resource potential. The remarkable thing is that this basic set of policies continued virtually unchanged until the middle Fifties, without ever being reviewed or reconsidered. In the Fifties a change was finally made in this policy, but primarily because of the *outside* stimulus that came from observing that in the United States and Western Europe there had been a radical shift in the fuel balance to oil and natural gas.

Routinization of Growth Processes. A closely related feature of the development strategy was a routinization of growth processes. Many students of the Soviet-type economy have been impressed with the simplicity and crudity of many decision-making procedures and how little these changed over time. Accounting and statistical forms and concepts established in the Twenties underwent little change for a long time. Bonus formulas and incentive funds, once laid down, continued with the same names and coefficients for many years. Criteria for decision making, rules for evaluating success, and the whole price system have exhibited a most unusual rigidity and permanence. In any collection of laws dealing with bookkeeping, the rights of managers, arbitration, or any such matter, one can see that many statutes and instructions have remained in force for long periods. For all the revolutionary changes the regime made when it was first established, it thereafter seems to have settled into a very rigid and unchanging pattern of decision making. The explanation for this is easily understood. Routine was both a defense against independence at lower levels and a device to make lower-level jobs relatively simple and undemanding in terms of initiative or creativity. One of the obstacles to development is a complex of problems related to the weakness or absence of a technical-entrepreneurial elite — people who have a vision of the future and the managerial and technical skills to create it. The problem in development is to find ways of encouraging the emergence of such people, or a substitute for them. The Soviet system economized on this kind of resource by locating decision making at the top and building an infrastructure to execute decisions with relatively little latitude for independent decision-making power. The structure is reminiscent of military organizations, which someone once described as "designed by geniuses to be run by idiots."

This approach has a certain rationale, best examined perhaps in a concrete example. The Russians long produced a very limited line of tractors and agricultural equipment, emphasizing big crawler tractors copied from western models, large combines, and the like. The approach was to copy western models, set up a few giant plants to produce them, and then pour out the same models for years. The planners' motivation in following this line was that it greatly simplified things and saved resources. Given a shortage of people with the skills to design equipment, they copied instead of designing their own and, to economize on these skills still further, they wanted to avoid changing models. There is a similar rationale on the production level, since a learning process is involved for the workers and it is costly to repeat it. The production system built on output increases and cost reductions was full of incentives that reinforced the inclination to keep original models in production and fully utilize the capacity of the

factory. The same considerations apply at the level of use —
training people to use the tractors and equipment, and setting
up a system for producing, stocking, and distributing spare
parts, would have been much more complicated if they had
produced a variety of models and replaced them frequently.
On the other hand, this approach clearly had costs. Heavy
combines were ineffective for some crops, and in damp or small
fields. For certain kinds of jobs, the right kind of tractor was
unavailable, so that users often had to use a 60-horsepower
crawler tractor to pull a manure wagon. Machinery designs
were optimized for certain kinds of work; other kinds were
left to hand operations or undertaken with unsuitable models.
The policy of not changing models meant that modernizing
improvements were postponed until a total traumatic overhaul
at infrequent intervals.

Numerous other illustrations could be offered of this predi-
lection for routinization and sweeping strategic decisions. For
each of them we could argue that, despite the costs, it may
well have been a rational response under the circumstances.
One interesting question to be taken up later is how the balance
of costs and advantages of this approach may have changed
as the Soviet economy grew and raised its general technical
level.

We have described this routinization as a specific Soviet
response to a standard problem characteristic of all developing
countries. What are some of the other obstacles familiar from
the economic development efforts of other countries, and how
have the Russians dealt with them?

Capital Accumulation — Social Overhead Capital

One of the central problems suggested by the general literature on economic development is that of raising the rate of
capital accumulation. As already explained, many of the features of the Soviet-type model can be interpreted as devices
for taking the investment-consumption decision out of the
hands of the population and putting it in the hands of the
bosses of the SPE. But there is another aspect of the capital
accumulation problem for which the Russian answer is both

distinctive and instructive in helping us to interpret their achievement: the issue of social overhead capital. A number of the investments that need to be made at an early stage in development have long gestation periods and high capital output ratios. A long gestation period means that a project absorbs capital over an extended period of time before it begins to add much to output. A high capital output ratio means that the number of dollars' or rubles' worth of resources invested in a project is relatively high compared to the annual value of its output. Transportation systems are often thought to have both these characteristics. Half a railroad is of little use; indeed, until a railroad is connected into a network, until all the ports and the feeder roads are in operation, the transportation system cannot play its developmental role of commercialization, integration, and specialization very well. Moreover, when the transport system is complete, the total investment it represents will be high in relation to the annual value of the service it produces. There are offsetting advantages — once built, the system may be able to take on a growing burden without much additional investment, and it is likely to last for a very long time. Those, however, are future benefits, and the cost of creating the system must be borne today. Many other kinds of investment needed in a development program have similar characteristics: power stations, water management facilities, housing and other urban amenities. Also, the intangible investment in human capital is prolonged over a considerable period of years before there is much payoff in the form of a more literate and skilled work force.

In understanding how the Russians dealt with the social overhead capital problem, it is important to remember that the Soviet Union inherited a rather large capital stock from the period of tsarist economic development. The distinctive contribution of Soviet planning was to greatly intensify the utilization of this stock of overhead capital and to restrict very stingily any additions to it. Consider the two examples of housing and transportation.

Development in the Soviet Union, as in any growing country, meant a shift toward the nonagricultural sectors of the economy and, as a corollary, urbanization. Indeed, most of the increment in the Soviet population between 1928 and the present has shown up as growth in the urban population. If these 50 million people had been provided housing merely at the same level the previous urban inhabitants had enjoyed, a tremendous portion of the total investment outlay would have been required just to put roofs over their heads. With urbanization on this scale, the Soviet planners were not able entirely to avoid investing in housing, but they did manage to keep housing investment very low by simply intensifying the utilization of the existing housing stock. As we saw in Chapter 4, the share of total investment devoted to housing was far below that of most other countries. The consequence of this policy appears very clearly in the declining amount of housing space per urban resident, which fell steadily from over 6 square meters per capita in the Twenties to about 4 square meters in 1940. (In the United States, housing space per capita is about 18.6 square meters.) Only in the Sixties did the Soviet figure once again reach the preindustrialization level, and by the beginning of the Seventies it was up to about 7.5 square meters.

In the transportation sector also, the Soviet planners inherited quite a large stock of capital, especially in the form of railroad line and rolling stock. Tsarist development policy had been based on railroads, and although the mileage per square kilometer was considerably below that of more developed countries, a reasonably complete network of rail transport facilities existed in 1928. Soviet planners deliberately attempted to limit investment in transportation. They decided not to build a highway network, but to rely mostly on trains for transport. However, they made very sparing additions to the railroad network, limiting themselves essentially to a few additions connecting raw-material producing regions to the rest of the country. The planners also shaped regional development policy to this end by emphasizing regional self-sufficiency. The demand for transportation induced by industrialization did increase very rapidly, but the Soviet system was able to handle this transport burden, in large part by intensifying the utilization of the existing capital stock. The output of a freight transport system is measured in ton-kilometers; a ton-kilometer is the movement of one ton of freight one kilometer, and is thus a measure that takes into account both dimensions of transportation work. One measure of intensity of capital use is ton-kilometers per kilometer of track in existence. This figure rose very rapidly during the first couple of decades of Soviet industrialization, and by the mid-Fifties was 8.9 million ton-kilometers per kilometer of railroad line, compared to 2.8 in the United States. Other important components of railroad capital are locomotives and freight cars, and in both these cases the Russians were able to achieve large output increases with much less than proportionate increases in the numbers of cars and locomotives in service. A good measure of how intensively freight cars are used is "turnaround time" — the average number of days between successive loadings of a freight car. This dropped in the USSR from about 10½ days in 1928 to 6½ days in the mid-Fifties. Compared to the essentially stable U.S. figure of 14-15 days, this indicates the great effort the Russians made to keep freight cars loaded with freight and moving. For locomotives, an analogous indicator is average daily run, which the Russians managed to raise from 85 miles per day in 1928 to 178 miles per day in 1955. Again, comparison with the U.S. figure of about 150 miles per locomotive per day suggests an intense effort to keep locomotives at work. The reductions in these indicators, and the high performance compared to the United States, are evidence of the emphasis placed on improving intensity of utilization as an element in the Soviet strategy of saving on transport investment.

At one point it was thought that the Russians would eventually have to pay for the failure to invest in the transportation system. The levels of intensity reached in the Fifties were so high, relative to that of railroad systems elsewhere in the world, that it looked as though the mortgage to the future had at last come due, if the railroads were to continue to handle increasing amounts of freight. These predictions have proved wrong, however, and the explanation is an interesting illustration of how technical progress has assisted Soviet growth. To understand this point, a short detour is needed to explain some characteristics of different kinds of railroad systems.

The American system moves freight across its network in very heavy, rather fast, but quite infrequent trains. When you are next stopped at a railroad track while a train is passing, count the cars and notice the capacities printed on their sides. Normally there will be well over a hundred cars, each with a very high carrying capacity. Jumbo cars are in use today that can carry over a hundred tons of freight, but the *average* freight car capacity on the American railroads has been over 50 tons for a couple of decades. An alternative kind of system is that common in Europe, which dispatches smaller trains, with much smaller total freight loads, much more frequently. English trains, for instance, look to Americans like toy trains. A Soviet railroad economist once hypothesized that the Russians could achieve extraordinarily intense utilization by combining the high frequencies of European systems with the heavy train weights and high speeds of the American system. By the Fifties the Russians were a long way from attaining this desirable result, since Soviet train weights and speeds were still appreciably below those of the U.S. system. And those performance characteristics seemed out of reach because of the low power of locomotives. The system during the Thirties and Forties had been operated with fairly simple, small, rugged, standardized steam locomotives, far less powerful than American locomotives. But the introduction of powerful American-type steam locomotives was impossible because their higher axle loadings could not have been handled without massive investment in upgrading the road bed — adding heavier rails, providing better ballast, making stronger bridges, and so on.

At this point, however, technological change came to the rescue, when a shift to electric and diesel locomotives offered a way out of the impasse. It is possible to build these types of locomotives with much greater tractive power but with relatively light axle loadings since, compared to the steam locomotive, they can be designed with a much larger number of driving wheels. By making this shift the Russians were able to continue to intensify still further the utilization of their roadbed and avoid heavy additional investments through the Fifties and Sixties. The average train weights and speeds shot up very rapidly after the program of dieselization and electrification started, and by the early Seventies Russian trains were achieving 80 percent of U.S. freight train weights and matching

U.S. freight train speed. So the USSR is close to achieving the desired hybrid high-intensity system.

In evaluating this part of the strategy, we ought to mention that it has imposed some costs. Poor housing has been one of the most depressing features of the Soviet citizen's life, with associated costs in morale, motivation, and productivity. The railroad policy has had the adverse effect of spawning too much regional self-sufficiency, and as an offset to investment savings in railroad capital it has forced the accumulation of extra-large stocks elsewhere in the economy. The system gets its impressive performance partly by strengthening the hand of the railroad against that of its clients. Unit trains, and prohibition of less-than-carload shipments force customers to hold larger inventories; heavy penalties against those who hold cars over long for loading or unloading force shippers into extra expenditures to do this work rapidly. But, overall, it seems an ingenious way of dealing with the social overhead capital problem. The mortgage may still come due, but its partial postponement by these expedients has been an important factor in aiding development.

Population Growth

Another of the standard obstacles to economic development is population growth. Developing countries, even if they successfully overcome all other obstacles, may still find their successes nullified by a "population explosion." Most underdeveloped countries start out with a high birth rate offset by a high death rate, so that actual net population growth is small. It is characteristic for economically underdeveloped countries to have a birth rate in the range of 40 per thousand, and a death rate of 30–35 per thousand, so that the net population growth is 1 percent or less per year. Economic growth, with its corollaries of education and public health measures, improved sanitation, higher consumption levels, and better nutrition, brings the death rate down dramatically, say to 15–20 per thousand. But the birth rate is likely to decline more slowly, so that net growth may shoot up to 2 or 3 percent per year. This makes it hard for output per capita to grow fast enough to improve living standards and also provide for sufficiently rapid rises in the capital stock to raise productivity.

Soviet Population Dynamics.   Soviet industrialization began with a situation typical for underdeveloped countries. In 1913, even after two decades of tsarist industrialization, the birth rate was reported as 47.0 per thousand, and the death rate as 30.2 per thousand. Another indication of the premodern demographic situation was a high infant mortality rate of 273 — i.e., of every thousand babies born that year, 273 died before reaching the age of one year. In 1928, when the great push started, the birth rate was 44.3 per thousand and the death rate had fallen to 23.3 per thousand. As Table 6.1 shows, this trend continued during the Thirties, with a net increase of about 20 per thousand, or 2 percent per year.

Table 6.1   Soviet Demographic Trends, 1913–1969 (per thousand persons)

	BIRTH RATE	DEATH RATE	NET INCREASE	INFANT MORTALITY
1913	47.0	30.2	16.8	273
1928	44.3	23.3	21.0	182
1937	38.7	18.9	19.8	170
1939	36.5	17.3	19.2	167
1950	26.7	9.7	17.0	81
1969	17.0	8.1	8.9	26

Not until the Fifties and Sixties did the decline in the birth rate overtake the fall in the death rate to bring the net increase below 1 percent per year. If we look at the demographic situation in more detail, however, we find that the Russians did not have as high a rate of population growth as these figures imply. Indeed, during the first three decades of their industrialization drive (1929–1959) the population grew at a rate of only about .6 percent per year. The resolution of this puzzle is that the birth and death rates given in Table 6.1 are for more or less normal years, and that other years saw various population catastrophes that kept population growth far below the rates that the net increases of normal years suggest. There were very large numbers of excess deaths and very large birth deficits in the years for which the Russians have not provided statistics (the Twenties and Thirties and during World War Two). These excess deaths and birth deficits were the result of starvation, the disruption of family life, purges, and the disastrous conditions of World War Two and its aftermath. World War Two also gave rise to large emigration, which kept the rate of population growth down.

This relatively low rate of population growth probably made a significant contribution to economic growth. Though it involved some wastage of human capital, it avoided a large diversion of output into consumption needs, and so permitted more investment than would have taken place otherwise. It also made it possible to avoid investment in such activities as housing and urban facilities, which have high capital output ratios and hence a low growth payoff. Third, it made it possible to keep the structure of output biased against agriculture and consumer goods sectors in which the growth of productivity has been slow, and toward more progressive sectors. Finally, it meant a rapid growth in the ratio of capital to labor, with the attendant possibility of utilizing new technology and raising productivity. To put the point in perspective, consider the following: If population growth had been at the rate of 1 percent in the three decades after 1929, the population on January 15, 1959, would have been about 231 million, or about 22 million greater than was the case. If the rate of growth had been 1.5 percent per year (still below the natural rates of increase implied by the birth and death rates for the late Thirties), the 1959 population would have been 266 million, or 57 million more than was the case. Considering how difficult a time the Russians have had housing, feeding, and clothing the 208.8 million people on hand in 1959, one can appreciate how millions more people would have undercut their ability to make the capital investments, and the research and training expenditures, that have been a crucial ingredient in the rate of growth actually achieved. And spreading this smaller investment over a larger labor force would have made it much harder to engage in the kind of technical upgrading that has taken place.

Population Growth in Eastern Europe. The Eastern European population situation differs somewhat from that of the Soviet Union. In East Germany and Czechoslovakia, the demographic transition had taken place well before Soviet-type regimes were installed. In the less urbanized and industrialized countries, birth rates had not fallen quite so much, and there was still a high infant mortality rate that offered some potential for rapid growth; but these countries, too, were well started on the demographic transition at the time they embarked on Soviet-type development strategies. During the communist period, birth rates have continued to fall in all of them faster than death rates, and the net increase has fallen accordingly. Today, with the exception of Rumania, all have population growth rates below 1 percent per year. But as with the USSR, this has happened without policy intervention on the part of the planners, except insofar as they have aided the natural desires of the population to limit family size by making abortion relatively easy.

On the whole, the lesson their experience teaches would seem to be that dealing with the population explosion problem has very little connection to distinctive features of the Soviet-type strategy. If the conditions are right, the population problem is amenable to some policy control via abortion policy, but that can be independent of other elements of the development strategy.

Foreign Trade

Another area of controversy in development policy is international economic relations. The basic question is how open a position the developing country ought to take toward the rest of the world, regarding both the inflow of foreign capital and technology, and trade itself. The issue also appears in the guise of sectoral development priorities — whether to orient investments toward import substitution or to concentrate on those industries in which comparative advantage can generate export-led growth. Autarchy may be useful for protecting infant industries and removing the threat of foreign competition and control, but going it alone introduces the dangers of depriving oneself of foreign funds and technical knowledge and of diverting the country's resources into lines of production in which it is not efficient or competitive. We discussed the main features of Soviet-type foreign trade mechanisms in Chapter 5; here we need only relate them to development strategy. In their approach to development, the Russians clearly opted for a closed, rather than open, economy. Somewhat paradoxically, this goal was approached in the first phase, during the First Five-Year Plan period, by a notable expansion of trade and importation of foreign technology. But the imports of this period were aimed at creating the production capacity that would eliminate the need for future imports, and after the First Five-Year Plan trade was sharply curtailed. The most distinctive thing about the Soviet approach is that it had in the foreign trade monopoly a far more effective instrument for isolating itself from world market forces than the tariffs and financial controls other developing countries resort to. The main lesson of Soviet experience would seem to be that development is possible in isolation, though it is difficult to untangle the positive and the negative influences of this policy on their growth, or to evaluate it apart from the fact that Russia is a very large country with a rich and varied resource base.

For the Eastern European countries, the situation was different – instead of being isolated in the face of a hostile capitalist market, they could approach the tasks of development within the framework of a socialist world market made up of comradely socialist partners. In fact, they were far from successful in finding a strategy for wresting from this situation the putative advantages of openness in development. Such capital flows as took place were conditioned more by political than developmental considerations, so that some of the weaker countries were financing development in the larger ones, and the biggest flow – aid to China – was halted by a political falling-out. Internally, these countries adopted the original Soviet investment policy of developing heavy industry to attain autarchy through import substitution. Ironically, this policy did not give the intended results; given the weakness of their domestic raw material base, it only shifted their dependency to primary products. And, as argued in Chapter 5, the emphasis on *gratis* intra-group transfer of technology condemned them to fall behind technologically. Altogether, the development experience of the Soviet world would seem to convey eloquent warnings of the dangers of autarchy, and provide good arguments for the stimulative effects of exposure to the international market.

A Model of the Soviet Strategy

Thus the key to the traditional Soviet-type approach to growth, in Eastern Europe as well as in the USSR, was its concentration on mobilizing and increasing the inputs to production. It concentrated on these as the central elements of policy and of system design, relegating many of the other considerations important in development to secondary status. The strategy has worked, but there are some problems concealed in it that militate against its indefinite continuation. We can best understand these by considering in a highly simplified but explicit way the relationships between some of the main magnitudes in the growth process.

Consider first the kind of growth illustrated by the following example:

	1st year	2nd year	3rd year
Output during the year	100	110	121
Capital stock, beginning of year	300	330	363
Investment during the year	30	33	36.3

The example is constructed on the assumption that output in any year is proportional to the stock of capital on hand at the first of the year. Thirty percent of the year's output is invested, i.e., added to the stock of capital, so that the next year's production is based on a larger stock. (All these magnitudes are considered net of depreciation.) Note that the capital stock, output, and investment all grow at the same rate, and that this rate is constant over time. These features are independent of the particular capital-output ratio and rate of investment we assume. In any given year the three magnitudes are in fixed proportions because of our assumptions, and the rate of growth is constant because the rate of growth of the capital stock (i.e., the ratio of this year's investment to the capital stock at the beginning of the year) is a constant determined by the two other constant ratios — the share of investment in total output, this output in turn being in a fixed ratio to the capital stock at the beginning of the year. If growth worked like this, it could proceed forever at a constant rate, and with an unchanging division of the national income into investment and consumption. And the higher the rate of investment, the higher the rate of growth.

But real-world growth and, specifically, growth under a Soviet-type strategy, does not work like this. In the real world, growth in output is based in part on growth in the labor input, as well as on capital input, and a good part of it is accounted for by productivity increase. In the Soviet record, as we have seen, output grows faster than the labor force, but less rapidly than the capital stock. In contrast to our model, this must mean that investment is growing faster than output, and hence must be rising as a share of total output — as indeed we have seen to be the case. In this situation, the relative rate of growth of the capital stock and output is determined by two kinds of linkages. The capital stock may grow faster than output because the share of investment is rising, but output may be growing more slowly than the capital stock because it is retarded by lagging growth of labor inputs and productivity. We may think of the rate of growth of output as determined by two counteracting forces — the drag of low growth in labor input, versus the pull of growth in the capital stock. The strength of this positive influence is dependent on how rapidly the share of investment can rise, and on the ease with which the extra capital can compensate for the deficit in new labor inputs, i.e., what economists call the elasticity of substitution of capital for labor.

Thus it is plausible that Soviet-type growth might work well if there were a lot of labor to draw on, so long as the planners had the power to keep forcing up the fraction of the total output of the economy diverted to investment, and so long as they did not run into heavy penalties in substituting capital for labor in the input recipe used for getting increments in output. But a growing economy would inevitably run into trouble on all these fronts. The growth of labor inputs depends on the possibility of mobilizing underutilized labor, as in agriculture, and people not in the labor force — but these reserves are not infinite. Sustaining the high rate of growth of the capital stock depends on a continuous rise in the share of the national income invested, and there may be some limit to this figure as well. Also, the experience of socialist planners has been that the amount of capital that had to be thrown into the breach when inputs of labor could not be much increased has come to be alarmingly high. Furthermore, under this strategy growth seems to take the form of making more steel to make more steel mills to make more steel, in a never-ending spiral that does little to raise per capita consumption, which socialist as well as capitalist economists acknowledge as the goal of economic growth.

When rates of growth began to decline all over the communist world in the early Sixties, a number of Eastern European economists made a diagnosis similar to that outlined above. They characterized the strategy they had been following as one of "extensive growth," and were much worried by the implications of trying to sustain growth by continuing that strategy. It was this realization that roused their interest in reform, as a way to shift to a strategy of "intensive growth" that would be based more on productivity increases and less on input increases. This would be partly a matter of adopting new patterns of resource allocation, with less emphasis on investment. It was seen as a way of backing out of the trap of channeling all the increments into capital, a policy that prevented them from increasing consumption — which might have helped improve the *quality* of the labor input through better incentives to offset its slow *quantitative* growth. But any shift to an intensive-growth strategy would also require fundamental changes in the functioning of the system. To achieve the productivity increase that was to substitute for massive infusions of capital would seem to require very great changes in the system of incentives and decision making.

Soviet economists were slower than the Eastern Europeans to discern and acknowledge these implications of their growth model, but they have now recognized that this is what lies behind their slowdown also. The Ninth Five-Year Plan (for 1970–75) embodies a decision to shift from the extensive-growth strategy to one that places more emphasis on productivity as a source of growth and less emphasis on investment.

We will return to the issue of how the economy is reformed to effect such a shift in strategy in Chapter 7. But first, let us look at a couple of other variations of the Soviet development strategy — the Chinese and the Cuban — to show how it has been modified in new settings.

Chinese Adaptation of the Model

The new communist leadership of China started out in 1947 as a reasonably faithful emulator of the Soviet strategy. The Chinese situation differed in certain important ways from that of the Soviet Union at the beginning of its industrialization — some advantageous, some highly unfavorable. As followers, the Chinese did not have to go through the long period of debate, experiment, and learning the Russians had experienced, and the existence of other socialist countries much more advanced than China meant that they could hope for economic and technical assistance. The Chinese also had a more favorable political and organizational position in relation to the peasants. With extensive administrative resources and experience in the countryside, the Chinese planners were able to collectivize without the open war with the peasants and the accompanying wholesale destruction the Russians had blundered into.

On the other hand, some features of the Chinese situation were extremely disturbing for long-range growth prospects. The most important was a very unsatisfactory ratio of land resources to population. The Chinese population in 1949 was about 540 million. Although the total land area of China is large, cultivable land *per capita* is only about one third acre, compared to nearly two and a half acres in the Soviet Union. With this kind of pressure on the land, the Chinese population lived very close to subsistence and Chinese agriculture produced virtually no surplus. It will be remembered, on the other hand, that prerevolutionary Russian agriculture produced a considerable surplus, as demonstrated by the very large grain exports managed by both the tsarist and Soviet leaders and by the fact that before collectivization a large portion of Soviet agricultural output was converted into animal products. Also, the Chinese began at a significantly lower level of development. Their per capita output of most important industrial commodities in 1947 was less than ten percent of what the Russian economy of 1926 produced. The inherited stock of social overhead capital was small; they had nothing like the tsarist railroad network. The Chinese had come much less far in developing a technical and managerial elite — poor as the Russians were in this respect, the Chinese were considerably less well off.

Despite these differences, however, the Chinese undertook what was basically the Soviet-type strategy. They raised the share of investment in the gross national product and allocated it mostly to industry, especially heavy industry. They moved to collectivize agriculture and to squeeze out of it whatever surplus was possible, both to provide food for the urban population and to export in order to earn foreign exchange. They undertook a large program of importing capital goods to create a modern urban industrial sector. They also set up a typical Soviet-type administrative and planning system, though in the Chinese economy, because of its more primitive level of development, this administrative system dealt with a much smaller portion of the total economy. The Chinese slighted agriculture perhaps even more than the Russians had. There was really no prospect of mechanizing Chinese agriculture, and they were spared the Soviet-style investment-by-default to replace slaughtered draft animals. Neither did they invest resources in the indirect ways specifically important for Chinese agriculture, such as fertilizer production. In the special conditions of China, such as multiple cropping, very old lands, and extensive irrigation, this is one measure that could have significantly raised agricultural output.

This approach was followed for the first ten years — to 1957 or 1958 — and the Chinese achieved significant success under it. Output grew quite rapidly — in the estimation of western experts, at something over 6 percent per year. The share of investment in GNP was raised by six to seven percentage points, to perhaps as high as 22 percent of GNP. A considerable flow of output was diverted to export needs. A lot of new capacity was built, and they came a long way toward building a Soviet-type administrative structure. Extremely important in this regard was the material and technical aid received from the Soviet Union and Eastern Europe. The Russians had promised, and during this period delivered a considerable fraction (about half) of, a planned complex of 300 or so major industrial plants that would constitute the core of a modern industrial sector — automobile and truck plants, chemical factories, refineries, steel mills, and transport facilities.

It appears, however, that despite these successes the Chinese found the situation quite discouraging by the end of the first decade. Certain intractable problems began to be revealed. The earlier success was partly the temporary result of reconstructing a badly disorganized economy. Aid from the Russians was beginning to decline, and the Chinese faced the prospect of repayment. During this period they had made no significant progress in getting agriculture onto a new technical level or in raising its productivity. Whether they were emboldened by their successes or made desperate by their continuing problems, the Chinese leaders now initiated a radical shift in strategy in the form of the "Great Leap Forward," which was intended to overcome the obstacles and redouble the successes. From an economic point of view, the essence of the Great Leap Forward was an effort to mobilize a resource they had in abundance — labor — and make it contribute more than before to growth. People were organized into very large communes and administration was decentralized to these communes. Basically, the idea was to mobilize local resources and to try to convert them by means of small-scale production into output of some sort, such as pig iron, consumer goods, raw materials, fertilizer, or capital investments in soil and water conservation. The resources of the agricultural sector were to be used more intensively to provide additional output, to be devoted both to raising its own productivity and to making possible a still larger net transfer of goods to the modern industrial economy and for export. But all this was done under the constraint of providing no more material inputs or incentives to the agricultural population, and there was accordingly a great emphasis on political zeal as a replacement for economic incentives.

The Great Leap Forward was an unequivocal disaster. One serious consequence was a break with the Russians. The Russians clearly advised the Chinese against the Great Leap Forward and, when their advice was ignored, withdrew their aid, cancelling deliveries of industrial equipment and withdrawing all their technicians. In the long run, this deprived the Chinese of a crucial ingredient in their growth processes and, in the short run, it inevitably disrupted the operation of the modern industrial sector. The Great Leap Forward also more or less destroyed responsible administration. It disorganized agriculture and, in combination with a couple of years of bad weather, eventually led to a very serious food crisis in 1960 and 1961. It finally became clear to the Chinese leaders that the Great Leap Forward had been a mistake, and in the early Sixties they began again on the basis of still a third strategy. The new approach accepted much less ambitious goals for the modern industrial sector, devoted more resources and attention to improving agriculture, and honored more soberly the importance of economic calculation and incentives. The combination of agricultural failure and the break with the Russians also made necessary a complete reorientation of their trade program from socialist to western countries, and an alteration of its composition by cutting capital good imports considerably and importing grain to make good the food deficit to which stagnant agriculture had led. The new strategy was successful in reinitiating growth, but was interrupted in 1966 by a new paroxysm, the Great Proletarian Cultural Revolution, which finally gave way to a new period of more orderly advance after 1969.

What has happened to output, investment, and other economic magnitudes during the vagaries since 1959 is difficult to say, since the Chinese gave up publishing economic statistics at the time of the Great Leap Forward. But if we look at the period as a whole, the really important thing stands out perfectly clearly: The population has grown very rapidly, i.e., from about 540 million in 1949 to 583 million at the beginning of the First Five-Year Plan in 1953, and to perhaps as much as 800 million in 1971, (though there is great uncertainty as to just how large the Chinese population is today). Meanwhile, agricultural production has barely managed, or not quite managed, to keep up with population growth, though a several-fold increase in industrial output has permitted GNP as a whole to outstrip population growth slightly.

The Experience of Cuba

Another instructive case of attempted transfer and ultimate revision of the Soviet model is Cuba — a nation at the opposite end of the size spectrum from China, with only about 7 million people at the time of the revolution.

In the first couple of years, the Cuban revolutionary regime had confused goals and vague ideas about how to reorganize the economy. Uppermost in their thinking was the aim of combating imperialism and social injustice, with no clear idea of how they would manage the economy. It was only after Castro became thoroughly disillusioned with the United States over the embargo that he came to call himself a communist, and began to base Cuban economic policies on the experience of the communist countries. Beginning in 1961 and 1962, the Cubans began to institute Soviet-style planning, importing a group of experts from Czechoslovakia who drew up Soviet-style plans, and moving toward a Soviet-type institutional structure. Even then, they maintained some differences from the Soviet strategy, especially in retaining a large private sector in agriculture. To the extent the Cuban leaders had any idea of development strategy or sectoral emphasis, it was dominated by the notion of diversification as a path to economic independence. They were insistent on reducing dependence on sugar, and on foreign trade generally, and on giving great emphasis to import substitution. This policy flowed from some purely domestic ideas about the evils of sugar monoculture and U.S. imperialism, but also reflects very closely the standard autarchic policy of the other socialist countries.

The outcome of these years of drift and experiment with Soviet-type strategy and planning was an economic disaster. The absence of data, Cuban inexperience, and the absence of technically trained people (a good part of whom had emigrated in response to the revolution) meant that the economy could be run by administrative means only clumsily. Efforts to raise the rate of investment and to create new industrial sectors depended on importing the capital goods and some of the raw material, while the one sector that could pay for these imports had been badly crippled — sugar production declined from a prerevolutionary level of about 5 million tons to 3.8 million tons in 1963. And the program as a whole was excessively ambitious — the Cubans planned to make big investments, raise the level of welfare of the rural poor, maintain a significant military force, provide social services and education, and undertake a big housing program. These misguided efforts did not pay off: production fell while commitments were rising. Rationing was introduced in March 1962, and by 1963 it was clear that the program would have to be altered. The new strategy, fully introduced in 1964, was to postpone industrialization for a while and reorient the economy once again to sugar, accepting heavy dependence on trade. Castro set a sugar output target of 10 million tons for 1970, and got commitments from the Eastern European countries to buy very large amounts in payment for the imports the Cubans depended on. This was a remarkable commitment to sugar, which if accomplished would restore sugar to the dominant place it had in the economy before the revolution, when it accounted for about a quarter of GNP produced. The system of planning was not changed along with the strategy, however. It was to remain centralized, and the new strategy was to be implemented by direction from above. The Cubans did not learn very fast how to make this system of central planning work. It remained heavily politicized — Castro was free to indulge his own hobbies and to set up special projects, run by people reporting directly to him, which had priority over everything else in resource allocation. Cuban administration has always been ambivalent on material incentives. Another Cuban peculiarity has been a failure to institute even the degree of financial decentralization implied by *khozraschet*. Most enterprises paid all their revenues into, and paid all their expenditures out of, the central treasury. This leads to poor financial discipline and little regard for economic calculation.

The new strategy seems not to have worked any better than the previous one. The 10 million ton sugar goal was missed badly, with an output of 8.5 million tons. What is worse, the commitment to the sugar program damaged the rest of the economy grievously by drawing off the labor and other inputs needed to operate it. The sugar strategy was predicated on exporting large amounts of sugar to pay for imports that would support industrialization, but failure to meet the output goal made it impossible to meet these commitments, and the Cubans have been able to operate their economy only through the other socialist countries' willingness to continue to send large amounts of unrequited exports.

Cuba has been in deficit in its trade with the socialist countries from 1962 on, and the cumulative amount of this deficit had reached over two and a quarter billion pesos by the beginning of the Seventies. Considering that Cuban national product was running at 6–7 billion pesos per year in this period, this represents a substantial flow of foreign aid — something like 4 percent of national product every year.

Nor have these sectoral troubles been balanced by general growth success. According to their own statistics, overall output has risen in some years, but for the period as a whole it has remained virtually stagnant. This is easily understandable in the light of the failure of the two major sectors — agriculture and industry — to grow strongly. The index of agriculture output computed by the Food and Agriculture Organization shows output below that of the prerevolutionary period in six of the eleven years after 1959, with no growth for the period as a whole. There has been an increase in industrial output of only a few percentage points a year, and due to its small share in total output this has not been able to lift the overall growth performance. This failure to increase output appreciably is all the more discouraging when we note that the population has continued to grow strongly during this decade, from 6.7 million in 1959 to 8.7 million in 1972, a rate of growth of

.

about 2 percent per year. Cuba is in the middle stages of the demographic transition, with birth rates fluctuating around 30 per thousand, and one suspects that it will be hard-pressed to manage any increase in per capita output.

So whatever the successes of the revolution in achieving the social aims it set for itself, and in asserting its independence from the United States, its economic results have been most disappointing. It is nothing like what the other countries have achieved, though we might want to write off part of these years as years of learning and consolidation of the regime, and expect that Castro and his regime may still manage to get growth going one of these days.

Sketchy though these capsule histories are, they permit us to draw several important conclusions about economic development under communism. First, whatever its successes in the USSR, the Soviet strategy obviously cannot work miracles. It has achieved its successes by mobilizing reserves and directing them to growth objectives, but when a society lives as close to the margin as the Chinese do, there is very little for it to work with. And in such situations the neglect of agriculture the Russians practiced cannot be afforded.

Second, hopes for diversification and self-sufficiency based on the kind of industrialization the Russians experienced are unrealistic in a small country. Seven million people is just too small a market, especially when important mineral resources and fuel are lacking. Such a country must specialize, take advantage of its special resource situation, and trade. And when a country's comparative advantage is in agriculture, the inherent ineffectiveness of Soviet-type planning in managing agricultural production makes it an intolerable handicap. Also, it is reasonably clear that whatever disadvantages there may be in economic dependency, they are as likely to emerge from dependency on socialist brother nations as from dependency on the capitalist world market. Cuba is, inescapably, a client state of the USSR, and very vulnerable to economic pressure.

Both the Cuban and the Chinese cases suggest that the efficacy of the Soviet model in generating growth is much diluted when blended with romanticism. It worked in the

Soviet Union because the leaders were willing to oppress the peasants and to be hard-boiled about incentives and performance. The Cubans have not been, and they have so far failed to prove that one can count on revolutionary enthusiasm to get output to grow.

Both Cuba and China, the latter most dramatically, underline the independent significance of the population issue. The Russians and Eastern Europeans evaded population pressure by accident or good fortune; the Chinese and Cubans have not, and this factor is important in explaining the difference in the success achieved.

Finally, looking back over the Eastern European variants, as well as the Chinese and Cuban, there has now been so much divergence from the Russians' policies under Stalin that it makes almost no sense anymore to think of the socialist countries as following a standard Soviet development strategy. It is more profitable to think of them as distinctive strategies, in which the common genetic inheritance has been overshadowed by adaptations to varied situations.

III

Reform and the Future of Socialist Planning

7

The Rediscovery of Economics

The bosses of the socialist economic systems had arrived by the Sixties at a point at which they were ready to consider reform seriously. Concern about economic perform- ance — whether in terms of growth, innovation, the multiplica- tion of objectives, or a desire to humanize socialism — made them willing to question some basic features of the model and to consider changing them. The function of the remaining chapters is to ask several related questions about the reform of the model that had evolved under Stalin and that had for so long been identified with socialist planning. What does reform involve? What concrete efforts have been made so far to change economic policies and institutions? What is the future shape of socialism toward which these reforms are tending?

It is clear that reform involves two quite distinct aspects — analytical and institutional change. A reorientation in thought and doctrine — a change in the way people conceive and understand how an economy functions or might function — is an indispensable first step. Only after this has been accom- plished can institutional tinkering be given some direction and policy changes be made with an idea of what they are intended to accomplish. The function of Chapter 7 is to consider the revolution in economic thinking that has taken place in the socialist world in the last decade or so, and Chapter 8 will review and evaluate the institutional changes that occurred during the Sixties. As we will see, these changes have so far been less than revolutionary, and seem not to have solved the traditional problems. In Chapter 9, we will try to identify the obstacles to reform and the unresolved issues, and to speculate on what kind of system might emerge in the future.

The Revival of Economics

As we have suggested, economics as a scientific discipline has generally played a subordinate role in the design and operation of the Soviet-type economy. Once the Stalinist model was established and functioning in the Soviet Union and in Eastern Europe, the regimes did not rely on economists for professional advice, and economists came to be an intellectually subservient group. Their function was primarily to deal with the political economy of socialism and to provide an ideological justification for the system. Socialist political economy did not offer much in the way of concrete advice useful to policymakers.

A typical Stalinist book on economics, or a Soviet journal article, is full of discussions of the "laws" of socialist political economy, doctrinal statements on why the national income must include only material production, assertions and conjectures that the means of production must grow faster than the means of consumption in an expanding economy, and so on. It is notably lacking in such standard economic ideas as scarcity, allocative behavior on the part of decision makers, incentives, choices, criteria for optimization, and the like.

This situation is not difficult to understand if we keep in mind two factors. First, the Stalinist approach was based on a kind of strategic vision that did not involve much thinking in terms of economic variables and economic choices. The overall strategy was clear, and the possibility of alternatives at the micro-level was more or less overlooked. Second, Marxian economics could not in any case be very helpful since it does not really concern itself with the central issue of

economizing. If we see the planners' problem as one of economizing or making the right choices, Marxian political economy
is of little use. It is basically true, as has been said, that there
is no micro-economics in Marx. Marxian economics does not
concern itself with the problem of allocation, and the ideas
it offers on the subject of value are rather useless since they
are divorced from any concept of allocation. Marxian economics broke off from the mainstream of economic thought at a
time in the history of the science before it had been understood
that the issues of value and allocation are inextricably inter-
twined. And, after all, Marx's value theory was directed at
and designed to elucidate quite a different kind of question
than choices about what and how to produce — the single issue
of how value affects class relationships and political power.
In this situation, the role assigned to economics and economists
was mostly one of explaining the virtues of socialist planning
and the contradictions of capitalist exploitation.

One of the most fascinating things about Soviet economic
planning, however, is the way in which practical planning
problems led Soviet planners and, on occasion, economists to
try to create a theory of economics that would be useful as
a theoretical basis for planning decisions.

The Capital Intensity Problem

One of the most interesting and instructive of these is the
experience with the capital allocation problem. As explained
earlier, in the Stalinist model no charge was made for capital,
and prices did not reflect the capital costs of various kinds
of output. Allocation of capital among major sectors was one
of the principal instruments of the strategy, and there was a
presumption that any mechanical or decentralized approach
to making this allocation was inappropriate. Also, Marxian
economic theory had always treated the income earned on
capital as an exploitative form of tribute extracted from labor,
and ridiculed the idea that it was due to the contribution to
production of capital itself. At the practical level of implementing planning decisions, however, the question of the capital
intensity of a given project could not be evaded.

Capital intensity is the value of capital tied up in some production facility in relation to the value of its annual output. The more dollars' worth of resources are tied up in capital per dollars' worth of output per year, the higher the capital intensity. The planners responsible for designing factories or machinery, choosing between traditional or automated production lines, or designing railroads, for example, constantly find that if they could have permission to commit more capital to these projects, the cost per unit of output in terms of current operating costs would decrease. Consider, for instance, the problem of a project maker in the electric power industry who must decide whether an assigned increment of generating capacity should be met by building a steam station or a hydroelectric station. When he estimates the costs for the two alternatives, he may find something like the situation illustrated in Table 7.1.

Table 7.1 Alternative Projects for a New Power Station

	STEAM STATION	HYDROELECTRIC STATION
Capacity	50 thousand kilowatts	50 thousand kilowatts
Initial investment	50 million rubles	100 million rubles
Annual operating costs	25 million rubles	20 million rubles
Fuel	10 million rubles	0 million rubles
Labor	10 million rubles	5 million rubles
Depreciation	5 million rubles	10 million rubles
Other	0 million rubles	5 million rubles

The hydroelectric station will require an initial investment of 100 million rubles, compared to only 50 million rubles for a steam station of the same capacity. But once this investment is made, the operating costs per kilowatt-hour of electricity produced will be appreciably lower forever after. Note that since depreciation has been figured in as one of the costs, one can assume that this station or a successor, financed from the depreciation allowances, can remain in operation indefinitely without additional investment. The hydro station will have no cost for fuel and there will be savings in other items, such as labor, as well. This possibility of cutting future operating costs by increasing present capital investment in a project occurs in many other situations. It should be noted that in the usual situation there are not just two alternatives, as our example suggests, but a whole succession of variants for any project, offering a more or less continuous trade-off between investment requirements and operating costs. Where along this continuum is the optimal capital intensity?

This problem as formulated by a firm in the capitalist economy would be different from our example in an important respect. In the capitalist economy there would be an interest charge for capital, and interest payments would be one element of the annual operating costs. Increases in the capital intensity of a project add to annual operating costs in the form of interest charges, and increases in capital intensity are carried to the point where the savings in operating costs are just offset by the additional interest payments to which the extra investment commits the firm. In the calculation in Table 7.1, the project maker has not included interest as an operating cost since for most of Soviet history there was no interest charge for the use of capital. In the traditional Soviet model, investments were financed by means of interest-free grants from state sources. The absence of an interest charge in the Soviet economy is based on Marxian economic theory. According to Marx's theory of value, capital contributes nothing to production; to a believer in Marxian theory, it would therefore seem absurd to require payment for the use of capital once the power of the capitalists is overthrown.

This Marxian interpretation of capital and interest is erroneous; capital is productive in the sense that the addition of capital to a given process increases the output. Moreover, capital is scarce and some rule is required for allocating it to the most productive uses. In the capitalist economy the interest charge serves both as a payment for the productive services of capital and as a means for rationing it. Unless the prospective user of capital finds that it will increase his output or cut his costs enough to be worth the interest he must pay for it, he will forego using it — and, indeed, cannot obtain it. Thus the rate of interest is a means by which capital is rationed out to those uses, and in those amounts, that will maximize its overall productivity.

In the Soviet economy the basic circumstance that capital is both productive and scarce still holds. It is true that in the Soviet system there is no need for the state to pay interest to persuade people to save; the state can compel savings by various fiscal and pricing devices. But the problem remains of assuring that capital be used in the best way, that the project maker in the example above not choose the hydroelectric station if the extra 50 million rubles that it requires could be more productively employed elsewhere. Thus we return to the question of the rule decision makers should follow in deciding how far to move toward the more capital-intensive variants of any project. Clearly, it will not do just to tell them to choose the variant that will minimize operating costs. The response would be that the sum of investment resources requested for all the projects being considered would far outstrip the amount available. If the irrationality and the extra work of an arbitrary allocation by some higher-level decision makers is to be avoided, it is necessary to adopt a rule that each decision maker can apply on his own; in Soviet planning practice there gradually emerged what is called the "payoff period" approach. In considering possible variants of a given investment project, the project maker asks how long it will take for the savings in operating costs in the more capital-intensive variant to recoup the additional capital investment it requires. In the example mentioned above, for instance, the hydroelectric power station requires 50 million rubles more investment than a steam station of the same capacity, but its annual operating costs are 5 million rubles less. The payoff period for the additional capital investment would thus be ten years. To guide project makers in these choices, it was customary to establish the rule that additional investment in such cases is justified only if the payoff period for the additional capital investment does not exceed some stipulated number of years. The number of years stipulated has not generally been uniform, but varied from industry to industry.

A moment's reflection will reveal that the payoff period is essentially the rate of interest turned upside down. A recoupment period of five years, for instance, means that the return to the additional capital invested (the return being measured as the value of resources saved) amounts each year to 20 percent of the investment. Or, in other words, the productivity of the capital in this case is 20 percent per year. If the authorities set a rule for plant designers that the payoff period must be no more than five years, they are in effect saying that capital should not be used unless the return to it is at least 20 percent. Thus the condemned rate of interest is brought in through the back door. In the early postwar years, the anti-Marxist implication of this practice was realized and it was officially condemned by the Marxist theoreticians. There followed a long controversy in which the necessity for some such device for capital allocation was made clear and, in the end the payoff period approach was accorded legitimate status. In going through this evolution, the Russians have not declared Marx wrong in his labor theory of value, but they have come to realize that the theory must be ignored when it conflicts with the demands of rationality in this practical problem.

Legitimation of the payoff period approach was only a partial solution, however, and left unsettled such questions as what the normative payoff period is to be, and whether it should be uniform for all sectors or differentiated among sectors. Soviet practice has generally been to accept different payoff periods in different jurisdictions, essentially those that had evolved over time in the underground tradition. To understand how this question *ought* to be settled, it is convenient to think about how variants might be chosen if the process were centralized. Suppose the planners had decided on the output increases for each product and asked the project makers to come up with several projects for each of the factories, transport facilities, etc., needed to produce these outputs and send them in to the Gosplan. A listing of the minimal-capital variant for each project would generate a total investment requirement less than the total amount of investment resources available. The next step would be to ask how the uncommitted capital investment resources should be allocated to move to more capital-intensive variants of the different projects. The question would be how far to go in modernizing one project to save labor, authorizing additional investments in equipment in another to reduce input consumption, or suggesting that the civil aviation planners choose more modern but more expensive airplanes that could reduce fuel expenditure per passenger mile. The easiest way to make these decisions would be to figure the payoff period for each proposal for increasing the capital-intensity of the original projects, and then rank them, the ones with the shortest payoff period at the top of the list. One could then simply go down this list, approving projects until all the available investment resources were committed. We might reflect that, if the planners had known in advance what the payoff period on the last project authorized turned out to be, much trouble could have been saved by announcing that all project makers should use this as the normative payoff period. They would then have arrived at the same choices on their own as would be decided centrally.

There is a straightforward implication here that there should be a uniform normative payoff period for the whole economy. In the centralized procedure suggested, it would be foolish to pass over a project high on the list to approve deepening the capital intensity of one farther down the list with a longer payoff period. And if, in a decentralized procedure, decision makers in different parts of the economy were to use different payoff periods, the same error would result.

A second difficulty with the payoff period approach is that project makers have come up against several problems that it cannot handle conveniently. Consider again the two variants for an electric power plant. Anyone looking for arguments against the hydroelectric plant might well object that its investment requirements are not fully accounted for in the calculation. If it is chosen, society would be committed not just to investment in the dam, but also to additional investment in the cement industry whose output will be used in constructing the dam. The proponents of the hydroelectric project might answer that not all the investment costs of the steam plant are reckoned either, since if it is chosen there will assuredly have to be additional investment in the coal industry. This could become a very elaborate competition, as the two sides catalogued all the investments needed in industries supplying investment goods or current inputs for the two variants, and the extra investments needed in the industries supplying them. This is a parallel to the input-output interdependency considered earlier, and it would be a mind-boggling endeavor to trace all the associated investments (or *sopriazhennye vlozheniia,* as the Russians call them) entailed by any set of project-making variants. But why does the issue arise? It would never occur to anyone contemplating an investment in a market economy to worry about the investment required in the supporting industries. Nor need we worry about it in his stead — those costs do get taken into account implicitly, since the prices of all the inputs (and the inputs to those inputs) already include the interest charges that all the producers pay on the capital they use. The conclusion is that it is not enough to use the payoff period as a surrogate for the interest charge just to choose between project variants. To avoid the problem of associated investments, interest should actually be paid on capital, and prices for various goods set at a level to include an interest charge on the capital involved in producing them. Indeed, the problem is much broader — such charges are necessary to make prices suitable indexes of social cost for *any* kind of calculation, not just investment calculations. An interesting illustration of the confusion caused by the absence of a charge on capital is found in foreign trade. As explained earlier, there is a shortage of raw materials in the socialist bloc, and all countries are reluctant to produce more of these goods for export. Their reluctance is founded in part on the argument that these are capital-intensive industries, and that any country that commits itself to these heavy investments is reducing the overall growth-effectiveness of its investments, since it will have to stint investments in sectors in which the ratio of output to investment is higher. At the same time, it would be facilitating growth in the recipient countries, which will make repayment with the products of industries that can be expanded with less capital investment. So there are cases in which raw-material exporters require the receiving country to provide some of the investment. The confusion and acrimony over this issue would be greatly lessened if it were clearly understood that with economic prices, including among other things a charge for capital, the problem vanishes.

Finally, the payoff-period approach is not applicable to problems of bringing outlays made at different times to a common time basis, as in the following case. Suppose the plan requires that a rail link be constructed between two regions, and that it must be able to handle projected traffic of 10 million kilometers by the end of the present plan period five years hence. Eventually, say ten years beyond that date, capacity will have to be four times larger, and to handle that larger volume of traffic the project makers realize that doubletracking will be necessary. They consider whether to do now some of the roadbed work required eventually for doubletracking, since a saving can be made if it is done while the equipment is in place and there is an ongoing organization. Suppose the alternatives are to do this work now at a cost of 50 million rubles, or later at a cost of 75 million rubles.

This doesn't quite fit the payoff-period framework; here, as there, the problem is to evaluate an extra outlay made today in the light of future savings, but here the saving is a one-time affair, rather than a stream in perpetuity as in the payoff-period calculation. The same sort of considerations apply, however. The hesitancy about committing the 50 million rubles flows from the fact that these resources could be used somewhere else to make savings *now*. If the normative payoff period is twenty years, somewhere in the economy that 50 million rubles could save 2.5 million rubles' worth of resources per year. And if the saving made in the first year were invested, there would be savings of 2.625 in the second year, and so on. Only if these sacrifices are smaller than the 25 million rubles saving from early construction of the roadbed is the latter justified.

It is hardly possible to avoid using the interest rate explicitly here, as in the formula that a bourgeois economist would use to calculate the total cost of the early outlay variant as 50 MR $\times$ $(1 + .10)^{10}$ for comparison with the 75 million rubles cost of the other variant. In that case, one might as well drop the payoff period concept entirely and adopt rate of interest as the most convenient way of taking account of the opportunity cost of capital in all contexts. The Russians finally reached that point in a landmark decision made in 1969, and the idea of interest as a measure of the opportunity cost of capital is now generally accepted by socialist planners, even though they still call themselves Marxists. These economies have still not established the right kind of institutions for implementing the new understanding. We will discuss in Chapter 8 how they have coped with the interest rate in the reform measures actually adopted. The important point is that they are now groping toward more rational ways of getting the opportunity costs of capital registered in decision making. Once the issue is understood analytically, the way is open to reform the rules.

The capital allocation problem is an excellent illustration of how responses to the practical problems of planning have forced socialist planners and economists over the years to give up some Marxist simplicities and move toward an interpretation of economic questions not much different from that of world mainstream economics. The capital allocation controversy has been a particularly productive area, since it has led them inexorably to such central concepts of economics as the idea of scarcity, the notion of opportunity cost, and the idea of imputation of value to any resource that is scarce and constitutes a limitation on the achievement of planners' goals.

Opportunity Costs and Administered Prices

Practical administrative exigencies often led planners in Soviet-type economies to correct insights about pricing in a wide variety of situations. One interesting article, for instance, discussed the problem of pricing the raw materials for vegetable oil production. In accordance with the usual Marxian emphasis on cost as the source of value, the prices set on the two kinds of seeds might be set according to the average cost to the producers. Such an error in pricing causes serious administrative difficulties. Suppose, for example, that the prices, oil content, and processing costs of the two kinds of raw material are as shown in Table 7.2 on the following page. Assuming that the oil produced from the two kinds of seeds is more or less the same, the cost of a ton of oil differs considerably between the two kinds of raw material. To produce a ton of oil from sunflower seed will require processing 5 tons of material, which will cost 200 rubles for the seeds

Table 7.2 Illustrative Opportunity Cost Calculation

	PRICE	OIL CONTENT AS PERCENT OF WEIGHT	COST OF PROCESSING A TON OF SEEDS	COST OF OIL
Sunflower seeds	40 rubles/ton	20 percent	10 rubles	250 rubles/ton
Cottonseed	35 rubles/ton	25 percent	12 rubles	188 rubles/ton

and 50 rubles for the processing. To produce a ton of oil from cottonseed will require processing 4 tons of seed, at a total cost of 4 × 35 = 140 rubles for the seed and 48 rubles for processing. Sunflower seed is therefore "disadvantageous" from the point of view of the producer, and if he has any choice in selecting his inputs, he will refuse the disadvantageous material. Or, if a firm uses a mixture, its cost performance will depend on whether the mixture it actually processes conforms to the mixture originally planned. Since the administrative system will not generally operate with sufficient finesse to allow for variations from plan, a plant that processes a mix different from plan may be penalized for poor cost performance, or rewarded for above-plan cost performance, when in fact these results are due only to a shift from the planned input mix. To eliminate both these kinds of problems, therefore, it quickly occurs to the price setters that different kinds of oil seeds should be priced so as to make them equally advantageous to enterprises. Assuming that the price of oil is 200 rubles, then, the price for sunflower seeds ought to be set at (200 – 50) / 5 = 30 rubles and cottonseed at (200 – 48) / 4 = 38 rubles. It would be then a matter of indifference to the processor which one he gets, and cost results will be more or less independent of changes in mix. This is an application of what western economists would call the idea of opportunity cost, and illustrates why the values of goods must reflect their usefulness to the user as well as the relative costs of producing the goods. Of course, there may be contradictions between these standards, as in this case, where relative values based on opportunity cost are out of line with the relative cost of production.

Such a contradiction would, however, be eliminated by reducing or halting production of the seeds whose production cost is above their value, as determined by the opportunity cost approach, and increasing the production of the other seeds. It might not be necessary to go to extremes in this switch, since as the output of sunflower seed was reduced and its culture limited to the most suitable areas, its cost might come down. This illustrates that quantities and prices are interdependent in any general equilibrium approach to optimizing the way society used its resources. Socialist planners have frequently been led by administrative instinct to the idea that prices should be set to reflect opportunity costs as seen by the user, but their Marxian blinkers usually prevented them from grasping the implications for decisions about quantities.

In the Fifties the accumulation of these insights, together with the change in the general intellectual environment after Stalin's death, culminated in a real revolution in economic theory and doctrine in the USSR and Eastern Europe. It was a revolution that discarded many of the mistaken ideas of Marxian economic theory and replaced them with standard economics as it is understood in the west. This revolution is fascinating as an episode in the history of economic thought, and obviously has great significance for understanding the reform measures that have already been taken and for assessing the possible direction future evolution of the economic system of the socialist societies may take.

This revolution owes a great deal to a willingness on the part of the regime to loosen the idelogical restraints on discussion of economic issues. In the late Fifties economists were permitted to consider once again some of the central problems of planning, a role that Stalin's repression of economics had ended in the late Twenties. Economists responded timidly at first, but then with an accelerating enthusiasm for creative investigation. Eastern European economists were generally bolder than the Russians, though their freedom to deal openly with economic issues would not have been possible without the change within the Soviet Union. The willingness of the communist regimes to permit this freedom of discussion was no doubt prompted by the growing complexity of running their economies by administrative approaches and by an unmistakable deceleration in economic growth. One aspect of the new climate was the possibility of looking outward again toward the rest of the world; when economists did so, they were fascinated to find that some new ideas in western economics were admirably suited to dealing with their planning problems. The Soviet receptivity to new ideas was further enhanced when the economists found that two of these ideas — input-output and linear programming — owed a great deal to Soviet contributors. Adoption of the new ideas could thus be accepted as a return to their own heritage, rather than a copying of bourgeois ideas.

Soviet and Eastern European Experiments with Input-Output

The feasibility of the original Soviet approach to drawing up a balanced plan at the center has been badly undermined by growth. As the economy becomes larger the balancing job takes more effort, becomes more frantic, and results in more costly mistakes. Several Russians have made eloquent predictions that, unless something is done, the annual balancing process will become less and less workable and the burden of staffing the planning offices will become intolerable. One way to improve and speed up the balancing aspect of annual planning is input-output; it will be useful at this point to describe what the Russians and Eastern Europeans have done along these lines and to speculate on whether input-output can solve some of the problems. In the process we will need to take a somewhat fuller look at input-output to see how it works and what its limitations are.

Once the interrelationships between different sectors have been laid bare in an input-output table, such as Table 2.1, it is possible to extract from the system a mathematical model of production interrelationships. Remember that the uses shown represent two different categories — final demand and intermediate demand. Each intermediate demand can be interpreted as the product of two factors — for example, the number of tons of steel required for the machinery industry is the product of multiplying the millions of dollars' worth of machinery to be produced by the number of tons of steel required per million dollars' worth of machinery output. Final demands are autonomous — i.e., they are determined by considerations outside these input-output relationships. The main condition to be satisfied in the system is that the output of any industry be large enough to cover both kinds of demands. To take steel as an example, a statement of the following form can be made for each industry: "The total output of steel needs to be just large enough to supply whatever steel is needed for all intermediate users (each of these needs being expressed as the output of the using industry times the amount of steel needed per unit of its output), with enough left over to cover the demands of households, government, and other final users."

Translated into symbols, this statement takes the following form:

$$X_1 = a_{11}X_1 + a_{12}X_2 + a_{13}X_3 + a_{14}X_4 \ldots a_{1,13}X_{13} + \text{Final Demands},$$

where X stands for the total output of some industry (*which* industry being indicated by the subscript) and the a's are input coefficients. For example, a_{13} means the amount of the product of industry 1 required per unit of output of industry 3. If industry 1 is the steel industry and industry 3 the automobile industry, then a_{13} stands for the tons of steel needed to produce one automobile. In this equation, each X represents an unknown, i.e., the level of output for that industry. In the input-output matrix of Table 2.1, there would be thirteen such unknowns. Since a similar equation can be set up for each industry, there are as many equations as there are industry output levels to be determined. Once we have specified the desired final demands, the set of equations can be solved to find the output level required for each industry. This required set of output levels may or may not be feasible, depending on the capacity limits of each industry and on some overall constraints, such as labor. The procedure then is to experiment with alternative combinations of final demands to find the best one among all those that are consistent with these capacity constraints. With computers it is possible to carry out this exploration of feasible alternatives very rapidly, even for very large systems. Input-output thus seems a close enough analogue to what the central planners are already doing to make it a feasible replacement for their present trial-and-error balancing. At the same time it would be much faster and more flexible.

Soviet economists have been experimenting with the construction of input-output matrices for the Soviet economy since the late Fifties. The construction of an input-output table is a complicated endeavor, involving a tremendous job of data collection and of finding satisfactory definitional compromises to fit the complexities of a real economy into this rather abstract scheme. The Russians have prepared a succession of input-output tables of increasing size and refinement. The latest stage in their experimentation is to use the input-output table to generate the levels of output and its allocation implicit in the plan targets for some future year, and then to check these against the plan worked out in the actual planning process.

The Eastern European planners have been equally fascinated with input-output and indeed have probably done as much or more work with it as the Russians. In addition, all these countries have made an effort to acquire the computer capacity needed to do their balancing by input-output techniques; the Russians, for example, have installed a large British computer in Gosplan for such work. These tables have been used extensively both to construct preliminary balanced estimates and to reform prices. Indeed, there is only one step remaining to be taken, namely, to transfer the actual operational annual balancing procedure onto the computer with an input-output approach. This part they have been reluctant to do.

Actually, the importance of input-output may be less in the impact it has had on the Russians' planning procedures than in its influence on their thinking about the process of planning. First, input-output has made planners and economists willing to call on mathematicians, a contact Stalin had denied them, and has been the principal pretext for their striking up an acquaintance with computers. Second, it offers some clarifying insights as to how planning should be conceptualized. The input-output framework has made it possible to distinguish more clearly the respective provinces of the political leadership and the economists, and to separate political and economic issues. For example, there has always been a tendency on the part of the strategic decision makers at the top to think in terms of sectoral outputs. As examples, Stalin had the simple-minded idea that the way to make the economy grow was to expand steel output, and Soviet ideology has always glorified priority for the machine building sector as the key to growth and technical progress. The input-output framework makes it clear that the question of how much steel to produce is partly a question of priorities, which is a legitimate concern of the leadership, but also partly a purely technical question. The input-output framework makes it clear that the top-level decision makers should concern themselves with the final outputs of the economy — consumption, investment, defense, foreign aid, and the like — and then let the technicians take over to figure out how much steel output those goals for final demand will require. As another example, the grand strategists of socialist growth always conceived their strategy in part as emphasizing "industry B," producing the means of production, over "industry A," producing the means of consumption. The attempt to construct an input-output table makes it clear that these ideas are quite meaningless and useless for thinking about growth strategy. The coal industry produces essentially one kind of good, some of which is used as a means of production, and some of which is used for consumption, as its row in an input-output table demonstrates. The electronics industry produces some goods that go to other industries, some that go to investment, and some that go to consumption. Growth strategy ought to be concerned primarily with the relative claims of investment and consumption on the economy's final output. The proper procedure is to start here, and then to work through the input-output table to implications for the growth of the textile industry versus the growth of the rubber industry, rather than trying to specify industrialization strategies in terms of gross output directly. Of course, once the Stalinist strategy was adopted in the First Five-Year Plan, with its disastrous implications for consumption, the regime did not like to discuss the question openly, and speaking in terms of industry A versus industry B helped confuse the issue.

Finally, input-output has served as an introduction to mathematical methods in general, and especially to linear programming. This is particularly important because linear programming was the instrument through which all these progressive insights were finally transformed into a real revolution. The progression from input-output to linear programming proceeds as described in the following section.

Linear Programming

Input-output has some very serious limitations as a planning device. Implicit in the input-output description of economic relationships are some peculiar assumptions about production, the important one here being that the production of a ton of steel takes a fixed menu of inputs and that no substitution of one input for another is possible. That may be satisfactory as an approximation, but it is not really true. To produce a kilowatt-hour of electric power, for instance, substitution of one fuel for another is possible — one can reduce the expenditure of coal per kilowatt-hour by using more natural gas. Thus input-output is an unrealistically restrictive framework. Suppose that balancing by means of input-output shows that electric power is a bottleneck because there is a shortage of coal. The input-output approach will not suggest that the bottleneck could be broken by substituting gas for coal. Input-output is thus solely a balancing technique, and completely ignores some of the important aspects of optimizing the allocation of resources and choosing the most efficient methods of production.

Another mathematical technique, known as linear programming, resembles input-output in many ways but is different in precisely this respect: it acknowledges that there is more than one technique for producing electric power (or any other output) and that these techniques differ from each other by different input coefficients. Electric power can be produced in hydroelectric stations with one set of coefficients, in gas-fired thermal stations with another, or in coal-fired stations with still another. The linear programming approach broadens the balancing process to consider not only the levels of output of each commodity required but also, for each, the combination of alternative technologies that should be used to adjust to the limited availability of particular inputs or the capacity for producing particular inputs. In short, linear programming provides a framework for explicit optimizing in a way that input-output does not. And, as has been said earlier, the traditional Soviet model, because of its strategic approach and Marxian ideological underpinnings, was not concerned with optimization. Adopting an explicit theory of optimization was

bound to have revolutionary consequences. Once linear programming came to be understood and accepted, there was no
turning back. How such a change could be made is a fascinating
story, worth dwelling on for what it shows about intellectual
revolutions in the Soviet context.

One of the strongest factors favoring the acceptance of linear
programming was the startling discovery that it had been
invented in the Soviet Union before it was invented in the
west. The original discovery of linear programming in the
Soviet Union grew out of a practical planning problem, in much
the same way as other changes we have described. In the
Thirties planning officials in the Central Plywood Trust in
Leningrad came to the mathematician L. V. Kantorovich with
a problem that had arisen in their plywood-producing operations. One of the basic processes in the making of plywood
is to rotate a log in a stripping machine that cuts off a continuous
thin sheet of material; these sheets are then laminated to make
plywood. The production plan for the trust designated a certain
assortment of different kinds of logs to be processed in this
way; the goal was to process as large a volume, in that
assortment, as possible. The trust had several different kinds
of stripping machines, each of which could work on any kind
of log, but with different productivities, as indicated in Table
7.3.

Table 7.3 Productivity of Different Machines by Log Type (m³/hour)

MACHINE TYPE	TYPE OF LOG				
	1	2	3	4	5
A	4.0	7.0	8.5	13.0	16.5
B	4.5	7.8	9.7	13.7	17.5
C	5.0	8.0	10.0	14.8	18.0
D	4.0	7.0	9.0	13.5	17.0
E	3.5	6.5	8.5	12.7	16.0
F	3.0	6.0	8.0	13.5	15.0
G	4.0	7.0	9.0	14.0	17.0
H	5.0	8.0	10.0	14.8	18.0

Each cell in Table 7.3 shows the volume of wood that can be processed, per hour, when a particular type of machine works on a particular type of log. Note that each of the machines is more productive when working on certain kinds of logs than on others. Note also that as one moves down the list of machines, those lower in the list are more productive than those higher up, no matter what kinds of logs they are working on. But there is a phenomenon visible in the table analogous to comparative advantage in international trade. For example, machine type H has a 25 percent productivity advantage over machine type A when it is working on log type 1, but only about a 12 percent productivity advantage when dealing with log type 5. Or, looked at another way, by shifting machine type A from log 1 to log 5, its productivity can be increased by more than five times, whereas the analogous productivity increase for machine type H is only about three and a half times. At the same time, however, it will not be possible to assign each machine just to the kind of log it handles best, since that might provide more capacity for some kinds of logs than there are logs of that type to be processed, while failing to process the requisite amount of other kinds of logs.

In thinking about this problem, Kantorovich first undertook to set it out in the kind of symbolic notation familiar to a mathematician. He expressed the problem as one of finding a plan or program specifying how much of the available time of each machine is to be devoted to working on any given type of log. These he designates h_{ik}, with the i's indicating the kind of machine involved and the k's designating the type of log. Thus, h_{c4} will indicate the fraction of total work-time available on machines of type C that will be assigned to working on logs of type 4. In the program we are working out, some of these coefficients will end up being 0, indicating that the machine in question does not work on the kind of log in question. Others may be 1, indicating full-time assignment to that kind of log; in other cases, they may be fractions. For instance, we might have $H_{d1} = .5$ and $H_{d4} = .5$, indicating that machines of type D work half the time on log type 1, and half the time on log type 4.

This set of coefficients could clearly be called a plan, since it indicates in operative detail how the productive capacity of the trust is to be used. The problem is to choose these coefficients so as to satisfy other requirements. The first of these is the goal of the trust to maximize the total amount of wood processed in the given proportions. This is expressed as:

$$\frac{\sum\limits_{i=1}^{n} h_{i1}\alpha_{i1}}{P_1} = \cdots \frac{\sum\limits_{i=1}^{n} h_{im}\alpha_m}{P_m} = \text{max}$$

where α_{ik} are the productivity coefficients from Table 7.3. Thus the numerator of the first term signifies the total cubic meters of log type 1 processed on all machines. It says: multiply for each machine its output per hour by the part of total time it will work on log type 1, and add that for all machines. This will give the total amount of log type 1 processed. The expression as a whole says that these sums of the amounts of each type of log processed must be proportional to the shares of different kinds of logs in the plan (the p's) and the whole output should be a maximum. Second, the program must not assign any machine to work more than the total time available; this condition can be expressed as $\sum\limits_{k=1}^{m} h_{ik} \leqslant 1$. Finally, these program coefficients cannot be negative. This is an obvious common-sense statement that a machine cannot be assigned to a given kind of work for a fraction of the time less than zero. But for the mathematician's purposes this condition must be set down explicitly, and it is expressed as $h_{ik} \geqslant 0$.

Writing down the problem was only the first step and solving it was rather difficult, since it was not one for which mathematicians had already worked out a standard solution process, or algorithm. The basic difficulty is that there are many sets of coefficients that will satisfy the last two conditions, and the problem is to find the one from among this very large number that will maximize the throughput. Kantorovich designed an algorithm for finding this best program that involved introducing some auxiliary numbers, which he called multipliers (by analogy with the Lagrangean multipliers of calculus). By altering these multipliers in a systematic way, he guaranteed a consistent movement toward the final solution. We will have more to say about these multipliers later.

One of the most interesting features of Kantorovich's work is that he realized that many problems planners faced could be fitted into this framework and solved by his technique. He apparently made a great effort to interest planners in the introduction of this method, to virtually no avail. He failed either to get planning agencies interested or to persuade economists that this was something relevant for their consideration.

At this point, however, let us leave Kantorovich's example and recapitulate the basic idea of linear programming in somewhat different terms — specifically, in the kind of terms in which it was later expounded when it was reinvented and developed in the west. All linear programming problems have certain features in common. They all aim to find a "program," that is, a set of values for certain *choice variables,* which in different contexts may be levels of activity of a particular process, outputs of a particular commodity, amounts of a particular input to be used, and so on. In Kantorovich's problem, these choice variables were the amount of time each machine was to spend on each kind of log. A linear programming problem always has an *objective function,* which is some linear function of the choice variables. In Kantorovich's problem, the objective was to maximize throughput in the given proportions; that is what the first equation poses as the goal. (Some linear programming problems may have an objective function that seeks to minimize something, like cost.) The pursuit of the objective in any linear programming problem is limited, of course, by a set of *constraints.* In Kantorovich's problem, the constraint was that whatever the assignment of a given type of machine to different kinds of logs, the total of its time committed could not exceed 100 percent. Also, in linear programming problems it is generally important to specify non-negativity conditions for the choice variables, as we did in specifying that in Kantorovich's problem $h_{ik} \geq 0$.

Another interesting feature of linear programming problems is that they always come in pairs. For any problem like Kantorovich's, which is described as a "primal" problem, one can construct a "dual" problem which involves some rearrange-

ments of the variables in the primal problem and the introduction of some new variables. For example, in Kantorovich's
problem the dual involves finding a set of "shadow prices"
which impute to whatever resources constituted the constraint
in the original problem the full amount of whatever value the
objective function indicated as the maximand. The multipliers
that Kantorovich introduced to find a solution to his problem
were these shadow prices, although he did not understand at
the time their full meaning or the whole theory of the dual
and primal problems. Also, his algorithm for finding shadow
prices was not necessarily one that would be used today. The
idea that there is a set of shadow prices that imputes the value
of the attained objective to the scarce resources is intuitively
understandable. After all, it is the constraints that set a limit
on the achievement of whatever goal is posed by objective
function, so that it makes sense to attribute to these scarce
resources whatever achievement the operation of the program
generates. In short, the linear programming problem exhibits
in a kind of microcosm the basic ideas of scarcity, the interrela-
tionship of allocation decisions and value, the notion of opportunity cost, the notion of value as an index of scarcity in relation
to goals sought, and all the rest. That is, it reveals all the
essential ideas of the theory of value.

And although the problems Kantorovich originally envisaged were small-scale local allocation problems, it requires
no great effort of the imagination to conceive of the whole
economy as involving something like a linear programming
problem. The goal of the planners is to maximize the total
output of the economy, but their ability to do so is limited
by the scarcity of some resources. To set up this planning
problem as a linear program would, of course, involve a very
complicated statement; nevertheless, even to think in these
terms suggests in a very compelling way that the basic notions
of opportunity cost, value, allocation, and the like developed
in this microcontext are applicable on an economy-wide scale
to all production and to all resources.

Inherent in this is a general appreciation of the fact that
value is conditioned by scarcity, so that any input into production, and not labor alone, may have value and may make a

contribution to the value of a product. Thus, accepting linear programming means to accept the idea of an opportunity cost for capital, and the idea that natural resources have a value and should be priced to help conserve them.

Once this pathbreaking step was taken and given license to be discussed, Soviet economists moved on fairly quickly to acceptance and appreciation of most of the ideas of western economics. Kantorovich's ideas were originally formulated primarily in a production context, assuming that what was to be maximized was already given by the planners. But as soon as the mathematical economists began to think about this kind of problem on a national scale, they rather quickly came face-to-face with some perplexities as to the ultimate goal of production — what should be the objective function for the whole economy? They rather soon reformulated Kantorovich's models into a dynamic context — i.e., growth models — and in these the major issue is how investment that will enhance consumption possibilities in the future should be traded off against more consumption today. This introduced the issue of the criterion of optimality, i.e., the common denominator in terms of which these two goals can be compared, and Soviet economists quickly saw that the end of production is not more production, but consumption. This ultimately leads to the problem of a theory of consumer behavior, and some ideas about utility. Socialist economists have to be very careful in talking about this, since the utility theory of value is an idea that the Marxian economists considered as a heresy to be stamped out. But the very approach leads to this question, and it can hardly be ignored.

We need to explain that this revolution is still incomplete, in the sense that not all socialist economists accept it and that much of its basic conceptual apparatus is still incomprehensible to the politicians, statesmen, ideologues, practical planners, and administrators. Nevertheless, this new school now has a firm hold on the minds of those now learning economics, a secure institutional position in the universities and research institutions, and access to the channels through which new ideas are disseminated. A Soviet economist of this school now finds no barriers to discussion of technical economics with his bourgeois counterparts, compared to the situation in the past, in which neither could have understood what the other was talking about.

In describing the evolution of this new theory, it is important to note the contribution that the economists in the smaller countries of Eastern Europe made. The new economics probably found a quicker response among them than it did in Russia; they experimented with input-output earlier, they wrote articles critical of Marxian ideas earlier, and they were more creative in extending the implications of the new ideas. There are several explanations. For one thing, they were much influenced by the need for improvements in foreign trade. Their economies were more dependent on international trade, and the kind of wastes they suffered when they did not have good prices were more obvious and costly to them. For another, in these countries there were many more survivors of an earlier tradition — people who had learned their economics before the communist period. Notable among these was the well-known Polish economist Oskar Lange, who had made an impressive career in the west before returning to Poland to participate in the socialist experiment. They were also, perhaps, less isolated from the world literature in economics. We know very little about the interaction between the Eastern European economists and the Russians, but there are reasons to believe that the former played an important role in educating the Russians.

Conclusion

To conclude, it is interesting to review how this revolution was made, considering how heretical the new ideas seem. Several things have made it possible. One is that the new economists are right, and have useful ideas to offer the people who are trying to make the system run better — something that cannot be said of the traditional economists. A second factor is that the new economists made their revolution more or less by invitation and by accident. Kantorovich has frequently been attacked for his ideas, but his defense has always been that there is nothing for which he can be blamed, since the problem was raised by "life," not by him. The practical planners brought the problem to him as he stood innocently on the sidelines, and it was not his fault if the application of the ideologically neutral, value-free tools of mathematics revealed that implicit in the problem were such ideas as scarcity and opportunity costs for capital. And in general, the new theoreticians have tried to minimize any political, ideological, or institutional interpretations of their work. They all claim to be good Marxists, to accept the Marxian theory of value, to believe in socialism, and so on. These theories have no implications about the subjects of class relations, the political structure, socialized ownership of the means of production, or other basic features of the socialist political-economic order. They are also very careful to steer away from the issue of goals — their technical apparatus is value-free, and they have no quarrel with the right of the leadership to set goals for the society. Indeed, they like to say that only in a socialist society can these ideas achieve their fullest flowering; they confer an advantage on socialism that should be eagerly exploited. The issue on which the new economics faces the most embarrassing ideological problem is the central point that the value of anything results from the tension between goals and resources, rather than from the amount of labor embodied in it, as Marx would have it. But this problem is evaded fairly neatly by completely divorcing "value" as postulated by Marx from shadow prices, which should be thought of only as a set of technical indices to help decision makers gauge the worth or cost of any action in terms of helping to fulfill the plan.

The theoretical revolution is still incomplete, since there is no agreement about how to translate the new theories into a new approach to planning. The linear programming revolution is thoroughly ambiguous in this regard. On the one hand, it suggests that planning might at last be made perfect and optimal by conceiving the formulation of the national economic plan as a linear programming problem, to be solved at the center with computers and communicated to those who are to carry it out. On the other hand, in the prices of the dual it offers a prospect that if the shadow prices can be found (and they can always be found very simply as an aspect of solving the problem) the plans and commands of the administrative model can be abandoned. It will be enough to announce the shadow prices, and to tell everyone to do his best to increase the value of output and cut costs in the light of those prices. Likewise, the new economists have not yet been given a very prominent role in efforts to reform the institutions, partly because they do not yet have a concrete program, and partly because there is a very large number of other groups that have interests to protect and enhance in the process of reform. We will explore in Chapter 8 the issues that are involved here. For this chapter, however, the conclusion can be summarized as follows: By the beginning of the Sixties, the time was ripe for acceptance of the new vision that Kantorovich had developed, and a real revolution in economics as a science had taken place. Mathematical methods had won respectability, and a certain security as well, especially as they began to find practical application in planning, such as input-output planning and operations research.

A considerable number of economists came to appreciate that optimal economic decisions and correct prices are related, that demand is a factor that should be taken into account, that there are other scarce resources besides labor, and that they make a contribution to the value of what they help to produce. Above all, they had acquired a theoretical basis for the idea that an economy could be decentralized, and decisions guided by economic signals such as prices and evaluated by such synthetic indicators as profits. If there existed accurate indices for how much a ton of coal was worth, how much investing a million rubles in a given project cost society in terms of foregone opportunities, what the value of land was, how valuable a ton of steel was in relation to a ton of aluminum — considering the resources that each took and the ways they could be substituted for each other in use — then the producer no longer needed a plan to tell him what to do; he could decide for himself by adding up the costs of inputs and the value of outputs for any contemplated action, as indexed by prices, and decide whether the benefits were worth the costs.

This revolution has probably gone far enough so that it is

impossible for it to be repressed, or for the ideologues to order a retreat to Stalinist obscurantism in economics. Such a thing could be done only at the cost of destroying a generation of economists, and creating a new coterie of parrot and zombies, as Stalin did earlier. But the leaders today are too well aware of the need to improve planning to make that kind of foolish mistake.

8

Reform of Planning and Economic Institutions in the Sixties

The revolution in economic thought described in Chapter 7 is only a prelude and accompanying motif to reform of the Soviet-type economy. If these insights are to have any effect on the functioning and performance of the economy, there must be some change in the institutions and procedures that affect decision making. The purpose of this chapter is to survey the changes that have taken place so far.

The Sixties might be characterized as a decade of economic reorganization in the socialist camp, when the USSR and all the Eastern European countries undertook, or at least considered, fairly extensive changes in the planning system as it had originally developed in the USSR. There were some antecedents. The Yugoslavs, as a consequence of their political conflict with the Russians, had already decisively rejected the Stalinist model and marked out their own "road to socialism." The chronicle of the Yugoslav reform is a long one, but already in the early Fifties they had proclaimed a fairly concrete idea of what they wanted to do. It abandoned the main feature of the Stalinist model — central plans developed and administered though a hierarchical bureaucracy — in favor of decentralized decision making in a market environment. A special element in the Yugoslav vision was that the working class should play an important role in economic decision making at that decentralized level through the institution of workers' councils in all firms. Progress toward these goals was erratic, but by the end of the Sixties Yugoslavia had come far enough toward realizing them that it is now better to think of the Yugoslav economy as a market economy with some anomalous features than as a planned economy with some decentralization. Some other revisionist programs were mooted in the Fifties, as in a set of reform measures proposed in Czechoslovakia and Poland. The original model's patentholders themselves experimented with some changes, as in Khrushchev's 1957 reorganization, though their tinkering never touched its core institutions.

Between 1963 and 1968, however, all the European socialist countries made a decision to introduce reform plans generally intended to decentralize economic administration. In some cases the projected reforms were never seriously implemented. By 1968 the Bulgarians had abandoned many of the reform measures earlier approved and were moving in the reverse direction of centralization. The Soviet reform was limited from the beginning, and instead of moving on to more radical steps, as its proponents had envisaged, it was not even fully implemented in the announced form. In Poland, reform was a casualty of an intraparty battle for political power, never pushed as a serious enterprise on its own merits. The East German reform was one of the more limited, but was carried out more or less consistently with the original blueprint. The most far-reaching reform programs were those of Czechoslovakia and Hungary, but the Czechoslovak movement collapsed with the Russian invasion, leaving the Hungarian effort as the only reform to move seriously away from the Stalinist model and to survive into the Seventies.

It is unlikely that the urge for reform is sated. The issue of improved performance is certainly not resolved, and we should be surprised if serious new efforts at economic reform are not made again. But at the beginning of the Seventies, the situation is more or less stabilized and clear enough that we can attempt to describe what the reformers were trying to do, analyze their programs critically, interpret why they succeeded so incompletely, and draw some conclusions from this skirmish about the future of the long-run campaign for modification of the Stalinist model.

Centralization and Decentralization

In view of the great variety of measures that have been taken in trying to reform the socialist economies, we will find it much easier to analyze and interpret them if we first discuss what decentralization and centralization mean, what ambiguities the concepts involve, and what the requirements are to achieve them. In the abstract, reform means better decisions about the use of resources, which in turn depend on better information and rationalized incentives. It is often assumed that these results must be sought in the socialist countries by decentralizing the present highly-centralized decision-making system of those societies. Our image of the fully decentralized system toward which they might move is something like the perfectly competitive model of the economics textbooks, or its close analogue, the market socialism model.

On the other hand, reform might mean more centralization, or better functioning with the existing degree of centralization. It is possible to imagine a parallel to the perfectly competitive model that might be called "perfect administration," i.e., an administratively organized economy in which all the frictions familiar in actual experience have been overcome, and the functions we discussed in Chapter 2 are carried out perfectly so that resources are used optimally.

The difference between a centralized system and a decentralized system can be thought of in terms of three main features. First, centralization implies a hierarchy, with decisions made at higher levels in the hierarchy. Any transfer of decision making to lower levels is a move toward decentralization, and the ultimate in decentralization would be to eliminate the hierarchy altogether and have all decisions made and coordinated by the lowest units of the former hierarchy. Second, in a perfectly centralized system actions at the bottom are based on docility rather than decision making. But as soon as there is any degree of decentralization, the question of the criterion guiding decision making at the lower level, and the associated problem of incentives, arise. And as the area of responsible decision making at the lower levels widens, the criterion must change accordingly. A third difference has to do with the direction and nature of information flows. In a centralized system, economic decisions are made, and coordination achieved, through vertical flows of information. In the administrative economy, interdependent decisions about steel output and tractor output, for example, are coordinated at the center on the basis of information sent upward by tractor producers and steel producers, and these decisions are then passed downward. Note also that much of the information passed around in the Soviet-type system is what the Russians call "addressed," that is, it is directed to a particular executant or decision maker.

In a decentralized model of economic coordination, on the other hand, decisions about how much steel to produce or how much steel is to be used in producing tractors would be made through communications and interactions directly between the people producing the steel and the people producing the tractors. The content of messages in a decentralized system differs by being more impersonal, and might be described as broadcast information. That is, it takes the form, "We stand ready to sell, to anyone who is interested, steel of certain characteristics at such and such a price."

The following paradigm may help to illustrate these ideas. A fully centralized system would collect information about consumer priorities and total resources available, and might conclude, let us suppose, that the socialist society should produce one million yo-yos for its citizens in the coming year. Obviously, this implies a corollary need to produce a million yo-yo strings. In making the plan, the central planning board would collect information about the capacities of the different plants, the amount of material needed per yo-yo string, etc., and would then pass down appropriate targets to the various units of the system. The textile industry would be ordered to make available a certain amount of material to be made into yo-yo strings. Each yo-yo factory would be assigned its share of the million yo-yos to be produced and would be authorized to obtain the necessary strings from one of the string factories. The target for a million yo-yo strings would be allocated among those factories and each would be authorized to employ a certain number of people, purchase a given number of pounds of material for strings, and so on. Note that all the significant communications here go up and down the hierarchy.

In a system of perfect administration, this yo-yo plan would be "perfect" in the sense that the resources would definitely be available; it would be wasteful to suggest that the yo-yo string producers overfulfill the plan. There is no room for decision making by enterprise directors — no choices need to be made according to some criterion of what is best. Their incentive to carry out these perfectly feasible orders to the letter would be to earn their salary, or an understanding that if they did not do so they would be shot.

In the actual Soviet-type economy, things are more messy. The exchanges of information between the yo-yo string factory manager and the center are less conclusive. There is some flexibility about how many yo-yo strings can be made out of a pound of material; it is not known for certain that the target is feasible; it may turn out that the promised inputs do not become available; and it is understood that it may not be out of order to produce some extra strings because the yo-yo target may also be overfulfilled. The system operates by telling the manager that he should fulfill the plan as given, and that if he does so he will receive 43 Brownie points redeemable in money. But knowing that it may not be feasible to fulfill every number in the plan exactly, the plan carries a tacit codicil to the effect that if the manager does not meet these planned numbers exactly there will be some adjustments in the Brownie points he earns. He might be promised 3 extra points for every thousand yo-yo strings above the target, and docked 5 points for every thousand below the target and 2 points for every ruble spent on labor beyond the sum authorized. The manager copes with day-to-day decisions — quality, whether he should try to scrounge some extra material through the black market, whether to try to overfulfill the plan by hiring more labor — by keeping an eye cocked to the effect his actions will have on the Brownie-point total. Note that his decision area involves lateral communications with other economic units, involving such matters as hiring more labor or dealing in the black market.

The real-world situation is complicated further by the fact that there can be intermediate levels in the hierarchy. For example, the yo-yo factories and the yo-yo string factories might both be subordinated to a Yo-yo Trust, and their actions co-ordinated at that level, though the interactions with the textile industry and the wood-products industry would have to be made at a higher level.

In a fully decentralized system, an enterprise director would have virtually no information exchanges with the center, except that in a socialist society it might be the center that held him to account for his stewardship of society's property. His information would come almost exclusively from lateral communication and interactions. These would tell him how many strings he could sell at what price, the cost of different kinds of material, and how much labor he could hire at various prices. He would then process this information into a decision as to how many strings to produce, and what inputs to use, according to some criterion. In a socialist environment, he might be told to seek the greatest possible difference between the cost of his production activity to society and its value to society, and this criterion would be made operative by relating his Brownie-point payoff to it.

This example touches on most of the variables the economic reformers think about working with. One option is to decentralize, which would mean (1) relegation of decisions to lower levels in the hierarchy; (2) appropriate reformulation of the decision-making criterion; and (3) the creation of a system to generate the appropriate new kinds of information. Any changes in these three dimensions obviously have to be properly coordinated. It will do no good, for example, to give enterprise directors more decision-making latitude, and to tell them to be guided by the goal of maximizing the difference between the cost and the benefit of their actions to society, unless steps are taken to create a system that will give them accurate information about the costs and benefits of these actions to society.

But the example also suggests that another option in reform is to gain more effective control over whatever degree of decentralized decision making now exists by reformulating the success criterion, or improving communications and information-processing capacities at the center. One could even contemplate the possibility of increasing the degree of centralization.

There are some important ambiguities in our discussion of the centralization-decentralization issue. First, decentralization as a principle of reform begs the question of what the basic decision-making unit should be. It is not clear that decentralization of the Soviet model would require moving decisions to the present "enterprises" of that system. Though we think of the market economy as decentralized, there is a great deal of administration in it. In the market economy, provision of the right number and sizes of truck tires to go on new trucks being produced is achieved through lateral communication and bargaining between truck and tire firms. But the number of *wheels* to go on those trucks is coordinated with the number of trucks by administration within the truck firm. The enterprise as it now exists in the socialist economy is a far different phenomenon from the capitalist corporation, and agglomerates within itself a rather different collection of functions. It is possible that effective reform should not only move decision making down from the top, but also centralize decision making by bringing existing enterprises into much bigger agglomerations.

A related ambiguity has to do with the question of which decisions should be decentralized. It may not be appropriate to decentralize all decisions. Even if the evidence seemed to demonstrate that it would be desirable to decentralize most decisions about current operations — input mix, output level and mix, and personnel policies — it might still be argued that decisions about major additions to capacity should be made at a higher level, say at the level of an industry, where the decision maker might be in a better position than existing producers to gather the information on future demand, or on technological trends that are important for this decision. In addition, a higher-level decision maker could plan the location of new capacity with regard to regional development goals or other considerations that it would be hard to build into the local decision maker's criterion, or that would not be reflected in the information he gathers from lateral contacts through the market. Reformers have to consider simultaneously whether any given area of decision making can be best improved by decentralizing it or by centralizing it more effectively, and whether there is any unit in the hierarchy that can take it on, or whether they may not have to reorganize the decision-making units along with relocating the decision-making power.

This, then is the terrain over which the goal of economic reform is being pursued, and an appreciation of its complexity helps us to understand the issues the reformers have to consider, the bureaucratic interests involved, and the difficulty of setting up a reformed system with the kind of coherence of design that will enable it to function effectively. Among other things, this description of the problem makes clear that it is too simple to think of reform only as decentralization, the use of capitalist ideas, or movement toward market socialism. Nor is it correct to think of the reformers as faced with a choice between the two possibilities of market socialism and the perfect administration model based on computers. The outcome is likely to be more complicated than either of these models, and, indeed, the economists, planners, and officials in those countries do not see reform in terms of these clearcut alternatives. These people show varying degrees of sophistication in their appreciation of the nature of the task, and not all of them would describe it in the kind of terms we have used. But those who are debating the theory of an "optimally functioning economic system" look at it in much this way. Indeed, that is what they mean by an optimally functioning economic system, or by the idea of a reform based on the "systems concept" that has so impressed them in its application to complex programs like the space effort.

Decentralizing Aspects of the Reforms

A great many of the actions the reformers have taken represent a movement toward a more decentralized economy, and we would like to provide here just enough illustrative material to show concretely what this involves.

Moving Decisions Downward. First, in those areas where decision making was already most decentralized and market-like — the relationships of the SPE with urban households and collective farmers — they have lessened somewhat the degree of interference. In 1956 the Russians dismantled the system of labor controls, and ever since they have been trying to adjust the wage structure to make it conform to the rules described earlier. The consumption good that was handled in the least market-like way was housing — the amount provided was far below the amount desired by households, the price was heavily subsidized, and housing space was distributed not by market methods at all, but by rationing. The smaller countries of Eastern Europe moved perceptibly away from this Stalinist tradition by raising rents to approximate the real costs, to let housing be distributed more freely, and to permit more of it to be financed. The Russians did not follow that lead but did, legitimate new institutions that could implement the consumer desire for more housing, namely, private housebuilding and housing cooperatives. They made it easier for individuals to lease land on which to build private housing, provided credit, and permitted the formation of cooperatives, which could procure land, borrow, and contract with construction organizations to build housing for their members.

Under the reforms, the bosses of the SPE have greatly reduced the "petty tutelage" they formerly tried to exercise over collective farm production decisions. In the USSR they abandoned much of the detailed planning, and gave the collective farms control over the tractors and other agricultural machinery that had formerly been managed by the machine-tractor stations. The main command retained was deliveries, but large changes were made in the general level of prices, and in relative prices, so that deliveries were more nearly consistent with collective farm interests. This is also the case in Eastern Europe.

The big reforms of the Sixties, however, involved the running of the SPE, and in most cases were undertaken to give enterprises more autonomy in decision making. Many of the changes have to do with the current output level and its composition. One of the earliest was the experiment in the USSR in which two plants — the Bol'shevichka and Maiak apparel factories — were to make their own output plans, without any directives from the center. They were supposed to make the plan on the basis of orders from their customers, rather than from the center — a model illustration of a shift from vertical to lateral communication. In the New Economic System that the East Germans introduced in the Sixties, central material balances were retained for some outputs, but for all others plans fixing output targets and allocating output among customers were drawn up not at the center, but at lower levels. Bulgaria also reduced the number of products covered in the central balancing process, and Czechoslovakia and Hungary abolished almost all central rationing of outputs.

A second general category of decisions handed over to enterprises was in foreign trade, especially in the Eastern European countries. By the mid-Sixties most countries had undercut the foreign trade monopoly somewhat, and granted direct trading rights to firms and associations. The East Germans left to enterprises the job of negotiating their own export commitments, subject only to a general indication from above of what their total foreign sales would be. There was less loosening of decisions about imports, though as an incentive to fulfill export plans, in most of these countries, enterprises were permitted to retain some part of their export earnings, and authorized to spend this foreign exchange on goods they wanted. Hungary, as one aspect of her comprehensive reform, went virtually all the way to letting enterprises determine their own export plans and generate most of the decisions as to what should be imported. The Soviet Union was quite conservative in this area, but it did do one interesting thing — allow enterprises to enter into contracts with foreign firms in agreements for technical cooperation in development of new products; earlier, such contracts were always made at higher levels.

Enterprises were given a considerably expanded authority to choose their current input mix. Their ability to exercise more choice in choosing material inputs was enhanced by the freeing of output decisions on the part of producers; East German clothing firms, for example, negotiated the styles, quality, and patterns of their textile purchases directly with the weavers. The number of decisions about the labor force that had to be negotiated through vertical communication with the center was cut considerably. Most observers agree that these economies tend to use labor very wastefully, and one of the goals of reform ought to be to motivate the managers to reduce costs by cutting the labor force. But the reformers have been somewhat inhibited by a fear of generating unemployment, and of losing control over the relative wages in different industries. Hence they have tried to keep such indicators as total employment, average wage, and total wage fund, but have universally given the enterprise more freedom in choosing the composition of its labor force. In some countries they were content to set labor force ceilings only, and in the Shchekino experiment in the USSR, now being widely adopted, the manager of the enterprise was permitted to fire laborers and to use some of the resultant savings to raise the average wage rate for the remaining workers above the prevailing standards.

Investment decisions were cut loose from central control in a variety of ways. In addition to the investments approved at the center, enterprises may now make investments in many cases on the basis of funds borrowed from banks, or out of newly augmented funds under their own control. In Hungary, by 1970, about 50 percent of all investment was financed through the banks, rather than from the treasury. The bank may have a total investment plan, but within this total decisions about its allocation are negotiated laterally between enterprises and the local branches of the bank, rather than at the center. In the USSR, an enterprise's depreciation funds, which had formerly been put into a central pool for capital financing, were put into an enterprise controlled fund to provide a local source to finance capital investments. The new freedom with investment funds is subject to two difficulties that are not yet fully settled. In situations in which material balancing has been severely weakened, management seems likely, in the absence of some aggregative controls, to use the new freedom to undertake large investments, which may lead to problems of excessive demand — a problem Yugoslavia, Hungary and Czechoslovakia have all experienced. Where the central balancing system has remained very tight, the enterprises may find their new independence somewhat meaningless, since they may have difficulty turning their investment funds into investment goods.

The reforms have also everywhere given enterprises *more latitude in deciding how to handle assets*, once acquired. In the past there were usually numerous restrictions on the enterprise's freedom to sell off either circulating or fixed assets (largely because of a fear that it might be tempted to provide equipment or materials to black markets), and an effort was made to regulate not only the total inventory holdings of the firm, but their composition as well. Many of these restrictions have now been removed. Before the reforms, a part of the depreciation funds accumulated by Soviet enterprises was rigidly earmarked for repair of existing assets, a restriction that prejudiced the choice as to whether existing assets should be repaired or replaced. This earmarking has now been eliminated.

New Success Criteria.   The reformers in all countries attempted to focus the attention of management on the goals of cutting costs or increasing the value of output, or on both, to increase profits. There was a trend toward payoff formulas that emphasized these as the ingredients of success. But it would be a mistake to say that profit was made the sole, or even dominant, criterion of success. A careful study of the East German reform found that managers looked on profit more as a constraint that had to be met than as an objective to be maximized. In the Soviet reform, output increases were retained as the main success criterion in many branches, or were included along with profit in a complex payoff formula. In some countries, growth in export sales might be made so important in the payoff formula that it could become the dominant goal. This failure to embrace profit wholeheartedly as the success criterion is a reflection of the reformers' lack of desire to go as far as the market socialism model in decentralization.

Price Reform. The third element necessary for decentralization — altering the information system — was sought through a price reform. The Soviet Union and all of the Eastern European countries carried out during the Sixties a general overhaul of their price systems. This is where the new economics discussed in Chapter 7 has had its most practical impact. The generally accepted rationale for these price reforms was that the prices of various commodities ought to be in line with their costs if they were to serve as appropriate guides for decentralized decision making. Among other things, this meant that price should include a charge for capital and some allowance for the contribution of natural resources; every country except Rumania has introduced an interest charge for capital. The USSR and Hungary have introduced explicit rent charges for natural resources, and the others have introduced pricing techniques, such as zonally differentiated prices, that serve some of the functions of a rent charge.

Let us consider how one might go about overhauling the price system of a socialist economy, since that will offer a useful framework for discussing both what was done and what deficiencies still exist in socialist pricing. Suppose that the initial situation is one in which some products earn high profits and others losses, in which there are neither capital nor rent charges, and in which the profits bear no relationship to the amount of capital or natural resources employed in various sectors. Suppose, to be concrete, that in the Polish economy the existing price of coal is so low that the coal industry consistently incurs large losses while the prices of electricity, textiles, and many other commodities are set high enough to earn large profits. The price reformers first consider the price for coal on the basis of last year's results, as summarized in Table 8.1.

Table 8.1 Report of the Polish Coal Industry for Last Year

Sales	100 million tons	@ 10 zlotys/ton	= 1,000 million zlotys
Material costs			
Electricity	200 million kilowatt-hours	@ .5 zlotys/kilowatt-hours =	100 million zlotys
Pit props	10 million m³	@ 10 zlotys/m³ =	100 million zlotys
Fuel	75 million gallons	@ 2 zlotys/gallons =	150 million zlotys
Spare parts	10 million units	@ 10 zlotys/unit =	100 million zlotys
Other			100 million zlotys
Depreciation			50 million zlotys
Wages			500 million zlotys
Total Costs			1,100 million zlotys
Loss			100 million zlotys
Total value of capital used in the industry			2,000 million zlotys

They want to raise the price of coal enough to turn the loss into a profit equal to a 5 percent return on the capital invested in the industry, i.e., 100 million zlotys. It seems that raising the price to 12 zlotys per ton would accomplish this goal. Upon reflection, however, we can see this will probably not be satisfactory. Since the price reform will change the prices on all other goods including pit props, electricity, and spare parts for machinery, the total cost of materials needed to produce 100 million tons of coal may rise. In that case, a price of 12 zlotys per ton could still mean losses for the coal industry. Alternatively, the cost of materials might fall, in which case 12 zlotys per ton would generate a return of more than 5 percent on the capital invested in the coal industry.

To deal with the problem, consider that the information in Table 8.1 might be stated differently. For example, the last column might be written as follows:

$$\begin{array}{c}\text{Value of}\\\text{coal output}\end{array} = \begin{array}{c}\text{cost of}\\\text{electricity}\end{array} + \begin{array}{c}\text{cost of}\\\text{pit props}\end{array} + \begin{array}{c}\text{cost of}\\\text{fuel}\end{array} + \begin{array}{c}\text{cost of}\\\text{parts}\end{array}$$

$$+ \begin{array}{c}\text{cost of}\\\text{other material}\end{array} + \text{depreciation} + \text{wages} \begin{array}{c}+\text{ profit or}\\-\text{ loss}\end{array}$$

We could make some substitutions in this equation (from the two middle columns of Table 8.1) to make it read as follows:

$$P_c \text{Tons}_c = P_e + \text{Kwh}_e + P_p m_p{}^3 + P_f \text{gals}_f + P_{sp}\text{units}_{sp} + 100 + 50$$
$$+ 500 - 100 = 1{,}000$$

The problem of the price reformer is to change the last equation, introducing a new price for coal such that instead of a loss of 100 million zlotys there will be a profit of 100 million zlotys. Unfortunately, he can't determine the new price for coal that will satisfy the equation without knowing what all the other prices mentioned in it will be. But the price setters will be facing an analogous equation as they move through the economy trying to set new prices for every sector or product. By simply accumulating all these equations they will, in the end, have enough equations to make it possible to find all the unknown prices simultaneously.

There are some other issues to be kept in mind here — ensuring that the total value of the goods to be sold to households at the new prices matches the sum of the wages mentioned in each equation, and that the profit going to the state matches the goods to be disposed of by the state at the new prices. Let us pass over those issues here; there is a problem at the end of the book through which you can explore these questions on your own. Our concern here is to point out that an approach something like that just described has been used in several of the Eastern European countries to generate a new set of reformed prices.

If price reform had been carried out only on this basis, one would have to rate it as a rather poor performance. One of the insights of the new economics is that the value of commodities cannot be determined by looking at the cost side alone, as this approach does, but must reflect demand considerations as well. It will be recalled from Chapter 7 that input-output can balance, but only linear programming can optimize. Similarly input-output can provide a set of mutually consistent prices, but to get prices indicating how valuable commodities are in light of their ability to contribute to some objective, a linear programming approach is needed. The Hungarians have experimented with such methods in their price reform and, more importantly, all of the Eastern European countries have made some effort to utilize linear programming techniques in a restricted way to get shadow prices for goods entering foreign trade.

In practice, the input-output approach was used only to give the framework of a new pricing system, i.e., to determine how the general price levels for whole industries should move. In setting the relative prices for closely related commodities within industry groups, the reformers *have* used widely the idea that prices should reflect value to the user. In numerous cases, prices of substitutes were made proportional to their value in use, as when prices of different grades of tires were set in proportion to their service lives and the prices of different kinds of fuel were set in relation to energy content. As another example, the prices on old and new models of a machine might be set to allow for the savings the user could achieve with the new model. In other words, the price reformers have introduced in a much more systematic way the general principle described earlier in the example of relative prices for different kinds of oil seeds.

Lack of Coherence in the Reforms.   To conclude, there is no doubt that there has been a significant decentralizing component in the reform, but it seems equally clear that it has had a far less revolutionary effect on behavior and performance than was hoped. Perhaps it did not go far enough, or it may take more fundamental changes in the political order to make bureaucrats act in an enterprising way. We will return to this issue later. But part of the explanation for the limited results of reform is surely that there was a very imperfect congruence between the three aspects of decentralization described earlier. The relegation of decisions to lower levels, the reformulation of the success criterion, and the shift from a vertical to a horizontal communication system were very imperfectly co-ordinated. First, though the reforms instructed managers to minimize costs and provided much more economically sophisticated measures of the costs of inputs to society than had existed before, the system of physical allocation was retained almost unchanged in the USSR, and for some commodities was unchanged in all the countries. This meant that decisions about the inputs a producer would receive were still being made to a very large extent through the traditional vertical channels of information exchange. Second, to the extent that enterprise directors did have a new freedom of decision making, the new price system was still a very imperfect medium of lateral communication. Most prices in most of the countries were not a matter of negotiation in lateral interactions between decision makers; they were based on the situation as seen from the center and were thus not subtly reflective of the value and costs to society of the various kinds of goods. This is a complex matter, but two cases will illustrate the problem.

In the Bol'shevichka experiment in the USSR the producer was supposed to choose his output assortment on the basis of orders from the retailers. But the more popular lines and models were not necessarily those most profitable for the plant, so that it was caught in a contradiction between the success criterion of profit and the sensitivity it was supposed to show to the demands of the consumers. To eliminate this problem, obviously, the negotiations between producer and buyer should deal not only with what kinds of things to produce but also with the price at which they should be exchanged.

An example from the Soviet oil industry shows how imperfectly the new economists' insights were captured in their translation into concrete pricing decisions. The price for crude oil was set more or less at the cost of the highest cost fields, say 20 rubles per ton. This is as it should be, since the price, considered as a message, broadcasts the fact that anyone who makes a decision that requires the production of another ton of oil is committing society to the expenditure of 20 rubles' worth of resources. But some producers have the advantage of exploiting fields where the cost of much of their oil is below this price, and it would be a mistake to let the resulting profits be interpreted as good performance, justifying bonuses. Hence a rent charge was levied to extract this surplus. But the rent charge was expressed as a charge per ton of output, rather than as a lump sum, which meant that the effective price to the producer was the 20 rubles (representing the value of the oil to society) minus the rent charge. If the rent charge for some producer is set at 4 rubles per ton, he gets 16 rubles of extra revenue for each additional ton of oil he produces and sells. Imagine that he has the option of getting more oil out of his field, say by acid treatment of the wells, at a cost of 18 rubles per ton. From society's point of view such an action would be desirable, since it gets something worth 20 rubles at a cost of 18 rubles. But if this producer is being judged by the criterion of profit, this expansion of output would be disadvantageous to him, since it would reduce his profit by 2 rubles for every extra ton. If the rent had been fixed instead as a lump sum, he would be motivated to expand his production to the point where the cost of the last ton produced was just equal to the value to society, i.e., 20 rubles per ton. Having accepted a rent charge as ideologically admissable, the price reformers failed to implement it in a way that would achieve Liberman's formula of making what was advantageous to society advantageous to the individual producer.

Strengthening Centralization

Many of the reform measures are in no way a move toward decentralization, but rather an effort to make the present degree of centralization work better. The biggest problems of a centralized system, it will be recalled, have to do with communicating information and processing it into evaluations and commands at higher levels in the structure, and with the structuring of incentives. Many of the measures taken by the reformers sought to improve these aspects of the system. Important gains can be had from an improved price system even without any notable decentralization of decision making. Even if decisions about the relative output of two different kinds of fuel are made at the center, the decision makers are in a better position to make the correct choices if they work with prices that reflect all costs, including interest and rent.

In many cases reform simply acknowledged that, although the central planners pretended to control some decision (such as the product mix of an enterprise), these decisions were in fact being made at lower levels as managers sought to optimize under the operative payoff formula, often with disruptive effects. Instead of introducing more controls to make sure the orders were followed, reform often meant an effort to improve local decisions by modifying the success criterion or the price system.

Even as some decisions were being decentralized, there was a concurrent effort to strengthen *central* decision making through the provision of more information-processing capacity in the form of computers, and by setting up more systematic and rational decision-making models for handling this information. Examples already mentioned are the use of input-output for balancing and linear programming, for such problems as drawing up locational plans for the new plants to be built in some industry. Another notable trend in these economies has been an effort to collect in a centralized fashion many new kinds of information important for centralized decision making that they have not bothered to collect before. Examples from the Soviet Union are the creation of a Conjuncture Institute to look at trends in aggregative terms, science and technology forecasting institutes, and agencies to gather information on consumer behavior. All of these kinds of data would be difficult or uneconomic for individual enterprises to collect on their own.

There has been extensive reorganization, difficult to characterize as either centralizing or decentralizing, which has as its aim an alteration in communications channels and a rearrangement of incentives. An important and instructive example is the effort to improve technical progress. The Soviet-type economies have had a very difficult time achieving technological progress. Though they devote a large volume of resources to research-and-development work, and make technical change ostensibly a matter of high priority, the actual achievement is relatively small. The diagnosis in terms of our earlier discussion is as follows: In the existing system, the creation and introduction of new technology is a highly centralized function. A great deal of information is gathered and passed up and down the hierarchical communications channels. The State Committee on Science and Technology draws up elaborate plans for a new computer, say, which assigns responsibility for design to some institute, responsibility for developing the necessary new components to another, and the production of an experimental model to another; sets a date for some factory to begin series production; and so on. In the nature of things, these participants in the process are likely to be found all over the industrial map. In an intricately complex project of this type, a breakdown anywhere can threaten the whole project. More importantly, there are crucial interactions that should take place between the participants, such as taking account of user needs in the design of the computer, ensuring compatibility among the various subunits of the system, developing software along with the hardware, and so on. In a centralized system, there is little motivation for this kind of lateral interaction to take place: it is always threatened by the incentive system, under which a firm that is supposed to supply special electronic equipment, say, will find that it can fulfill its plan more easily if it concentrates on other kinds of output. And when a new model of a machine is finally developed, the firm that is to produce it may find itself better off under the existing success criteria not to take on the disruptive task of producing it, but to stick with the old obsolete models already mastered.

How can this situation be remedied? One approach would be to decentralize the function of innovation and make it the responsibility of firms, rather than of the central planners. Unfortunately, it seems doubtful that this would work with most enterprises as they now exist in the planned economies. Many of them are too small to deal with the problem of technical forecasting, to spread the cost of that innovative work over an adequate volume of output, or to do efficient research. So the problem is one of reconstituting the hierarchy to create a new kind of unit to which this decision-making power could be assigned. In the Soviet Union, several devices have been used — one of the interesting ones being the consolidation of several small units into a new unit called the *ob'edinenie* or *firma*. One of the best-known of these is the Sigma firm in the Baltic republics, which produces computers and other electronic items. It was formed by merging several components suppliers, a design and research organization, and some production enterprises into a kind of combine that puts all the functions figuratively under one roof. Another similar case is the Electrosila firm in Leningrad, producing electric power-generating equipment, which absorbed the formerly independent design and testing organizations. The problem can be considered from the side of the research organization. These institutes often complain that they cannot interest producers in a new process or a new machine because they have not demonstrated the commercial feasibility of the idea in pilot plant operations or produced and tested a prototype. The enterprise feels that it cannot responsibly take on such risks, given its plan assignments. The answer would seem to be to agglomerate to the research-and-development organization some prototype production and testing facilities, to enable it to turn out a finished innovation ready to go into production. The great success of Soviet military aircraft is said to be explained by this kind of arrangement in the aviation industry. The designers, like Tupolev, have experimental production and testing facilities under their control, and can produce a prototype, demonstrate its usefulness, get it certified, prepare the production drawings, and correct miscalculations, which makes it feasible for a higher level of authority then to order a production plant to introduce it into its production program.

Apparently this is the kind of interaction that can best be handled by agglomerating many of the associated activities under one authority, rather than by lateral communication between independent units. But before it can be moved down from the high level at which it is now assigned — the Ministry or the State Committee of Science and Technology — it is necessary to do some centralizing to create a unit large enough to accept this responsibility.

Another illustration is found in the Eastern European reforms, where decentralization of powers has usually been not to enterprises but to a new unit — the production association — which has in many cases taken over some enterprise rights and responsibilities. These have been newly created in some of the reforms (e.g., the Rumanian centrales) while others strengthened existing units. These associations are large enough to do market research, carry on negotiations with foreign firms for export production, and the like. Since they are closer to the enterprise than the ministries they often replaced, they are in a better position to gain real operative control over enterprise actions, and in that sense represent a centralizing of responsibility. It seems likely that such intermediate bodies will win the major gains in autonomy from the reforms.

Conclusion

Summing up the experience of this decade of doctrinal innovation and institutional tinkering, we must ask what economic reform has accomplished. More broadly, thinking back to what has been said in earlier chapters about the modifications in Soviet precedents made by other socialist emulators, we may ask what has happened to the "Soviet-type economy" in this period?

First, there is now much more variety than there was at the beginning of the Sixties. Diffusion into different environments has altered the homogeneity that once justified the view that to understand the economic institutions and growth strategy of any communist country it was enough to have a clear picture of the Soviet model from which it was copied. This differentiation is partly, as exemplified in China and Cuba, a response to divergent resource environments that differentiated other countries' growth problems and potentials from those of the USSR. Implementation of these variant strategies has required considerable institutional departure from the Soviet example, as in the egalitarian wage policy and regional decentralization of much economic administration in China, and in the organization of agriculture in Cuba.

Economic reform, conceived of as decentralization or the adoption of market methods to improve resource allocation, has also contributed to the process of differentiation. Two countries — Yugoslavia and Hungary — have changed their institutions enough in this direction to "re-form" centrally planned economies into new kinds of systems for which that term is no longer quite appropriate. For the USSR and the other Eastern European countries, reform has led to more variety in the details of economic organization than previously existed, but in none of them has it been sufficiently radical to change the basic nature of the system, or to ameliorate significantly the traditional problems of the Soviet-type economy. Many reform measures have been intended primarily to make effective the centralized management that has until now been undercut by imperfections in the practice of administration, and even to increase the degree of centralization.

Decentralization efforts have tended to be partial and irresolute, partly because the advocates of reform lacked a coherent blueprint of the kind of system they wanted to build. Also important has been the caution of the political leaders and the opposition of vested interests. Economic reform rouses not just disagreement over how best to improve the functioning of an economy, but also a struggle over the distribution of power and influence. Economic reform inevitably has political implications (to which we will return in Chapter 9, which has made the leaders cautious about accepting the full program of changes the reformers envision.

Thus, the Soviet-type economy is still alive, if not necessarily well. In the Soviet Union economic reform has not touched the fundamental features that underlie our characterization of it as an administratively-run economy. Similarly, for the Eastern European countries other than Yugoslavia and Hungary, economic reform has not proceeded far enough to change them much significantly, or to alter the fact that they function basically like the Soviet economy.

9

Unresolved Issues and Possible Alternative Futures

The task of this final chapter should be to assess the significance of the Soviet-type economic system in relation to modern economic history and our ideas about economic systems. That these two perspectives are related is clear enough from the kind of questions we often ask about the Soviet system. For example, we wonder whether the Soviet model and Soviet strategy are best understood as an alternative to the kind of private-property, market-dominated system that exists in other advanced countries, or as a kind of transition system suited only to the needs of the early stages of economic development. If the latter, is it a uniquely effective and transferable approach to economic growth or only a tragic misstep in Russian history, never consciously designed for efficacy, more Russian than socialist? Can an economic system built to that design be adapted to deal with the novel challenges posed by advances in the level of output and technology, and a more open world? That is to say, is reform possible? Finally, can we get any hint from the reform experience, which has now extended over several years, about the kind of economic system it might become as it outgrows the matrix in which it originated? Will it converge to something like the western market model, or will it evolve differently?

The first of these questions has been fairly well dealt with in earlier chapters, and a simple recapitulation here should suffice. The system and the strategy of Soviet planning, in the form in which it was constituted by Stalin, seems to be a transitional model that has outlived its original rationale. Its virtues stand out, and its weaknesses can be overlooked only in a situation in which there are extensive resources to be mobilized and the goals of growth can be expressed in a simple set of priorities, and in a country large enough not to suffer overmuch from autarchic prejudices. If those conditions are not fulfilled, either because of growth itself or because the model is transferred to another setting, the benefits diminish and the latent defects come into sharper relief. Moreover, harking back to the discussion of the industrialization debate in Chapter 1, it is not so clear that the Stalinist approach was the only way or the best way the Russians could have chosen — Bukharin may have been right after all, and the victory of the Stalinist strategy a consequence of political immaturity rather than of its actual merits. However that may be, whether it has outlived its usefulness is hardly a question for debate. There is a clear consensus on that issue among the socialist planners themselves, accompanied by a willingness to seek a new growth strategy, and a new set of economic institutions to take better advantage of the stimulation of foreign trade, respond to the opportunities for growth inherent in a technologically dynamic world, release the initiative of the managerial elite, and honor with some sensitivity and flexibility the increasingly complex goal system that becomes feasible when output per capita rises to modern levels.

The internally felt need for extensive change has demonstrated itself beyond any need for us to argue it; the more important questions demanding our attention have to do with whether this system can change, and the direction of possible changes. As the discussion in Chapter 8 made clear, this process seems to have moved rather haltingly and uncertainly, and with considerable organizational reshuffling. The leaders have been cautious about tampering with the central institutions of the system, such as centralized planning of output and allocation, and are torn between trying to decentralize and to retain or strengthen the present degree of centralization. Those who follow the debate on economic reform in the USSR and Eastern Europe have become rather bored with it — there seems to be endless talk, a lot of minor tinkering, but little fundamental change. The changes get stalled or sabotaged in implementation, the characteristic problems seem to continue unabated, and the hoped-for rejuvenation of performance remains elusive.

Looking at these countries' experience with reform, one can discern a pattern in their treatment of economic reform. Poor performance — in foreign trade, in growth, in consumer service, in technical change — creates pressure for reform. At this point, some of the restrictions on objective analysis of problems are removed, numerous ideas for improvement are proposed, experiments are made, and eventually a concrete program of reform is undertaken. But these reforms are not comprehensive and coherent. There would seem to be a critical cluster of changes that need to be made simultaneously if reform is really to change things, but the reforms usually retain enough of the old system to cripple the impact of the changes that are made. Before long there emerge new problems, without much amelioration of the old ones. If pricing remains deranged, decentralized decisions lead to shortages and wastes. If investment decisions have been effectively decentralized, firms may respond with excessive investment, which leads to inflationary pressures and immobilization of resources in projects that cannot all be completed. If enterprises are pressured to cut costs, labor will be threatened with job insecurity, and there may be unemployment. The principle was never better expressed than in the Czech joke about reforming traffic patterns from left-hand to right-hand driving, but introducing the new system experimentally at first — for ten percent of the traffic.

As the next step in the reform pattern, there arises an argument in which the conservatives say the reform should never have been attempted, claim to have warned of the mess to which it would lead, etc. The progressives respond to this attack with a claim that the trouble is that the reform did not go far enough, that its implementation was emasculated by the politicians and gutted by the vested interests. Depending on the outcome of this battle, there may be a retreat to traditional centralization or a final victory for reform. If the progressive forces can mobilize sufficient support, they may get the system over the threshhold of real change in the system. So far this has only happened in Yugoslavia, though it looks as if the Hungarians may also have crossed the threshhold. The Czechs were definitely committed to moving to a truly decentralized economy in 1968, but were pushed back by the Russians. In all the other countries, some combination of circumstances has so far enabled the conservatives and vested interests to block fundamental change, and in some cases to roll back what reform had been made. This suggests two issues we might look at more closely, namely, the obstacles to change, and the requirements for a change big enough to affect performance significantly.

Roadblocks to Reform

One of the reasons the reforms have been incomplete is that they are always weakened in application by vested interests. It does not require deep analysis to show that many people owe their jobs to the present system — from the top of the SPE right down to the bottom. The positions of bureaucrats and planners confer important material rewards, as well as power and status. If we count on these people to design and implement the reform measures, they are bound to dilute their effectiveness. When the ministries were reintroduced in the Soviet reform of 1965, they were supposed to govern with a much lighter hand than they had in the old days, but the Soviet press is full of stories about the gradual extension of their petty tutelage. The new systems require at the bottom of the hierarchy a new breed of manager who can show initiative and think for himself in the new framework. Each reform effort faces the delicate problem of weeding out the old types who held their positions for political reasons and by virtue of a willingness to follow the command system; the reformers have always felt some inhibitions in this task. In addition, many people's livelihoods are tied to past decisions that a new model will reevaluate and rescind. The old system made serious misallocations of resources — locating factories in the wrong places, choosing obsolete technologies, producing domestically goods that ought to have been imported, and creating plants whose output fails to meet world market standards. So whenever a reform threatens to apply the test of profit, to rationalize prices, to test old decisions against the benchmarks of world technology or prices on the world market, peoples' jobs are threatened, and these fears can be used to enlist allies in the bureaucrats' fight against the discipline of a new system. In the USSR the new prices for oil showed the fields in Azerbaidzhan to be uneconomic; the Azerbaidzhan oil officials fought very hard to have the zonal price for Azerbaidzhan set at average cost for the region, with the profits of low-cost producers subsidizing the losses of high-cost ones rather than being extracted as a rent. If the price had been set at marginal cost in the region, this would have been so high as to provide effective ammunition for the argument that many of the Azerbaidzhan fields ought to be shut down as uneconomic.

The State and the Managerial Class

The problem of vested interests is perhaps a short-term problem that can eventually be overcome. More central to a long-run analysis of the possibilities of reforming the system is the issue of the kind of contract that should govern the relationship between the state and the directors of enterprises or other decision-making units. The question is whether it is possible to change things much without first fundamentally changing the relationship between the state and the managerial elite as a whole. Pursuing this question eventually leads one to fundamental questions about the political-economic order.

Many who have analyzed the performance of the Soviet-type economy have observed that one of its fundamental weaknesses has to do with managerial behavior — specifically, a kind of willful footdragging. Conceptually, at least, we can make a distinction between two kinds of wastes in the performance of Soviet-type economies. One flows from errors of decision making — plants located wrongly; production of too much of one commodity and too little of another; misallocation of resources such that one firm has too much capital in relation to labor, and another has too much labor in relation to capital. But another species of waste represents a kind of slack in the economy — the excessive inventories held by most enterprises, underutilization of capacity, failure to make innovations, managerial inertia that retains labor arrangements that require more labor than would some new plan. The common feature in all these weaknesses is inertia, or willful obstruction on the part of the controllers of the enterprise's activity. Nor is the phenomenon limited only to the enterprise; it can occur at higher levels as well.

This is a distinction virtually parallel to that one economist has made between efficiency proper and "X-efficiency." If one asks why two capitalist countries (say the United States and Great Britain) exhibit sharply different levels of resource productivity, it is difficult to argue that it is a result of a difference in economic systems. Both operate under a system in which the capitalists have to satisfy rules regarding the efficient combination of the inputs to maximize their profits; both operate with market price signals; and both have access to basically the same technological possibilities. One is left with a puzzle: why producers in one of these market economies achieve a much higher output per unit of resource input than those in the other country. The answer offered is that managers in the backward country simply are not forced by the climate of pressures and incentives to extract what they could out of the resources they use. This difference in productivity, caused by something other than departures from the rules we usually have in mind when we talk about economic efficiency, Liebenstein conceptualized as X-efficiency.

There is a lot of evidence to suggest that this kind of waste is quantitatively most significant in explaining the low productivity of resources in the Soviet-type economy. The big wastes are the failure to innovate, the search for an easy plan, simulation, hoarding, and underutilization of capacity. These are the kinds of reserves that managers are always exhorted to mobilize but that always seem to remain only partially tapped. This must be attributable to a lack of interest, an inertia, a stubborn refusal on the part of management to make the effort it might to mobilize the potential increment in output available.

To some extent, even the errors of centralization are attributable to the failure of management in the Soviet setting to behave in a responsible way and to accept the responsibilities that only they can discharge. Consider the following example. In the USSR there was at one point a serious imbalance between the output mix of petroleum refineries and the stock of internal combustion engines. The engine designers made decisions that resulted in a stock of engines that contained too many diesel engines and too few of the gasoline variety, in relation to the capacity of the refinery industry to produce gasoline and diesel fuel. Our usual reaction would be that this kind of situation might occur in the market economy, where people are making decisions about tomorrow in the light of market prices that reflect current rather than future scarcities, but that it ought not to happen in the planned economy, since a planner with responsibility for planning both investment and engine design should see that the two decisions are co-ordinated. But, contrary to these expectations, the market economy very seldom makes this kind of mistake, and the planned economy frequently does. The explanation is simple enough. The capitalist firms do not make these decisions in response to current market prices. The decision makers on each side — the engine designers and the refinery planners — know that they will be in their jobs for a long time and will have to live with their decision. So they make an effort to procure the information appropriate to the decision. The engine makers know that their ability to sell diesels or gasoline-engined tractors in the future will turn on the relative prices of gasoline and diesel fuel in the future, not today; thus they gather all the information they can on technological trends and future supply prospects in the fuel industry. Their lateral exchanges of information are not limited to current price information.

If we ask why the Soviet decision makers did not behave this way, the answer is obviously that they lack the commitment and involvement to accept that responsibility, and think in terms of short-term responsibilities. In short, their behavior is very much determined by the nature of the contract they have with the center or, ultimately, with the state. Somehow this contract does not succeed in motivating them to do these things; it is worth spending some time thinking about why. The terms of this contract, and the procedures for negotiating it, have always been weak spots in our understanding of the socialist economies. The problem is a gaping hole in the Lange model of market socialism, which merely assumes that enterprise directors will follow the rules set by the center, with little consideration of how this behavior will be enforced. Moreover, failure to appreciate the nature of this relationship has been a weak point of all the practical reforms so far carried out.

Recall the difficulties with the administration of the bonus function in the Soviet version of reform. One of the defects is that it envisages explicit targets for the success criteria, and payoff coefficients are variable depending on whether the targets are fulfilled, underfulfilled, or overfulfilled. The output target thus becomes a bargaining point in the plan making procedure. It may be to the advantage of the enterprise to secure an excessively low plan and overfulfill it, or vice-versa. Always lurking in the background is the traditional difficulty that it may be dangerous to propose ambitious plans or to overfulfill the plan. Under the new system, the danger would be that an enterprise which does so may be confronted with readjusted, discriminatory payoff coefficients in the next round. As long as management knows that its contract terms are subject to renegotiation at frequent intervals and that it is the weak partner in these negotiations, it is risky to reveal its true capacities or to exhibit initiative. It is very much in its interest to bargain over these terms and, as a way of getting easy terms, to try to prove its weakness by performing less well than it could.

This was a central theme in the analysis of a Czech economist I knew who had helped design some of the first reforms the Czechs experimented with, in his effort to understand their failure. He considered the most important lesson to be that the state must convince officials that its terms were "parametric." That is to say that their terms were to be taken as given, not subject to negotiation, and that however the enterprise might plead, threaten, rage, or even declare bankruptcy, they would not be changed. If the state did not make these terms parametric, the enterprise director considered it as important to try to influence them as to maximize under them. And the best way to get better terms, or an easier plan, was to argue his low potential and to substantiate the argument by as poor a performance as he could get away with.

One of the most perceptive Polish analysts of the Eastern European reforms concluded that no change in the success criterion, the bonus rates, or other elements of the payoff system will fundamentally change enterprise behavior as long as the institution of annual target-setting remains. His argument is that the director always faces the danger that if he proposes an ambitious target on his own and fulfills it, or responds to a profit-sharing incentive system by mobilizing reserves, he can expect that the next time around more will be expected of him. Managers fear that the response from above will always be biased, in the sense that in the next round of target-setting the pressure will be increased so much that the enterprises cannot fulfill the expectations and will risk losing all bonuses.

This issue of stability in the mutual obligations of state and enterprise arises in many contexts, and we will illustrate with one example from the Soviet reforms. One of the principles in the Soviet reform is supposed to be that the payoff formula remains fixed for a relatively long time. A very instructive example of what is involved arose in connection with rent payments in the oil and gas reform. The Russians always describe these as "fixed (rent) payments." This formulation is intended to emphasize that these payments will be established in advance and will remain unchanged for some time so that the producers will know where they stand; it is instructive that the emphasis is on the notion of fixity, and that the rent idea is literally parenthetical. However, this stability feature roused intense criticism from the producers, on the grounds that costs typically rise as an oil field moves from flush production to pumping and secondary recovery. Fixed rent charges meant that the producer would be progressively de-

prived of the possibility of good profit performance and bonuses as time went on. In an effort to overcome this problem,
an interesting suggestion was made by some producers that
the rent charge be varied over time in accordance with changes
in output per well, supposedly the main determinant of changes
in the unit cost of oil extraction. This can be interpreted as
an attempt to establish not only the terms on which performance is evaluated, but also the terms on which the original
terms will be renegotiated. Many analogous cases could be
cited; in their totality they demonstrate that how to negotiate
and renegotiate these contracts, how long the terms should
be fixed for, whether they should be individually negotiated
for each unit or standardized by group — such as all plants
in a given ministry or all plants of a given size — are vital issues.
The reforms have generally included a statement of intent to
keep the terms fixed for some extended period, but it appears
that they are in practice changed frequently and arbitrarily.

We can think of this bargaining process in which the annual
targets or payoff terms are fixed as a game in which the state
and the managerial class are the players. Many past problems
and the failure of the reforms can be explained as due to a
propensity on the part of the state to treat it as though it were
a zero-sum game, that is, a game in which the gain of one
side equals the loss of the other. The center approaches
bargaining on the assumption that it must guard against giving
away too much in bonuses, that it must not barter away state
income for incentive purposes. It is this assumption that
justifies annual reviews of targets and terms, the "ratchet
principle" of constantly increasing targets upward, and a
grudging and stingy attitude toward the division of above plan
gains.

But this is not a zero-sum game. A bargain could be negotiated that would give both the state and the managers a better
outcome. The managers stand guard over a very significant
potential increment to output; this extra output could be
generated with very little effort or real resource input, so that
the state could fully compensate management for its effort and
still benefit substantially. But there is some kind of defect in
the contract-making procedures that prevents management

from taking the bait, and the state does not succeed in coaxing these gains from the managers.

That potentially available output would seem to be what economists call a surplus or a rent. That is, it is an income in excess of what would have to be paid to the agents who can make it available, and the state ought to be able to capture most of this rent for itself. Why are socialist managers unwilling to release this extra potential for reasonable contract shares even if they know that the contract will be renegotiated? The crucial factor, surely, is that they fear that such an action will incite the state to arbitrary exactions in the future.

The problem finds an obverse expression in the security the enterprise enjoys in the administrative economy. Numerous commentators have suggested that decentralizing reforms cannot work very well until the center is willing to let business enterprises fail and die under some kind of bankruptcy and liquidation procedures. These exist, but are virtually never used. The Soviet economist N.P. Fedorenko thought that the reform would require that some enterprises be closed, but that idea was quickly put down. The importance of establishing the principle of bankruptcy if the reforms were to succeed was another of the themes to which my Czech friend continually returned. He thought that so long as the state did not dissociate itself from the enterprise sufficiently to accept its failure with equanimity, the enterprise would always find it more advantageous to bargain hard for easy terms than to work hard under stiffer terms. The enterprise often possesses what the game theorist Thomas Schelling has called the "coercive power of the weak," i.e., the credibility given to its threats by the fact that it has so little to lose compared to the stronger player.

Perhaps an essential ingredient in the final realization of a reform that will make the socialist economy more productive is a new kind of contractual relationship, in which the state retreats somewhat from its entrepreneurial pretensions, specifies its terms for longer periods and more on a class basis, and establishes a constitutional procedure for renegotiating the terms of contracts. All these would be guarantees of a "parametric" stance toward the managerial class and would disestablish the game situation that now exists. As Schelling notes, it is often a useful strategy for the player with the most at stake in this kind of game to bind himself and limit the range of responses he will consider as a means of undermining the coercive power of the weak.

Here, obviously, we are dealing with fundamental questions of the political order, as well as with aspects of the economic mechanism proper. I have used the words "class" and "constitutional" above in a neutral way, but it is not accidental that these words suggest political ideas as well. We have already referred to the caution of the political leaders regarding the degree of reform they are willing to entertain, and one wonders if it may not be that a change in the economic system radical enough to really improve its functioning would be unacceptable to the leadership as a threat to their political power.

We can think about this in Marxian terms; indeed, it would not be surprising to learn that some people in the socialist societies analyze it this way. In Marx's view of how economic systems change, the basic idea is that as technology advances, productivity rises, and wealth accumulates, the system of production relations outgrows the property relations, which become a fetter on the further growth of production. The bargaining relationship between the managerial class and the state, which we have described, involves power, property, and class interest. In the usual Marxian view, a ruling class never resolves these conflicts by voluntarily giving up its power, and this "antagonistic contradiction," as the Marxist theoreticians call it, can be solved only by a revolution. If we think about the role of the Party in the Stalinist development strategy, it certainly offers a parallel to the Marxian idea that the bourgeoisie was doomed to create its own gravediggers. To elaborate somewhat on various ideas that have been presented earlier, the role of the Party in the system was that of the board of directors in an all-inclusive structure in which political power and economic strategy making were tightly fused. Moreover, as the leaders of this organization, they interpreted their "planning" role (in the sense in which that term was used in Chapter 2's discussion of the administrative paradigm) very broadly as covering many issues of means, as well as ends, in resource allocation. Legitimacy for this dual role was argued on the grounds that only a dictatorial Party could enforce the discipline that catching up with and surpassing the advanced countries called for, and that economic planning and administration could not be left to the economists and managers but had to be shored up by the wisdom of the Party as the vanguard group. Stalin conveyed the strength of his belief in this point by annihilating the cream of the economics profession and a large part of the managerial-technical elite in the early Thirties. Today, development has undermined both those claims. Though the USSR has not yet caught up overall with the most advanced capitalist country — the United States — it has equivalent military expenditures, and has surpassed the United States in the size of its investment program. Hence it becomes implausible to claim that the Party has to exist to hold down consumption and divert resources into military and investment activities in order to protect the revolution from its bourgeois enemies and achieve socialist abundance. This would be a formidable job even for George Orwell's Newspeak. As for the other ground of the Party's legitimacy, growth has created a new managerial and technical elite, which calls into question the need for the Party to control everything from the center. And the increased complexity of the larger economy has forced the Party to license a new generation of economists to replace those destroyed in the Twenties, and increasingly to turn over to them the issue of how to achieve the goals the top leadership sets. For example, the Party is gradually surrendering to the economists judgments concerning one of the strategic variables of the Stalinist strategy — the allocation of investment by sector. The leaders have begun to see that this is only a technical issue, with which they need not concern themselves. But it is very difficult for the Party leadership to let the economic scientists settle what might be called a "constitutional issue," i.e., the design of the *structure and institutions* of a new and more efficient economic system, particularly if this might institutionalize power in the hands of the managerial and technical elite along the lines of the contract relationship discussed earlier. In the USSR, at least, this is where the Party seems to draw the line; it has shown in Czechoslovakia its willingness to defend this line in other countries as well.

This discussion would seem to cast the managerial-technical elite as the successor class, but we might note in passing that there is another candidate as well. It is often argued that the Russian revolution was not a proper socialist revolution since it was premature, that power fell into the hands of the Party to be held in trust for the proletariat, and that the revolution will be completed when power is handed over to the working class. Indeed, this is more or less the position that Lenin took. The Yugoslavs insist that economic reform must settle this piece of unfinished business, and their answer has been the distinctive Yugoslav institution of workers' control. This idea seems to evoke a warm response elsewhere. A spontaneous movement to establish workers' control was part of the aborted Czech reform, though the Russians have fought this concept as a heresy.

I am not sure it is wise to follow this line of thought to its apocalyptic Marxian conclusion that basic change cannot occur without revolution, and that in the meantime there is little possibility of reforming the economic system to improve performance. It seems more reasonable to expect that the Party will see it as a wiser course to retreat somewhat from its present monopolization of power in economic affairs. These leaders may be willing to continue to hand over to the managerial-technical specialists more and more decisions about how to use resources to achieve assigned goals, and perhaps even about how to organize the economy, contenting themselves with deciding the genuinely important questions, i.e., end-use priorities. And there is no reason the Party leaders cannot alter their priorities concerning end uses to cater more to the wishes of the population. They could exercise their authority over the allocation of resources among various end uses on behalf of the working class, even though they were adamant against putting the basic consumption-saving decision directly into the hands of households.

There is much disagreement about political development in Soviet-type societies, but many observers have interpreted the general political evolution of these societies as a process in which the Party retains its monopoly political position, but increasingly makes its decisions as a broker among competing interest groups, and is ever more prone to leave technical issues to the technicians. The scenario above is simply the expression of this general dynamic in the sphere of economic policy. Within this less dramatic kind of interpretation, what might we expect to happen to the Soviet-type economy? If it is a transitional form designed to cope with the problems of economic development, what is it a transition *to* ?

Future Evolution of Soviet-type Economies

First, this question is perhaps premature in regard to the more underdeveloped of the communist countries — those in Asia, and perhaps Cuba as well. They have moved away from the Stalinist model in various ways, but mostly in response to the peculiarities of their resource situation or political history. They are surely still capable of achieving results from institutions that are basically designed to mobilize and to effect gross structural changes.

Second, after the experience of the Sixties, the prospects for market socialism do not seem very bright. Only one country has succeeded in making this transition, and it is a discouraging reminder of how precarious this commitment is in socialist countries to find both political and economic liberalism under attack in Yugoslavia in the early Seventies. The Hungarians are managing a persistent movement in the direction of market socialism, but occasional twinges of friction with the Russians remind us that success in this transition is not assured.

Given that Soviet evolution may limit the possibilities for adopting market-type reforms, and *will* influence what other countries do, what kind of evolution might we expect within the USSR? The major variable would seem to be the relative strength of centralizing and decentralizing forces in the administration of the SPE. Present efforts can best be described as an attempt to improve the effectiveness of the present degree of centralization, and in this effort the policy makers are counting on computers and the insights of the new economists for help. There has been a struggle between two views about how to come to terms with the computer. One is that the computer and mathematical methods will at last make possible the dream of perfect planning, a computopia in which a giant complex of communication and computing facilities will permit previously inconceivable volumes of information to be collected at the center and processed into perfect plans. These plans would be optimal and enforceable because they were feasible. The intoxication of this vision of building a complete computerized planning system from the very beginning, and from the top down, has begun to wear off in recent years, however. The sobering reality is that it requires much more computing capacity than the Russians have in sight, and a meticulously conceived and incredibly complex model for processing data into decisions that is beyond their ability to design.

An alternative approach, therefore, is to start the shift to the computer at the bottom of the hierarchy. Policy is now aimed at introducing the computer into administration and planning first at the level of the enterprise, and building around it an "automated system of administration" for the enterprise. The concept hardly differs from the way capitalist firms use computers to take over record-keeping, calculation, and such decision-making and control functions as production scheduling and inventory control. The Russians are expecting a fourth of all the large enterprises in the major branches of industry to achieve something like this situation by 1975, a reminder that we are talking about processes that will extend over a number of years. The next step would be to integrate these *enterprise* systems into *branch* systems. The enterprise computers will report not just to enterprise management, so to speak, but also to the head office of the ministry in Moscow. But the volume of information that thus becomes accessible, the speed with which it is available, and the computing capacity to be added at the ministerial level will make it possible for the ministry's supervisory role to be much more active than in the past; indeed the ministry can take over much of the decision making. As an example, in the Soviet economy hoards of excess materials at some firms exist simultaneously with shortages in others. Once the ministries have the necessary data, they are likely to assume authority over inventories so that they can shift them among enterprises under their control and avoid allowing a shortage at one plant to interfere with meeting production targets. We could offer similar arguments for many other aspects of management as well. Despite enterprise objections, this increase in centralization seems inevitable with the coming of the computer. One ministry has already constructed such a system.

Once the branch systems are developed, the final step will be to link them to a fully centralized system of automated planning and management, in which the planners in the Gosplan would exercise the kind of control over ministries that the ministries had already established over enterprises. This slower approach thus also makes the computer the midwife to a highly centralized system. But the route to it would be different, and this may be a case in which even with a given goal in mind, the final outcome depends on the route by which the goal is approached. The present approach might make it possible for the ministries to aggrandize their power at the expense of the center at the same time they gain power at the expense of the enterprises. If the ministries have control over the design and development of the computer and information systems for their ministries, they will have built a considerable bulwark against control from the center. There will be an inherent tendency to design them for the needs of ministerial control rather than to fit into a subsequent overall control scheme. The Soviet Union and such countries as East Germany and Poland thus might end up with a system in which ministries, or the somewhat smaller combines and associations that are common in Eastern European countries, would have a high degree of autonomy and would settle many issues by interactions with each other directly, rather than through some central planning body. They would be analogous to large American corporations, which, incidentally, are a model viewed with favor by many Soviet management experts.

Such a system might have some of the characteristics Galbraith sees in an emerging "new industrial state" in American society — a concentration of power in the hands of the technical and managerial experts in the corporations; the decline of

competition and of control by the consumer through the
market; and an erosion of the power of the central government
to regulate these corporations, because of their size and because
the two structures acquire shared outlooks and interests. This
would be a kind of convergence in which neither the market
economy nor the administrative economy lose out to the other
in competition, but in which both evolve to something like
a common type in response to the needs of technology, bureaucratic organization, and high mass consumption. Some sociolo-
gists predict such similarities not just for the economy, but
for the society as a whole; they speak of the emergence of
a "postindustrial society" as the successor to all the classical
systems. (The Russians ridicule this prediction, though their
refutations do not seem very convincing.) Obviously, these are
very large questions, that cannot be settled or even adequately
discussed here. We have raised these questions not to make
predictions, but with the didactic aim of suggesting a hypothe-
sis to guide our thinking about the evolution of the system,
and to return to the themes with which we opened the book.
The Soviet-type economy is not merely an exotic arrangement
for resource allocation, but also a special political-economic
order that grew out of a particular historical situation and the
problem of economic development it posed. The nature of the
problem has now changed so that the system has become
unsuitable for dealing with present problems. But social systems can be changed only slowly and not always predictably;
the transformation of the Soviet-type economy to meet the
needs of the new situation will involve a complicated interaction of both political and economic processes.

Problems

Each of the following problems provides a set of data that can be used to illustrate and to exercise your understanding of a major issue covered in the text. For each I have posed the basic questions, but each is sufficiently complex to require elaboration and guidance from the instructor, and to support an in-depth analysis of the point at issue.

Problem 1.   Comparison of U.S. and Soviet GNP, 1955

Morris Bornstein once made the following comparative estimate of U.S. and Soviet GNP (having first estimated Soviet GNP in rubles according to western concepts). Without explaining in detail his conversion procedures, let us simply say that he was trying to approximate what the Soviet GNP figures would be if each of the goods and services comprising Soviet GNP were given dollar price tags and totaled, and vice-versa for U.S. GNP in rubles.

Why did Bornstein arrive at two such different answers for the relative size of the two economies' output? Which would you consider the better measure of relative size?

244   Problems

Table P.1   Comparison of U.S. and Soviet GNP, 1955

	RUBLE COMPARISON			DOLLAR COMPARISON		
	USSR (billion rubles)	United States (billion rubles)	USSR as per-cent of U.S.	USSR (billion dollars)	United States (billion dollars)	USSR as per-cent of U.S.
Consumption	840.8	4,045.5	20.8	105.1	269.7	39.0
Investment	263.5	540.4	48.8	52.7	77.2	68.3
Defense	144.6	192.0	75.3	36.2	38.4	94.3
Government administration	36.9	24.2	152.5	18.4	12.1	152.1
GNP	1,285.8	4,802.1	26.8	212.4	379.4	53.4

(1) Is it legitimate to put dollar prices on each element of Soviet consumption and then to total them to arrive at the value of consumption in dollars? Do you suppose that if the Soviet consumption-goods output in 1955 had been auctioned off to U.S. households as a replacement for the consumption goods they actually received in some five-month period in 1955 the resulting relative prices for different commodities would have been the same as the dollar prices that actually existed in the American economy in 1955?

(2) The dollar valuation shows Soviet defense expenditures as almost as large (94.3 percent) as U.S. expenditures. Consider whether that is plausible along the following lines. Bornstein does not disclose the underlying quantities of goods and services in the two defense programs, but we can use the U.S. budget for 1955 to reconstruct them schematically as follows. Of the U.S. defense expenditure of 38.4 billion dollars, about 10.6 billion dollars was spent on the 2.5 million persons in the U.S. armed forces, and the rest on goods, primarily military hardware. The Soviet armed forces numbered something over 5 million persons (let us call it 5 million); since Bornstein presumably included expenditures for them in his dollar total by computing them at dollar prices, they must have accounted for about 21.2 billion dollars of the 36.2 billion dollars he posits for the Soviet defense program. The remaining 15 billion dollars of the Soviet program was the dollar value of nonpersonnel

elements of expenditure, presumably also heavily dominated by military hardware. At the risk of some oversimplification, we might say that the relative amounts of manpower and machinery devoted to defense in each case were as follows (taking the U.S. physical amounts as 100):

	USSR	U.S.
Manpower	200	100
Machinery	50	100

Thus the Soviet commitment of resources to defense was twice as big as ours with respect to manpower, and half as big with respect to machinery. How ought we to average these two figures to determine the overall relative standing? What is the common denominator to which these inputs should be reduced? Can you think of any reason why U.S. prices for manpower and machines might not be a suitable weighting system? Would the ruble price system be any better?

Problem 2.   The Capital Intensity Issue

The new Five-Year Plan calls for three new gas pipelines, differing from one another in length and in the volume of gas to be transported, as shown in columns 1 and 2 of the following table. The job of drawing up a plan for each pipeline is assigned to a different project-making group. A standard Soviet handbook on pipeline costs gives the unit cost information shown in columns 4 and 5 for each of the different diameters the project makers can consider for each pipeline.

Using the information on total project costs shown in columns 6 and 7, figure payoff periods as a Soviet project maker would. What choice would each group come up with if the normative payoff period used in the pipeline industry is 9 years? Suppose the investment funds tentatively allocated to the Ministry of the Pipeline Industry will not permit more than 480 million rubles to be assigned for all three pipelines together. Is this consistent with the use of a 9-year payoff period as a criterion? How would the argument go if the Ministry reported to Gosplan that it must have more than 480 million rubles for these pipelines so that each group can choose the

Table P.2 Pipeline Investment Project Costs

	1	2	3	4	5	6	7
	THROUGH-PUT (10^9m^3)	LENGTH (km)	OUTPUT UNITS ($10^{12} \text{m}^3\text{km}$)	COST/OUTPUT UNIT (10^6 rubles)		TOTAL PROJECT COSTS (10^6 rubles)	
				Capital cost	Operating cost	Capital cost	Operating cost
Variants for Project No. 1 (being designed by Uzbek Office for Gas Pipeline Construction)							
A (529 mm pipe)	2.0	3,080	6.16	22.91	3.187	141.12	19.63
B (720 mm pipe)	2.0	3,080	6.16	24.64	1.453	151.78	8.95
C (820 mm pipe)	2.0	3,080	6.16	28.24	1.384	173.96	8.52
Variants for Project No. 2 (being designed by Leningrad Institute of Pipeline Planning)							
A (720 mm pipe)	4.0	2,248	8.99	16.52	1.690	148.55	15.20
B (1020 mm pipe)	4.0	2,248	8.99	18.99	.919	170.76	8.26
Variants for Project No. 3 (being designed by Technical-Economic Department of the Ministry)							
A (1220 mm pipe)	11.5	1,000	11.5	11.28	.935	129.7	10.8
B (1420 mm pipe)	11.5	1,000	11.5	13.21	.764	151.9	8.8

Problems
247

variant with the largest diameter pipe, since it is well known that large-diameter pipelines are technically progressive?

Suppose that the payoff period were set at 12.5 years. Now that an interest rate is acceptable, show that use of the equivalent "coefficient of effectiveness" of 8 percent would lead to the same choices as the payoff period approach.

Problem 3. Financial Balance and Price Reform

The accompanying Table P.3 presents the accounts of a simplified economy in two different versions — as operating

Table P.3 Data for Price Reform Exercise: I. Operating Accounts

Firm A		Firm B	
Revenue	Expenditures	Revenue	Expenditures
1,000R	M — 400R	500R	M — 300R
(40 units	(C — 50R)	(50 units	(A — 250R)
@ 25R each)	(B — 250R)	@ 10R)	(C — 50R)
	(D — 100R)		L — 100R
	L — 500R		P — 100R
	P — 100R		

Firm C		Firm D	
Revenue	Expenditures	Revenue	Expenditures
1,000R	M — 200R	500R	M — 100R
(100 units	(A — 150R)	(100 units	(A — 100R)
@ 10R)	(B — 50R)	@ 5R)	L — 100R
	L — 200R		TT — 200R
	TT — 600R		P — 100R

Households		State financial plan	
Revenue	Expenditures	Revenue	Expenditures
Wages	1,100R	P — 300R	Labor — 200R
1,100R	(C — 700R)	TT — 800R	Goods — 900R
	(D — 400R)	1,100R	(A — 500R)
			(C — 200R)
			(B — 200R)

Note: Enterprise A produces good A, enterprise B good B, etc. M stands for expenditures on materials, L for expenditure on labor, P for profit, TT for turnover tax, and R for rubles.

Table P. 3 (continued) II. Input-Output Flows

	Firm A	Firm B	Firm C	Firm D	Households	State	Gross output
Firm A	0	250 (10 x 25R)	150 (6 x 25R)	100 (4 x 25R)	0	500 (20 x 25R)	1,000 (40 x 25R)
Firm B	250 (25 x 10R)	0	50 (5 x 10R)	0	0	200 (20 x 10R)	500 (50 x 10R)
Firm C	50 (5 x 10R)	50 (5 x 10R)	0	0	700 (70 x 10R)	200 (20 x 10R)	1,000 (100 x 10R)
Firm D	100 (20 x 5R)	0	0	0	400 (80 x 5R)	0	500 (100 x 5R)
Households	500	100	200	100		200	
Profits and turnover tax	100	100	600	300			
Total	1,000 (40 x 25R)	500 (50 x 10R)	1,000 (100 x 10R)	500 (100 x 5R)	1,100	1,100	3,000

accounts, and as an input-output table. The reformers want
to introduce a new price system that will make the prices of
different goods a better measure of the cost of producing them.
Suppose they decide to even out the disparities in the present
markups over cost by treating the turnover tax and profit as
a single "accumulation" category, to be collected as 450R from
firm A, 250R from firm B, 250R from firm C, and 150R from
firm D. Calculate a new set of prices that will embody this
change, and show how all these accounts will look with the
new prices, assuming that all physical flows remain unchanged.
Be sure that everything balances as before, i.e., that households
earn just enough to pay for the goods they buy, and that the
state financial plan is balanced.

Do you suppose that the new prices will make any difference
(a) for state enterprises; (b) for the volume of investment; (c)
for consumption; (d) for micro-balance in the consumer-goods
markets?

Problem 4.   Opportunity Cost

A group of Czech project makers deciding what kind of
tractor models to produce set up the problem as shown in
the accompanying table.

Table P.4   Payoff Period Calculation for Tractor Design

	Variant A (with diesel engines)	Variant B (with gasoline engines)
Aggregate capacity in horsepower	Enough to do the job required in agriculture	Enough to do the job required in agriculture
Cost-to-build tractors	400 million crowns	320 million crowns
Fuel cost to operate/year	.2 million tons of diesel fuel @ 60 crowns/ton = 12 million crowns	.22 million tons of gasoline @ 100 crowns/ton = 22 million crowns

Suppose the normative payoff period in the tractor industry
is 9 years; which model should they decide to produce? One
member of the group says she doesn't trust the fuel prices

used in the calculation, and you are sent to the oil ministry to see what you can find out about gasoline and diesel fuel. They are pretty closemouthed, but you do get two bits of information:

a) In general from 1,000 tons of crude oil they get:

	which is priced at:	and hence is worth:
400 tons of gasoline	100 crowns/ton	40,000 crowns
300 tons of diesel fuel	60 crowns/ton	18,000 crowns
200 tons of residual fuel oil	50 crowns/ton	10,000 crowns
100 tons of waste and other products	100 crowns/ton	10,000 crowns

b) One of the engineers tells you that it is technically possible to take the 300 tons of diesel fuel and crack it to get 200 tons of gasoline and 80 tons of residual fuel oil, the other 20 tons being consumed as fuel in the cracking operation. This fuel is virtually the only cost of the cracking operation.

Using the concept of opportunity cost, explain whether there is an implication in your information that the original decision as to which tractor to produce was wrong. The essential question is whether diesel fuel is properly priced at 60 crowns per ton if gasoline is worth 100 crowns per ton.

Suggestions for Further Reading

This book is only an introduction to the subject of the economies of the socialist world. Many qualifications and interesting details have necessarily been omitted, and many problems not even mentioned because of limitations of space. For the interested reader, works in English that might be consulted for more information on some of the problems covered are listed below. Considerations of availability and completeness guided the selection.

Several books of readings provide a wide selection of articles otherwise difficult to assemble: Franklyn D. Holzman, *Readings on the Soviet Economy* (Rand-McNally, 1962); Morris Bornstein and Daniel Fusfeld, *The Soviet Economy: A Book of Readings* (Irwin, 1970); and George R. Feiwel, *New Currents in Soviet-type Economies* (International Textbook Company, 1968). Another general introduction, with an approach sufficiently different from the present book to make it a useful complement, is J. Wilczynski, *Socialist Economic Development and Reforms* (Praeger, 1972).

The origins of the Stalinist model are examined in Alec Nove, *An Economic History of the USSR* (Penguin Press, 1969). A more specialized study of the industrialization debates, on which the discussion in Chapter 1 has drawn extensively, is Alexander Erlich, *The Soviet Industrialization Debate, 1924–1928* (Harvard University Press, 1960). The early debates are also surveyed in Nicolas Spulber, *Soviet Strategy for Economic Growth* (Indiana University Press, 1964). A companion volume, *Foundations of Soviet Strategy for Economic Growth* (Indiana University Press, 1964) contains a selection of Soviet writings from this period, which are valuable for conveying concretely the intensity and imagination that went into these controversies. The special issue of policy toward agriculture and the peasantry is treated in various contexts in M. Lewin, *Russian Peasants and Soviet Power* (Allen and Unwin, 1968); W. A. D. Jackson, ed., *Agrarian Policies and Problems in Communist and Non-Communist Countries* (University of Washington Press, 1971); and James Millar, ed., *The Soviet Rural Community* (University of Illinois Press, 1971).

For a systematic examination of the Soviet model as an approach to economic development, and as a possible model for other underdeveloped countries, see Charles K. Wilber, *The Soviet Model and Underdeveloped Countries* (University of North Carolina Press, 1972).

Our discussion of planning has necessarily been schematic; more detailed and concrete descriptions of how the system works may be found in some of the articles in the books of readings already cited, and a Soviet text on planning available in English — I. A. Evenko, *Planning in the USSR* (Foreign Languages Publishing House, 1961) — is also useful as a description, somewhat idealized, of Soviet planning institutions and procedures.

Important western studies of growth in socialist countries include *The Real National Income of Soviet Russia Since 1928* (Harvard University Press, 1961), by Abram Bergson, the pioneer in this field; T. C. Liu and K. C. Yeh, *The Economy of the Chinese Mainland: National Income and Economic Development* (Princeton University Press, 1965); the publications of the Research Project on National Income in East Central Europe at Columbia University, summary results of which are available in Thad P. Alton, "Economic Structure and Growth in Eastern Europe," in U. S. Congress, Joint Economic Committee, *Eco-*

nomic *Developments in Countries of Eastern Europe* (Government Printing Office, 1971). The last work cited is one of a continuing series of studies on the socialist economies published each year by the Joint Economic Committee, which are valuable sources for detailed and authoritative appraisals of their current status.

The ideas of the designers of the distinctive socialist model developed in Yugoslavia are analyzed in Deborah Milenkovitch, *Plan and Market in Yugoslav Economic Thought* (Yale University Press, 1971), and an excellent review of Yugoslav economic policy and performance is available in the annual surveys of the Yugoslav economy produced by the Organization for Economic Cooperation and Development.

The literature on the Cuban and Chinese economies is extensive, but diverse in quality and definitiveness; some valuable introductions are Jan S. Prybyla, *The Political Economy of Communist China* (International Textbook Company, 1970); Carmelo Mesa-Lago, *Revolutionary Change in Cuba* (University of Pittsburgh Press, 1971); and René Dumont, *Cuba: Socialism and Development* (Grove Press, 1970). There has been virtually no scholarly study of the North Vietnamese and North Korean economies.

For a small sample of works dealing with international economic relations as an aspect of socialist planning and development, the following are interesting reading: Alan Brown and Egon Neuberger, eds., *International Trade and Central Planning* (University of California Press, 1968); Asha L. Datar, *India's Economic Relations with the USSR and Eastern Europe* (Cambridge University Press, 1972); Tibor Kiss, *International Division of Labor in Open Economies, with Special Regard to the CMEA* (Akademiai Kiado, 1971); John M. Montias, *Economic Development in Communist Rumania* (MIT Press, 1967); and P. J. D. Wiles, *Communist International Economics* (Basil Blackwell, 1968).

Analyses of the revolution in economic thought and of economic reform in Soviet-type economies have become an unmanageable flood. Good works for general orientation purposes are the Feiwel reader mentioned earlier; Morris Bornstein, ed., *Plan and Market: Economic Reform in Eastern*

Europe (Yale University Press, 1973); and John P. Hardt, *et al., Mathematics and Computers in Soviet Economic Planning* (Yale University Press, 1967). The most eloquent and lucid statement I know of the ideas of the advocates of reformed socialism is Ota Sik, *Czechoslovakia, the Bureaucratic Economy* (International Arts and Sciences Press, 1972). Works of two of the prophets of the new vision in economic thought are available in English translation: L. V. Kantorovich, *The Best Use of Economic Resources* (Harvard University Press, 1965); and V. S. Nemchinov, ed., *The Use of Mathematics in Economics* (Oliver and Boyd, 1964), which contains a sample of Novozhilov's ideas. A perceptive explanation of how the new economics may be used in fashioning a new approach to running the socialist economy is Michael Ellman, *Soviet Planning Today: Proposals for an Optimally Functioning System* (Cambridge University Press, 1971).

For anyone interested in following current developments in these economies, and in getting the flavor of how economic issues are discussed in those societies, there are several continuing sources of translated material. The *Current Digest of The Soviet Press,* published by the American Association for the Advancement of Slavic Studies, is a weekly publication containing English translations of important speeches, articles, and documents appearing in the Soviet press. It is available in many libraries in this country, and reading through a few issues of it is an excellent way to obtain an impression of the Soviet press. More technical articles from the Soviet and Eastern European economics literature are available in translation in two journals published by the International Arts and Sciences Press, *Problems of Economics and Eastern European Economics.*

Index

112560